# SOCIALISATION
# THROUGH CHILDREN'S LITERATURE
### THE SOVIET EXAMPLE

## SOVIET AND EAST EUROPEAN STUDIES

### *Editorial Board*

The National Association for Soviet and East European Studies exists for the purpose of promoting study and research on the social sciences as they relate to the Soviet Union and the countries of Eastern Europe. The Monograph Series is intended to promote the publication of works presenting substantial and original research in the economics, politics, sociology and modern history of the USSR and Eastern Europe.

# SOVIET AND EAST EUROPEAN STUDIES

*Books in the series*

# Socialisation
# through children's literature

## THE SOVIET EXAMPLE

## FELICITY ANN O'DELL

**CAMBRIDGE UNIVERSITY PRESS**

CAMBRIDGE

LONDON · NEW YORK · MELBOURNE

Published by the Syndics of the Cambridge University Press
The Pitt Building, Trumpington Street, Cambridge CB2 1RP
Bentley House, 200 Euston Road, London NW1 2DB
32 East 57th Street, New York, NY 10022, USA
296 Beaconsfield Parade, Middle Park, Melbourne 3206, Australia

First published 1978

Printed in Great Britain by
Western Printing Services Ltd, Bristol

*Library of Congress Cataloguing in Publication Data*
O'Dell, Felicity Ann
Socialisation through children's literature.
(Soviet and East European Studies)
Bibliography: p.
Includes index
1. Children's literature, Russian – History and
criticism. 2. Socialisation. I. Title. II. Series.
PN1009.R803    301.15′7′0947    77–91093
ISBN 0 521 21968 X

# Contents

# List of tables

TO MY PARENTS

# Acknowledgments

My interest in the Soviet Union was first aroused when I was a small child and a Russian visitor to my home showed me how to drink tea with jam. Later when I began to learn Russian I was fortunate indeed in my early teachers, Martin Weir and James Forsyth, whose own enthusiasm was a constant and delightful stimulus. James Forsyth, of the University of Aberdeen, later also gave prompt and helpful criticism of one of the central sections of this book.

This study began as work towards a doctoral thesis at the Centre for Russian and East European Studies University of Birmingham. As a post-graduate I was supervised by Geoffrey Barker. Meetings with him never failed to renew my vigour. I am greatly indebted to him for his helpful and thought-provoking comments.

This book could not have been produced without the help of many people. I owe much to many members of CREES, especially Michael Glenny, Michael Berry and John Dunstan who provided both information and encouragement when most needed. Especial mention must be made of Anthea Roth, the Centre Secretary, and Jenny Brine, the librarian, who always gave thoughtful and efficient help. The final stages were much smoothed by the practical help and advice of David Lane, Emmanuel College, Cambridge. I am particularly grateful to Stella Uttley for her typing. I should also like to thank all the Soviet friends who with invariable patience answered my questions and the officials who showed me round their institutes in a most welcoming fashion.

MacGibbon & Kee Ltd/Granada Publishing Ltd kindly granted permission to quote the poem 'I don't believe a thing today' from Markov and Sparks, *Modern Russian Poetry* (1966), pp. 817–19.

Finally I should like to express my appreciation to all those friends and relations who bore with me through the long tasks of writing and re-writing this book.

# Part I

## INTRODUCTION

# I

# Children's literature and social control

## *A traditional means of character-education*

In *The Republic*, Plato wrote:

Shall we allow our children to listen to any stories written by anyone, and to form opinions the opposite of those we think they should have when they grow up?!

We certainly shall not.

Then it seems that our first business is to supervise the production of stories, and choose only those we think suitable, and reject the rest. (Plato 1973:114–15.)

From earliest times those concerned with education and social control have been aware of the power of fiction. Jesus, Muhammad and Confucius all taught through parables. In England, ever since children's stories were printed, they have attempted to teach youngsters the Christian virtues of the type, and in the way, appropriate to the nature of the particular age. The Puritan era sought to alarm its children into honesty by such verse as this:

> The Lord delights in them that speak
> The words of truth; but every liar
> Must have his portion in the lake
> That burns with brimstone and with fire.
>
> Then let me also watch my lips
> Lest I be struck to death and hell
> Since God a book of reckoning keeps
> For every lie that children tell.
>             (Watts quoted in Thwaite 1972:54.)

In similar didactic vein the introduction to a Victorian children's story, *The Little Hermit*, ends:

The story teaches how God can, and often does, bring good out of evil, and should teach sufferers from any adversity to pray and expect that the trial may prove a lesson, which, however painful, shall produce in them the fruits of righteousness and peace. 'Remember thy Creator in the days of thy youth', saith the Word of God; and in thus remembering God will the youth be laying a sure foundation for future usefulness and happiness. (Ready 1853:vi.)

Highly goal-directed societies have always followed Plato and believed that poetry and stories can shape young minds and each has accordingly told tales aimed at moulding its young minds into the form desired. Even in less purposive societies, like most Western countries today, there are those who ask alongside the French writer on children's literature, Paul Hazard,

Tomorrow what will England be? To determine that, we can study the colour and composition of its ministry, calculate the rate of exchange of the pound, consult all the signs of the present. But let us not overlook the books and newspapers for children. If the English children continue to read and like what Nelson and Wellington read in their youth, England will not change. (Hazard 1960:143.)

This view attributes not just *a* major role but *the* major role to children's literature in the shaping of young minds. The faith which some in the West have in the influence of children's stories is demonstrated by the practice of 'bibliotherapy', mentioned by several American books on children's literature. In an article on the subject, Richard Darling says that 'bibliotherapy' may be preventative – a little vicarious injection with a problem in a story will inoculate against a hard case of the same kind of experience in the young reader's development – or it may be curative – bringing the reader similar experiences to his own in novels and showing him how fictitious characters cope (Trinkner 1962). Humorously exaggerating this trend, one children's writer draws a sketch of an American mother going to the library for a book for her son and being asked what his problem is. Does he need a book about delinquents or unmarried mothers? (Bawden 1974:11.)

Confidence in this method is great in many quarters – American judges have given book-lists to young offenders – but it seems that concrete evidence of 'bibliotherapeutic' effectiveness is as yet small. I cannot accept that the books which a child reads can have a deeper and more lasting influence on him than the nature of the political system of the society in which he is growing up, or than the colour and composition of its ministry. But I do believe that there is a connection between society and children's books. It is not simply that certain books may produce a Wellington, but that existence of a Wellington determines the sort of books that are written. The political system and social organisation of a society will, to varying degrees of explicitness, be reflected in the society's children's literature – just as they are in its educational system and its other methods of social control. It is, to some extent, a two-way process. Ideas certainly to some extent affect political and social systems, and children's literature – especially, perhaps, textbooks – is certainly one of the many formative influences on those who will conceive future ideas.

We can expect a study of the children's literature of a particular time or place to reveal much about the values and nature of the society which produced it, even if the society's authorities do not deliberately use children's literature to didactic ends. But as our theme is children's literature in the contemporary Soviet Union, we are dealing with a society that is both explicit and systematic in its use of literature as a means of social control and leaves the reader in no doubt as to how it desires to educate the minds of its future citizens.

### The Soviet view

The Russian language distinguishes between two types of education, *obrazovanie* and *vospitanie*. The former is concerned with knowledge, information and instructing, the latter with attitudes, morals and upbringing; and it is the latter with which we are dealing. *Vospitanie* has been variously translated, for want of an exact English equivalent, as 'upbringing' or 'moral training', but here the expression 'character-education' will be used as this term seems to cover most adequately the gamut of training in political, moral and social attitudes and behaviour which is implied in the Russian word and which we shall see expressed in Soviet children's literature.

That Soviet children's literature should have a degree of character-educational content is regarded as essential. A Soviet librarian typically declares:

Soviet children's literature has a strong affinity with literature for adults. They are related by a true and growing manifestation of reality, by the typical features of what is new in our way of life, by creation of images of our contemporaries, by optimism, by high artistic standards. All Soviet literature has a common goal: the education of the universal man, the moulding of his 'world-outlook', his moral outlook and his aesthetic values. (Medvedeva 1971:133–4.)

As Medvedeva reminds us, Soviet literature for children and for adults is obliged to conform – as, indeed, are all the arts – to the canons of the doctrine of socialist realism.[1] *Bolshaya sovetskaya entsiklopedia* (*BSE*; the *Great Soviet Encyclopaedia*) defines socialist realism as 'an artistic method, the basic characteristic of which is the just, historically concrete depiction of reality in its revolutionary development, and the most important task of which is the Communist character-education of the masses' (*BSE* 1957: Vol. 40, p. 180). Character-education is certainly not considered as a process that is completed and can be forgotten about as soon as the young citizen reaches his legal majority at eighteen. It is a lifelong process. Many in the West would regard adult literature as a chief casualty; a mandatory literary doctrine giving priority to moral elevation can often prove impoverishing.

The didactic element in socialist realism for adults results in at least three major requirements. Firstly, *all works must be optimistic.* Marx has proven the ultimate inevitability of the Good Society of which man has always dreamed, and so 'The art of socialist realism, consciously reflecting the inevitability of the triumph of the new over the old, of the revolutionary over the reactionary, is saturated with life-affirming strength, with historical optimism.' (*Idem.*)

A work of socialist realism is assured of a happy ending in that the forces of good will be seen to be conquering the forces of evil – although the actual hero of the work may come to an unhappy end.[2]

A second important aspect of the didactic world-view of social-

---

[1] For a detailed discussion of the origin, meaning and implications of this doctrine, see Vaughan James, *Soviet Socialist Realism*, London, 1973.

[2] See for example Vishnevsky, *Optimisticheskaya tragediya* (*An Optimistic Tragedy*, Moscow, 1933), in which the heroine dies but Communism is seen to triumph.

ist realism is that *man must be portrayed as being basically a social animal.* In the contemporary fiction of the West, on the contrary, man is seen primarily as an individual. A Soviet hero may initially be depicted as alienated from his society but, by the end of the novel or play, he will not merely be resigned to his fate, he will have become an active member of society realising that it is on the true and glorious path. One has only to compare the heroes of, say, Graham Greene, with those of a dedicated socialist realist, say Gladkov, to appreciate the difference of approach.

An extension of this basic tenet – that society rather than the individual is of central importance – is the official Soviet emphasis that modern literature must be for the masses and not just a cultivated minority as tends to be one main branch of literature in the West.[3] Thus Mayakovsky, it is argued, is dear and familiar to the whole Soviet people, while Eliot is intelligible only to an initiated elite. At best, this may mean that Soviet writers' works lack the pretentiousness and effeteness that is a hazard of the esoteric Western approach; at worst, it may mean that there is little place for genuine profundity.

All these points are summed up in a third Soviet concept implicit in the term 'socialist realism': *every work of art should have 'ideological content'.*[4] Soviet critics deny the value of literature that is pure narrative or seeks solely to entertain. The highest form 'ideological content' is 'Party content'[5] which implies a writer's identification with the goals and methods of the Communist Party. This necessitates the previously discussed optimism of social orientation of the work, as well as a whole-hearted acceptance of the Party's world-view, its approach to the past, the present and the future.

It would be expected that Soviet children's literature would be at least as controlled by the demands of the educators as is writing for adults. Certainly its primary aim is to educate; the aim of entertaining is only secondary. N. V. Chekhov, a scholar of

---

[3] Another main branch of literature in the West is sensational writing certainly aimed at mass consumption but produced with profit rather than education in mind and very different from Soviet literature for the masses.

[4] *Ideinost'* – i.e. a moral concern with ideas and principles.

[5] *Partiinost'* – i.e. a commitment to disciplined involvement in the struggle for progress as defined by the Communist Party of the Soviet Union (CPSU).

children's literature at the turn of the century who is frequently quoted by Soviet sources, wrote:

Children's literature, as a branch of general literature, lives and develops under one and the same influences as the latter does and it inevitably reflects the same social classes and their interests. But in its development there is one special factor. This factor is the pedagogical ideas and the pedagogical practice of the particular epoch. (Chekhov 1927:21.)

Indeed, all the educational features that we saw as being essential to a socialist realist novel – optimism, ideological content, positive heroes – are similarly required in children's literature, which thus must not try to escape its educative role.

In comparison with adult literature, there is, however, a certain shift in balance. The didactic element assumes an even greater importance, but, in deference to the youth of the readers, works are encouraged to be entertaining as well, to an extent that is not the case with adult literature.

It is stressed that stories must not be totally instructive and devoid of amusement. Dobrolyubov, the nineteenth-century radical publicist, declared that children's books must be 'in content rational but at the same time interesting', and this demand has been continued by Soviet theorists. For example, L. V. Zankova, a pedagogue, says: 'Reading a work of fiction should always bring joy, it should not turn merely into a process of study, often boring the children.' (Zankova 1967:40.) In principle, there is no conflict between the didactic and the entertaining. The problem is just that too great a stress on didacticism can easily lead to pomposity – which is not usually entertaining.

## Soviet and Western debate on theory and practice

### Fantasy

No one in the Soviet Union would publicly question the basic assertion that the primary aim of writing for children must be educational, although there is, indeed, some discussion as to what extent entertainment is itself educative through its development of the imagination and the aesthetic sense. The most important expression of that debate has been in connection with fairy-tales and fantasy. It is revealing here to consider the way such discussions on theory and practice relating to children's literature have developed in the English-speaking West and in the USSR. This should set our later analysis of Soviet children's literature into a clearer framework.

The treatment of fantasy in stories for children is one topic that has always aroused strong feelings. In discussion over the centuries of what literature unduly frightens or worries children, fairy-tales especially have come in for much fire. John Locke, for example, did not approve of them: the rationalists of the eighteenth century poured scorn on giants and dragons. Nineteenth-century critics wanted fairy-tales to point a moral. In the 1930s they were banished from American schools; around the same time in China, the Governor of Hunan Province banned *Alice in Wonderland*. In the introduction to the 1948 edition of Lucy Sprague Mitchell's *Here and Now Story-Book* it is declared that:

It is only the blind eye of the adult that finds the familiar uninteresting...Too often we mistake excitement for genuine interest and give the children stimulus instead of food. The fairy story, the circus, the novelty-hunting delight the sophisticated adults, they excite and confuse the child. Red Riding Hood and the circus Indians excite the little child. Cinderella confuses him. Not one clarifies any relationship which will further his efforts to order the world. (Quoted in Smith 1963:30.)

But, of course, fairy-tales have their numerous defenders, too – many of them illustrious. Bertrand Russell maintained that stories like 'Bluebeard' and 'Jack the Giant Killer' 'do not involve any knowledge of cruelty whatever. To the child they are purely fantastic and he never connects them with the real world in any way.' (Quoted in Trease 1964:46.) The chief argument of the fairy-tale's supporters is, however, the fairy-tale's alleged power to develop the imagination.

A type of story closely related to the fairy-tale is the animal fantasy. Some Western authors have harshly criticised stories which involve anthropomorphised animals. Margery Fisher, for example, speaks out very strongly: she finds 'no excuse for putting funny hats on hippopotamuses or making monkeys talk in bursts of facetious slang' and she sees inaccuracy, vulgarity and sentimentality as pitfalls of the writer of animal stories. She continues:

'Children can very easily be deluded by the stories they are given in their first years and silly books about animals are about the most corrupting influence they can meet.' She does, however, concede that good animal stories can be written if they are about a whole environment (she cites *Tarka the Otter* as a successful example of this) and if something is left of the original animal (Fisher 1961:51). One can sympathise less with the Chinese Governor's reason for banning *Alice*: 'Bears, lions and other beasts cannot use a human language, and to attribute to them such power is an insult to the human race. Any child reading such books must inevitably regard animals and human beings on the same level, and this would be disastrous.' (Trease 1964:45.)

When one descends from abstraction, one must recall that works using this device include *The Just So Stories*, *The Wind in the Willows*, the Winnie the Pooh books and Beatrix Potter's stories, all of which are widely accepted as good literature. Perhaps each book has to be judged individually; if some general theory can be constructed, it must certainly take account of the classically successful. Be all this as it may, animal stories consistently rank high in surveys of children's favourite reading.

A more modern development of fantasy has the rather alarming name of 'machine animism' in psychological discussions. This denotes stories which have inanimate objects as their protagonists. Goethe's 'Wandering Bell' is an unusually early example of this type of fantasy, which was made popular by Hans Andersen. One Western article on the subject divides such stories into two categories. Firstly, it considers those which are about animated dolls and toy animals; these it finds valuable in that the toys usually depend on a child and thus the young reader is partly compensated for his inferiority feelings towards the adults in his life. Secondly, it deals with stories with animated serviceable objects like trains or steam-rollers; these it condemns: they make men seem inferior to machines and represent a very narrow functionalist, technical ethos. Also they are an affront to the child's taste: 'He ought to be offended by an illustration showing a machine ogling at butterflies.' It seems more probable that he will simply find it amusing – but the author maintains that books of this type positively harm the child: 'He should be taught respect for life and for meaningful relationships with living human beings.' (Schwarcz 1966:76–95.)

What is the Soviet attitude to fantasy in its various forms? In June 1973, *Detskaya literatura* devoted thirteen out of its eighty pages to the fairy-tale. This was in honour of the Fourth Festival of the Fairy-tale held at Tobol'sk, the birthplace of Ershov, the author of *Konyok-Gorbunok* (*The Little Hump-backed Horse*), a delightful nineteenth-century fairy-tale. One of the contributors, expressing his enthusiasm for this tale, wrote:

Every one of us has his literary attachments. Some prefer Lermontov to Pushkin, Tyutchev to Nekrasov, Esenin to Mayakovsky, Turgenev to Dostoyevsky, Chekhov to Tolstoy: is that not so?...but all of us, differing as we do in our literary tastes and attachments, unanimously love *The Little Hump-backed Horse*. We love him from our early years, from childhood; we love him like childhood itself and I cannot imagine a Russian whose life could begin without this enchanting fairy-tale. (*Detskaya literatura*, June 1973:16–17.)

His fervour is echoed in the other articles in the journal, and the fairy-tale clearly enjoys adult as well as child favour in the Soviet Union. But this has not always been the case. One of the chapters of Chukovsky's delightful *From Two to Five* is called 'The Battle for the Fairy-tale' (Chukovsky 1963:114–39) and it records the stormy fate of the fairy-tale since 1917. Chukovsky begins by recounting how, in 1929, he started reading to some sick children in a sanatorium from *Adventures of Baron Munchausen*. The children responded with much hearty laughter and enjoyment but, all of a sudden, the woman who had been looking after them reappeared:

She snatched the book out of my hand and looked at it as if it were a toad. She carried it off holding it gingerly with two fingers while the children howled with disappointment and while I followed after her in a mild state of shock. For some reason my hands were shaking. . .

Then there appeared a young man in some kind of uniform and both began to speak to me as if I were a thief whom they had caught red-handed:

'What right do you have to read this trash to our children?'

And the young man went on to explain in an instructor's tone that books for Soviet children must not be fantasies, not fairy-tales, but only the kind that offer most authentic and realistic facts. (*Ibid.* 115.)

Chukovsky points out that the fairy-tale only serves to emphasise reality for the children – they would not laugh at Munchausen if they were not aware of his wild imaginings.

But Chukovsky's opponents could not be convinced. They were pedologists, members of a school of educational theory, since officially discredited, but in vogue in Russia at the time, and spoken of with scorn by Chukovsky as 'miserable theoreticians of child-guidance, contending that fairy-tales, toys and songs were useless to children of proletarians' (*ibid.* 118). Of their ideas about children's literature, he declared: 'To fear that some little fairy-tale will turn children into romantics, into incompetents for practical living – this fear can possess only those bureaucratic contrivers who, attending meetings from morning till night, never see a live child.' (*Ibid.* 128.) The major point made by Chukovsky is that, if children are not told fairy-tales, they will invent their own; he quotes numerous instances to prove this, concluding that, as this is a need for children, why not give them the many great fairy-tales which have been created throughout the centuries by writers of genius from all countries?

But the pedologists (who were supported in this by Lenin's wife, Krupskaya) would not accept this reasoning; they wrote their own stories and poems for children. One depicts a boy who, in accordance with pedological theory, finds fairy-tales counter-productive. A 'fairy' appears to him spreading out her 'magic carpet'. What was the boy's reaction to the fairy?

> His hands
> In his trousers
> He thrust,
> Snickered,
> Whistled,
> And said:
>> 'Auntie, you're fibbing –
>> And how!
>> Who needs you now
>> And your magic rug?
>> You can fool no one now
>> With this or any humbug.' (*Ibid.* 129.)

This extract from the memoirs of a Soviet woman, once at

school in Stalinist Russia, shows vividly the approach to fairy-tales at this time:

> For the October celebrations that autumn our class produced a small play in which a group of young Pioneers expelled the heroes of Russian fairy tales as 'non-Soviet elements'. The curtain parted on this drab little group of Pioneers. Their appearance brought no response from the audience. Then the group leader, a girl called Zoya Mechova, got up and made the introductory speech. She explained the old fairy tales about princes and princesses, exploiters of simple folk, were unfit for Soviet children. As for fairies and Father Frost, they were simply myths created to fool children.
>
> After her speech the colourful crowd of 'non-Soviet elements' came on stage. A sigh of delight passed over the hall and grew into a wave of applause...
>
> The trial began. Cinderella was dragged before the judges and accused of betraying the working class...Next came Father Frost, who was accused of climbing down chimneys to spy on people. One by one we were condemned to exile. The only exception was Ivan the Fool, who was set free because he belonged to the common people and was no traitor to his class. He was renamed Ivan the Cunning.
>
> To the great disappointment of the audience we were led away... Zoya Mechova made her summing up speech but nobody heard it. The children in the audience began to cry. 'Bring them back! Bring them back! Don't shoot them!' The uproar was deafening.
>
> (Gouzenko 1961:142–3.)

Soon, however, such intolerant attitudes were forced into retreat. Gor'ky was gaining even more influence in the literary world with the setting up of the Union of Writers. Gor'ky was a lover of the fairy-tale – as is shown both by his theoretical writing and by certain of his own stories – like that of Danko, who leads his fellows through a dark, unknown and fearsome forest by tearing out his own heart which is literally burning for love of them; he succeeds in lighting up their path, dying only once open ground and sunlight have been reached (Gor'ky 1895).

Writing in 1959, Chukovsky did not feel that the attitude which had caused him so much distress thirty years previously had completely disappeared. As a case in point, he mentioned his own story, *Mukha-Tsokotukha*, a charming tale which has as its heroes a fly and a mosquito. An opera was based on this story which, in 1956, provoked an indignant letter to *Literaturnaya gazeta*:

Such tales do not deserve to be put into music or even to be brought into the world. This story evokes in children a definite sympathy for a poor, undeservedly-suffering fly, for a 'brave' mosquito and for other parasites. And this is very strange: on the one hand, in our country, we carry on a systematic, relentless war against insects, and, on the other hand certain writers bring into the world works that strive to evoke sympathy for these parasites. (Chukovsky 1963:131.)

*Literaturnaya gazeta* refused to be moved – but the Committee on Children's Literature of the Union of Soviet Writers sympathised, much to Chukovsky's amazement and concern. They answered, saying:

You are right in the way you pose your question. Regrettably, some of our writers who work in the field of fairy-tales for pre-school children, actually, for the sake of charming them, make mistakes, assigning to harmful animals, birds and insects the qualities of real heroes. (*Ibid.* 134.)

Chukovsky ridicules this attitude by saying that:

One has to be out of his mind and completely alienated from the realities of life, when seeing in some little Vanya's arms a velvet toy bear, to take it away from him, fearing that because of it, when he becomes an Ivan, he will not aim his gun or use his hunting-pole at a live bear. (*Idem.*)

From the last few pages it has become clear that the fantasy story has had enemies and friends of very similar vein in both the West and the USSR. Judging by the large numbers of fairy-tales and animal stories published, Soviet authorities now agree with Chukovsky rather than with the 1956 Committee on Children's Literature. No longer do the enemies of childhood scream 'The revolution is in danger' whenever 'a children's publishing house put out new editions of *Hiawatha*, or the tales of Pushkin or Munchausen.' (*Ibid.* 130.) Certainly an anthology for children recently published in Moscow includes fairy-tales by Andersen, Grimm, Perrault and Ershov, numerous folk-tales from Russia, England, Slovakia and the Ukraine, as well as stories which anthropomorphise animals by Krylov, the nineteenth-century Russian fabulist, Tolstoy and Chukovsky himself, to mention only a few of the writers in a field which is extremely well represented in such contemporary collections (*Khrestomatiya* 1972). As Western and classical Russian tales are widely known, the illustrations offered below are chosen from Soviet authors.

Fairy-tales are in one significant way unique in the field of writing for Soviet children. It is now more or less accepted, as Chukovsky urged, that their primary aim is to entertain and that their function in the character-education process is the indirect and possibly somewhat nebulous one of development of the imagination or the aesthetic sense. This unfortunately takes them very much to the fringe of the present study, which has its focus on moral education but, since they are such a well-represented and popular element in the literature, attention must be drawn to the nature of the new Soviet fantasy story for children. An example is E. Vasil'evskaya's 'Tigrovy plemyannik' ('Tiger's Nephew'). This could be interpreted as a new embodiment of the age-old theme of 'pride comes before a fall' or as an indictment of cowardice – but one feels really that the moral content of this tale is merely incidental. It concerns a stripy cat who sees a picture of a tiger and decides that they are so alike that they must be related. He starts to put on airs with all the other cats of the neighbourhood, telling them that he is a tiger's nephew. They are all eager to meet his uncle and so set off on an expedition to the zoo. When finally they find the tiger's cage, having looked in amazement at some of the other animals, the stripy cat boldly walks up to it and says 'Hullo, Uncle Tiger, I. . .' but suddenly can say no more, he is too afraid. The tiger is so big and a roar like thunder is emerging from him. The cats all flee, led by the tiger's nephew. In his fear, he does not even hear what the tiger is saying to him – 'Grrrrrrrrrrreetings!'

There is much gentle humour in the personification of the cats:

In the evening the cats met on the roof and began to talk of this and that, each on his own favourite subject. The white cat reminisced about the delicious milk she had recently drunk – the stripy cat interrupted her. The ginger hunter-cat wanted to tell of his adventures but the stripy one cut him short. He didn't allow anyone else to speak, but was all the time exclaiming 'My uncle, the tiger!! My uncle tiger and I!. . .We drink only cream! We hunt only enormous wild animals! He and I.' (*Khrestomatiya* 1972:342–4.)

'Machine animism' literature is also popular in the Soviet Union today; there are, for example, stories of tanks with human characteristics; this technique has an early and pleasing precedent in some of the poems of Mayakovsky such as one in which he describes the unrequited love of one battleship for another (Mayakovsky 1963: Vol. 2, pp. 158–9).

But the fairy-story can be and is on occasion used more directly in Soviet character-education. This is commonly attempted in one particular way. The child's love for the familiar form of folk-tales is used to heighten his sense of wonder at the real-life marvels of the Soviet twentieth century. An example is Kassil's story, 'The Knights' (*Khrestomatiya* 1972:222). He begins: 'There is a folk-tale about how thirty-three knights emerged from the sea onto the shore. . .But now you're not going to hear a folk-tale. I'll tell you what truly happened: The fascists seized one of our towns on the sea-shore. . .' and he goes on to tell a war adventure story in the idiom of the folk-tale, referring throughout to the Soviet soldiers as *bogatyri*, the medieval name for heroic knights. A more curious example is called 'Lenin's Truth'; it is classified as a Belorussian folk-tale. It is written exactly like a folk-story – using, especially, the typical device of repetition. Two brothers live a wretched peasant life in the country and one day they set off to seek the truth. They enquire what the truth is of a landlord, a priest, a merchant and a factory-owner but are tricked by each of these. The older brother ends up working in a factory where the workers tell him that only one person knows the truth and that person is called Lenin. He journeys on to seek Lenin who does, indeed, tell him 'the truth' – that the workers must struggle to rid the land of landlords and merchants and factory-owners (priests are not included in this list). This truth was later borne out by the October Revolution, for the workers and peasants now live happily in their own land. This story is an example of the Soviet mixture of folk tradition and contemporary reality already encountered. It strikes the Western ear as bizarre but it is certainly an ingenious way of presenting the young child with a Soviet version of twentieth-century 'history' in a form which is immediately appealing to him because of his familiarity with the folk-tales of the past.

Whether Soviet children respond morally to folk-tales in the desired way is a matter which has caused some concern to Soviet investigators. Pre-school children were asked why they liked or didn't like the characters in some tales. At first their comments would usually be based on the external appearance of the characters – 'I like the Princess because she is well dressed', 'I don't like Koshchei because he looks frightening'. But after further educational work and retelling of the stories to the children, they would give more advanced answers – 'I like the tsar, Prince Ivan's father, because he ordered Ivan not to throw away the frog but to love it'. Thus it would seem that it is not enough just to read folk-tales and fairy-stories to children. To acquire any educational value they must be discussed with a person skilled in character-education (Karpinskaya 1972:35–7).

In 1958, an English commentator on Soviet children's literature, could write 'the fantastic, for better or worse, is absent' (Rapp 1961:447). Both the above and much of what is to follow show that this is clearly no longer the case. Not only have the old fairy-tales been reinstated but new ones are being created.

*Violence*

Another area in which there has been much controversy in the West as to what children should or should not be allowed to read is that of violence. Does it harm them to read of violence? Does reading of naughtiness – or even of evil – encourage them to be naughty or wicked themselves? Or, on the contrary, does it steer them away from actual anti-social behaviour by allowing them to sublimate their anti-social urges – to be 'naughty by proxy' as Margery Fisher expressed it (Fisher 1961:37)? Opinions have ranged between both possible extremes: the current consensus seems to veer largely towards a belief in the sublimatory values of literature. This, of course, raises problems of limits: should one include, a certain amount of incest, say, on the same reasoning?

Various reasons are put forward to defend the inclusion of violence in literature for children. Some support it on the grounds of realism, maintaining the impossibility of hiding evil from children in a world of mass media and suggesting that wretched disillusionment is in store for them if they read only of good. Approaching the problem somewhat differently, G. K. Chesterton saw a certain nobility in stories of violence. He wrote:

The vast mass of humanity, with their vast mass of idle books and idle words, have never doubted and never will doubt that courage is splendid, that fidelity is noble, that distressed ladies should be rescued and vanquished enemies spared...[Their literature] will always be a blood and thunder literature, as simple as the thunder of heaven and the blood of men. (Quoted in Tucker 1957:271.)

Geoffrey Trease, a left-wing children's writer, thinks that children are less confused if black and white are clearly distinguished (Trease 1964). One may question the value of such generalisations, however, since they are not based at all on research into what a child's actual response to reading about violence and evil in fact is.

The question of violence in children's literature is linked by many authors to a discussion of comics. While all British writers agree in condemning the most lurid American horror-comics, there is little American comment on children's comics at all, except for Josette Frank's defence of them. She refers to a group of psychologists who agreed that, while comics (like films, TV and radio) do not create fears, nevertheless, for certain children under certain conditions, they may bring to the surface anxieties which already exist (Frank 1954). At the other end of the opinion-scale, Bettina Hurlimann reports that horror-comics have turned twelve-year-olds, according to their words, into murderers. She reports with consternation that an analysis of 100 American comic-books and 1000 comic-strips showed 218 major crimes, 313 minor ones, 531 acts of bodily violence, 87 sadistic acts and so on. Under the guise of 'self-defence', detailed advice was given in these comics on such things as how to press somebody's eye out with the thumbs and how to kick somebody in the kidneys. She does not condemn all comics unreservedly, speaking with respect of the Reverend Marcus Morris, who founded the English comic *Girl* to 'prevent the Devil having the best tunes'. Nor does she scorn the comic-strip as a medium, comparing it to the telling of Bible stories in church mosaics and quoting John Steinbeck with sympathy as saying 'I think Capp may very possibly be the best writer in the world today' (Hurlimann 1967:166).

Geoffrey Trease, however, feels that the English press should not be unduly smug over its superiority to American comics. 'They [the Amalgamated Press] do not realise that the mere exclusion of murder, snakes and sex does not in itself produce healthy literature.' (Trease 1964:72.) He would concur with Germaine Greer and other writers of the Women's Liberation movement in condemning the dream world of the love comic (which many girls start reading while still children) and the adulation of pop heroes which is encouraged by most modern youth magazines. He does, however, praise some of these, especially informative ones such as *Animals* and *The Children's Newspaper*, which he regrets is the only British weekly paper for children dealing with current events.

On the whole, children probably enjoy comics as relaxation requiring no effort to read them, just as their fathers relax with the New York *Daily News* or the London *Daily Express*.

The Soviet approach to comics and to violence in children's literature is, of course, determined by the general Soviet attitude to literature. This must be optimistic and present positive heroic figures who can be admired and imitated by the readers. This Soviet theorists see as far more important than multifaceted realism. There is certainly no Soviet equivalent of Nina Bawden's book about a battered baby (Bawden 1973). Violence of the type found in the American comics described above is totally condemned:

In capitalist countries and before the Revolution here in Russia there flourished and flourishes a 'commercial', mercenary attitude to children's books. It is widely known to what extent comics cripple children's souls – they are attractive in appearance and most harmful in their content of tinned hatred for mankind, of vulgarity, of dangerous passion and of skilful technology of crime. Such works are let out onto a world market in editions of millions and they are hungrily swallowed by children. And, although leading people in the West have warned of the terrible harm of these publications, although statistical reports on child-crime modelled on these comics and the bloody series of gangster films and television productions have proved it, the social struggle to make healthy 'art for children' does not yield any effect, for it always stumbles against the powerful profit-motive – against which it is powerless. With pride we can say that things are different with us. (Smirnova 1967:9.)

But as we shall see there are instances where a certain depiction of violence is permitted. N. N. Yakovlev says that, when the child emerges into the adult world, 'he should not meet too many unexpected unpleasantnesses'. It is significant, however, that he says this only in an essay called 'Abroad through the Eyes of Soviet

Publicists' (in Aksenova 1971) for it is only into the treatment of life in capitalist societies abroad – and in pre-revolutionary Russia – that violence is allowed to penetrate. It might seem that there are also 'unexpected unpleasantnesses' of violence and injustice in Soviet adult life but, in the literature he reads, the Soviet child is tenderly protected from these. Life abroad and in tsarist times is allowed no such rose-coloured spectacles and there is certainly no attempt to shield children from violence or the dark side of life here. When considering the topic of violence in children's literature, Soviet theorists are thinking of its political implications rather than of any possible effects on the psychological development of the young readers. Violence and injustice are normally shown as being restricted to life abroad or to the Russian past, and they are presented as contrasting very strikingly with Soviet actuality. It may be stressed however that even the violence depicted in capitalist states never approaches the sensationalism of some Western comics. The other area where the dark side of life is permissible is in war stories. As we shall see these exist in great numbers but again it will be noted that, although violence is recognised as essential to a treatment of such topics, it is never glamorised or wallowed in as in some Western comics.

## Soviet children's literature and the character-education process

From the above it is clear that there is much that will be of interest in studying Soviet children's literature. It has already been shown that Soviet literature in general and Soviet children's literature in particular are used as methods of character-education. But is it in fact significant to study children's literature for insight into the whole process of character-education? After all, children's literature is only one aspect of character-education among many. Clearly, for most children, the roles of the home, the school and the peer group are dominant in the formation of character. It is, in my opinion, a significant area of study in that Soviet authorities take the whole process so seriously that all the agents of character-education are, as far as possible, thoroughly co-ordinated. In general, the values of children's literature will be identical to those proclaimed by the official youth movements and by the schools. This is, of course, in sharp contrast to the situation in Britain where the attitudes taught a child in his Cub Scout meetings are very probably not reinforced at his school and are certainly contradicted by his comics. In the Soviet Union, children's literature may not be the most significant influence in the shaping of young minds, but it deserves study as a typical representative of the whole character-education process.

This does not, of course, mean that all Soviet children are equally affected by the relatively unified and systematic methods of character-education to which they are subject. To a large extent this is because attitudes are not formed solely by overt or direct inculcation on the part of the older or wiser. They are also affected by a covert, often unconscious process whereby the child imitates or assimilates from the behaviour he sees around him. What he is explicitly taught has to filter through the perceptual screen of his own experience. I would hazard that, in all societies, there is some discrepancy between the official values which are taught to the child and those which are practised by his family and the adult world which he observes.[6] In looking at Soviet character-education through children's literature we are dealing with the overt process, but it must be remembered that there are covert influences as well which will affect the impact of overt character-education. The child reads that vodka is harmful but he sees his parents enjoying it. Inconsistency between textbook values and practised behaviour can only detract from the successful inculcation of the overt values.

Children's literature may be one specific agency of character-education but it occupies a particular position in that, in the USSR, it has very strong links with other agencies. Unlike the adult press, children's literature does not fit neatly into some category like 'the mass media'. It is far more personal and direct in that stories are usually initially told to the child by an adult. In the Soviet Union this process again is more thorough. We shall see, for example, how a Soviet child does not simply return his[7]

---

[6] A minor but apt example springs to mind from my own teaching experience. A boy said 'Hallo, blondie' to me as I passed, unaware that he could be overheard by one of the RI masters who immediately pounced on him and swore violently at him. More socially significant is the way medieval Christians preached gentleness and forgiveness but went on Crusades or the contrast between the public and the private Victorian sexual moralities.

[7] On stylistic, not sexist, grounds, the child will be referred to throughout as

book to a silent librarian and then choose a new one himself at
random. The librarian will discuss what he has just returned,
will look at his record card to remind herself what else he has read
recently, will encourage him to criticise the book to any other
children present and will advise what he should borrow next,
perhaps consulting the lists of recommended books issued by
school and youth movement authorities. We shall see how, in this
and in many other ways, children's literature in the USSR is not
simply an isolated subdivision of 'the mass media' although it
certainly *can* be considered as a subdivision there. It is also, however, in various ways closely intertwined with the agencies of
'education', 'leisure groups', 'peer groups' and in many cases, in
the Soviet Union as elsewhere, with 'the family'. As well as being
representative of the standard Soviet official value-system, Soviet
children's literature has, in this way, close practical bonds with all
the other major agencies of character-education and is thus
deserving of especial attention.

   Another point to be borne in mind when examining the children's literature of any society is that all the agents of character-
education exist within a given political situation and, as a result,
are subject to political authority. Contrasts between theory and
practice are not always a result of the weakness of human nature
or the difficulty of living up to lofty ideals. Sometimes, such contrasts are part of overt character-education and a matter of
deliberate manipulation on the part of the controllers of society
in order to legitimate and maintain their own authority. Stalin,
perhaps more than any leader before or since, made use of the
device of saying one thing and doing another. He claimed, for
example, that there was collective leadership and fundamentally
voluntary collectivisation. He had notable forebears. Machiavelli
wrote that it was essential for princes to have an honest, good
appearance but that for them always to behave in this way is
ruinous (Machiavelli 1972:99–102). Plato went so far as to pro-
pose the creation of a deliberate 'foundation myth' to explain the
'origins' of the organisation of the Republic. By categorising
people into men of gold, silver and iron – with gold in the blood
only of those divinely qualified to be Rulers – it should serve to

'he' and the teacher or librarian (both predominantly female professions) as
'she'.

increase their loyalty to the state and to each other (Plato 1973: 160–5). Similarly the concept of the Divine Right of Kings must have subdued many a potential revolutionary. In other words, a fiction – often with an important religious dimension – is a useful tool for social control. Although contemporary Soviet society does not carry this process to its Stalinist extremes, we shall find striking evidence of a 'foundation myth' in the children's literature examined.

'Foundation myths' have thus frequently been given a religious dimension. In less Machiavellian ways, morality has been derived from the sincere religious teaching of those whom people trusted as prophets. To use the Russian phrase, the 'accursed questions' of Death and Justice and the Purpose of Life were solved by the ultimate unquestionable of God and his infinite wisdom. This sacred answer gave social morality an order and a justification.

In the nineteenth century, when the theory of evolution usurped Adam and Eve and the findings of science began to shake people's faith, many tormented themselves with the question of how Right could exist if God did not. If there is no God, is not all permissible? Today, in most Western industrial societies, religious faith is no longer the norm; in the Soviet Union, religious belief is officially discredited. Both alike face the need to create a new character-education process – one that does not rely on traditional religious justification. In the Soviet Union, the problem has been thoroughly studied and an all-embracing programme of character-education has been systematically put into practice. In the West, there have been only few and isolated theoretical studies in the field and organised application of any available theory has been even rarer and more fragmented. Blinkered by comparatively superficial debates on whether homosexuals should be allowed to teach in New York schools or whether British children should wear school uniform or should stay at school for an extra year, we have avoided facing more fundamental problems. The increase in juvenile delinquency and in purposeless violence can be blamed in part on this negligence. We may not find that we agree with the principles of the Soviet value-system, we may disapprove of some of the methods used, but the Soviet Union has at least tried. We can only learn from study of both the positive and the negative aspects of its character-education process and it is hoped that the present work may prove to be at least a peripheral contribution to the discussion of the development of education outside the Soviet Union.

## The aims of this book

Having identified some issues fundamental to any discussion of children's literature, let me now state just what the present work sets out to do. It aims to identify: the specific role assigned to children's literature in Soviet society in the purposive socialisation of the child to officially approved norms; the content of the messages so conveyed and their relationship to key features of the nature of Soviet society; the degree of success with which they are transferred to the child; and those features of the character-education process in Soviet society which account for its specific successes and failures.

These aims will be approached in the following way. Chapter two sets out the officially approved value-system of Soviet society, as set forth in 'The Moral Code of the Builder of Communism' in the Programme of the Twentieth Congress of the Communist Party of the Soviet Union. It is essential to know which are the virtues that are stressed in theory in order to be able later to discuss meaningfully those which are emphasised in practice. This chapter also discusses Soviet theory on methods of overt socialisation.

Chapter three narrows in on the specific organisation of children's literature in Soviet society. It will consider the various official roles assigned to adults in connection with the production and dissemination of children's literature.

Chapters four and five are concerned with different specific aspects of the content of Soviet writing for children. The first major area to be studied is that of primary school reading books. These were felt to be an especially significant source of material because they are read by virtually every Soviet child of the appropriate age. Inevitably, they will have been produced with an especially careful eye to their character-education content by reason of their all-embracing captive readership.

Even in far less goal-directed societies than the USSR, text-books – particularly those in the humanities – are likely to reveal much about the society which has produced them. In his article entitled 'History as She is Writ', Roy Nash discusses the treatment of South Africa and India in British history textbooks for primary schools. Out of fourteen textbooks on the history of South Africa, only two suggested that the country had any history before European settlement and only four gave any account of slavery. In all the textbooks, British rule is unreservedly held to have brought nothing but benefit to both India and Africa (Nash 1972: 230–2). But more like Nazi Germany and contemporary China, the Soviet Union makes far more explicit use of its textbooks. No Soviet-style censor in Britain would have allowed even four crude references to slavery to escape his blue pencil.

The age group using the primary readers (seven- to ten-year-olds) is also particularly significant; as Durkheim maintains:

One can distinguish two stages in childhood: the first, taking place almost entirely within the family or the nursery school – a substitute for the family, as its name suggests; the second, in elementary school, when the child, beginning to leave the family circle, is initiated into a larger environment. This we call the second period of childhood; we shall focus on it in discussing moral education. This is indeed the critical moment in the formation of moral character. Before that the child is still very young; his intellectual development is quite rudimentary and his emotional life is too simple and underdeveloped. He lacks the intellectual foundation necessary for the relatively complex ideas and sentiments that undergird our morality. The limited boundaries of his intellectual horizon at the same time limit his moral conceptions. The only possible training at this stage is a very general one, an elementary introduction to a few simple ideas and sentiments.

On the other hand, if, beyond this second period of childhood – i.e. beyond school age – the foundations of morality have not been laid, they never will be. From this point on, all one can do is to complete the job already begun, refining sensibilities and giving them some intellectual content, i.e. informing them increasingly with intelligence. But the groundwork must have been laid. So we can appropriately fix our attention above all on this stage of development. (Durkheim 1973:17–18.)

For the reasons above, in chapters four and five attention is fixed on the second stage of childhood. To counterbalance the textbook analysis of chapter four, chapter five will consider out-of-school reading – in particular *Murzilka*, the most popular magazine for the under-tens. Both similarities to and differences from the school material of the previous chapter will be found. An additional historical dimension is added to the *Murzilka* section as it has been possible to look not only at issues for the late 1960s and early 1970s, but also at those for 1928, 1938 and 1958. This reveals much about the development of the Soviet character-education process and is a striking reflection of the differences in the nature of Soviet society in these significant periods (New Economic Policy (NEP), Stalin industrialisation and purges, Khrushchev reforms).

Chapter six is the final chapter directly concerned with the content of Soviet children's literature. Its aim is to draw together those aspects of contemporary writing for Soviet children which are particularly indicative of the nature of the society which has produced them. Such conclusions are drawn on the basis of both the material analysed in the two previous chapters and other extensively published stories and verses.

Having attempted to answer these and other questions, in chapters seven and eight, the available evidence is assessed as to the successes and the failures of the character-education programme.

When considering the Soviet Union, it is impossible to measure the impact on character-development of children's literature in isolation since the aims of the various Soviet methods of conscious socialisation are so closely co-ordinated. The methodology of chapter seven is, therefore, to discuss first the evidence on the successes of children's literature only in so far as it relates to the inculcation of desired reading habits. The following chapter then considers the results of the character-education programme in general in the light of several important pieces of Soviet research before assessing the degree of success attained in regard to each of the main Soviet virtues identified in chapter two.

Because of the relative paucity of previous work done in the West on Soviet writing for children, it has proved necessary to adopt a broad approach ranging over all the issues which seemed central. In some ways, this has proved satisfactory. It has raised most of the central issues of Soviet children's literature and character-education, some of which might well have been missed in more specific studies. It has been possible, for example, to contrast leisure reading with school reading and to begin to give a historical dimension to the contemporary problem. In other ways, the wide scope of this work has proved frustrating. It is realised that many aspects require further research in depth. It would, one suspects, be particularly enlightening, for example, to do a thorough examination over time of individual themes like the treatment of Lenin or of patriotism. It would have been especially revealing to have examined a children's paper such as *Murzilka* over a larger number of years than the limitations of this study allowed. It is hoped, however, that the present work will constitute an adequate and reliable starting-point for future, more specialised researches.

# 2

# Character-education and its theories

Its extreme goal-directedness is one of the most characteristic features of Soviet society. The Communist Party of the Soviet Union has defined aims for every sphere of social life and, through exhaustive planning and central control, all available means are mobilised to implement these aims.

Clearly, the attitudes of the people who actually make up society are the most crucial and the most problematic objects of control from above – far more so than, say, the economic institutions within the society. The Soviet authorities have, as could be expected, a detailed concept of the type of citizen whom they would like to inhabit the present – and the future – society. As with other aspects of Soviet life, plans in this area are outlined in the Programmes of the Communist Party of the Soviet Union and it is helpful to look at these to see which qualities the Party is explicitly seeking to encourage in the 'New Soviet Man' (to use the romantic phrase once popular in Soviet writing, now less common than the perhaps more prosaic 'Builder of Communism'). The wished-for attitudes and behaviour of the Soviet citizen have now been prescribed in some detail by the Party leadership. In view of the official importance attached to Soviet morality, it is necessary to consider in rather more depth its sources and its nature.

## The foundations of Soviet morality

There is one pronouncement in particular by Lenin about morality which Soviet theorists regularly quote as the basis of their beliefs. Answering critics who claimed that the Bolsheviks had no ethical standards, Lenin said to the Third Congress of the Communist Youth League (Komsomol) in 1920:

Is there such a thing as Communist morality? Of course there is. It is often made to appear that we have no ethics of our own, and very often the bourgeoisie accuses us Communists of having repudiated all ethics...We say morality is what serves to destroy the old exploiting society and to unite all the toilers around the proletariat which is creating a new Communist society. (Lenin 1963: Vol. 41, p. 309.)

This, then, defines the fundamental tenet of Communist morality which underlies the list of desired qualities in the Party Programme: whatever furthers the ultimate emergence of a Communist society is moral. In other words, a good man and a good Communist are synonymous.

Brzezinski and Huntington, the American political scientists, highlight this point when they comment on the differing connotations of the word 'ideological' for an American and a Russian. In prevalent American usage, it has a pejorative meaning. A man can be admired for being idealistic, but not for being ideological. To a Soviet Communist, however, 'to be ideological...is to be idealistic in a practical sense' (Brzezinski and Huntington 1964: 17).

The above passage from Lenin also highlights another significant element of the Communist ethic and one which distinguishes it radically from Christian morality. Christian values are considered as God-given and absolute. What is morally right now was morally right in the past and always will be morally right. To the Marxist, however, there is no timeless categorical imperative; for him, morality is part of the superstructure of a particular society and depends on its particular economic base – the productive relations prevailing in that society. The Hungarian Marxist philosopher, Georg Lukacs, writes: 'For every socialist, then, morally correct action is related fundamentally to the correct perception of the given historico-philosophical situation.' (Lukacs 1972:9.)

The relative rightness or wrongness of behaviour will thus vary with the social situation and actions can be judged only in their social context. Does it help in the advancement towards Communist society? *This* is the ultimate ethical question, rather than – Is it in accordance with God's eternal law?

Lenin rejected the claim that there was no such thing as Communist morality. Nevertheless, as the Western philosopher of ethics, E. Kamenka, points out, 'An anthology entitled *Marx on*

*Ethics* would contain no passages that continued to be strictly relevant for more than three or four sentences.' (Kamenka 1970:6.) As ethics were not a particular concern of Marx's own writings, Marxist ethics have been developed on the basis of his philosophy of society in general. Marxist philosophy is termed 'materialist', which means that it rejects any idealistic, mystical or supernatural explanation of the origin or purpose of life. The 'accursed questions' can – and eventually will – be solved by reason and science alone. From this materialist base comes Marxist–Leninist ethics. The idea of God is dismissed as little more than a 'foundation myth' arising out of a particular stage in the development of the productive forces and property relations, and man himself becomes the purpose of all endeavour. If mankind is liberated from all exploitation, class contradictions and false consciousness, then both society in general and every individual in particular will enjoy the conditions necessary to develop all potential to the full.[1] No village Milton will remain mute and inglorious because of restricting social circumstances. The ethical is defined as that which helps mankind progress towards that ideal state.

Soviet morality has developed this into a concept, termed 'socialist humanism', which is explained thus in a Komsomol handbook on the foundations of Communist morality.

The humanism of the socialist revolution of the communist transformation of all aspects of social life, consists above all in the creation of the real, material, and cultural conditions for the realization of the slogan 'Everything for the sake of man, everything in the name of man.' (*Osnovy* 1973:142.)

Man is to be honoured and respected in lofty language. Everywhere it is stressed, however, that, although this humanism is a descendant of Renaissance humanism, it is not simply an abstract doctrine of love for all men. The words 'intolerance' and 'irreconcilability' appear frequently in 'The Moral Code of the Builder of Communism', and it must be noted that:

To be a humanist means to distinguish the personality of a human being, and to respect its dignity. But can we ignore a person's concrete characteristics? Can we demand love and respect for a person

---

[1] For a more detailed discussion of the basis of Marxist ethics, see *Marxism in the Twentieth Century* (London, 1970) by Roger Garaudy, the French Marxist professor of philosophy, especially pp. 96–105.

if he is an egoist, an idler or a money-grubber? As a general rule, we give a negative answer to such questions, explaining justifiably that love and respect must be earned. (*Osnovy*: 144.)

Such negative characteristics are not only to be condemned; they must also be actively fought against when necessary. Socialist humanism does not praise violence for its own sake but it certainly is no Tolstoy-like doctrine of non-violence; it states directly:

Marxist ethics have never enthroned violence as an absolute. Marxists do not consider the hangman as the 'professor of morality', as Plekhanov put it. Marxist ethics maintain that violence and non-violence can be revolutionary only when they correspond to the purpose and that both can become reactionary if applied by metaphysics. (Angelov 1973:252.)

Once again, this passage illustrates the importance of purpose in Soviet morality – to the purpose all (including, certainly, socialist-humanist respect for the dignity of the individual) is subordinated. Violence can be tolerated when it furthers the revolutionary cause. Indeed:

Humanism demands that there be no mercy to those who threaten a destructive war, to those who encroach on the freedom and independence of other peoples; it allows no concessions to those who destroy public property or hinder the building of new relationships between people, to loafers, speculators and hooligans. (*Osnovy*: 153.)

The socialist humanist must, therefore, while feeling a positive love for his fellow men, also be implacable towards those who, in the Soviet view, exploit them. His attitude can be compared to the Christianity of Calvin rather than that of St Francis.

   The problems associated with any philosophy which justifies violence for a worthy end are evident. When can we be sure enough of the consequences of our actions to justify violence? Even if sure, who – when personally involved – can be sufficiently objective and just with regard to the relative merits of ends and means? Is there not a danger that the oppression used to end exploitation may, if abused, be as disagreeable as the exploitation itself? There may be grounds for the old joke which defines the difference between capitalism and communism: under capitalism man exploits man, but under communism it is the other way around. Doubtless a society which bases its behaviour on the premise that the end may justify any means is likely to be able to change more rapidly than the other extreme of, say, Jain culture, which rejects even the violence of killing a fly. But it also lays itself open to abuse by those who can command repressive power.

Soviet society thus extols an explicitly political morality based on scientific rationalism and called socialist humanism. Though it disclaims any absolute rules, none the less contemporary Soviet morality does prescribe certain qualities which it postulates as indispensable characteristics of the Builder of Communism. Elaborate claims are made for the powers of Soviet philosophy and morality, in language that often does not sound particularly rationalistic or scientific, for example:

Our revolutionary science – the ideological weapon of the Communist Party and its highly reliable compass – has also been, in combination with revolutionary practice, a powerful means for the formation of the best human qualities. What, by comparison, is the mystical 'philosopher's stone' that alchemists of ancient times sought, applying their sorcery! What is gold! We have in our hands a truly miraculous method of transformation, our 'philosopher's stone' – the philosophy of Marxism–Leninism, with which Soviet society rears a man whose spiritual and moral qualities are worth more than any treasures of the world...(*Izvestiya*, 19 September 1969.)

What precisely are the spiritual and moral qualities that are more valuable than any treasures of the world? The overlapping demands of 'The Moral Code of the Builder of Communism' can be classified into six main virtues, all of which find justification in the general features of Soviet morality and socialist humanism discussed above: collectivism, discipline, love of work, patriotism, proletarian internationalism and atheism.

### Collectivism

Soviet thinking about morality is purely socially oriented and this finds specific reflection in the kind of moral characteristics looked for in the model Soviet citizen. All the values implicit in the Moral Code are couched in fundamentally social terms. For example, love of work is not described as love of work *per se* or as love of work to the glory of God, but rather as 'conscientious labour for the good of society'. The Komsomol handbook on morality sums up the purpose of moral education as being 'above all, the turning of social moral needs into the personal moral values of every individual' (*Osnovy*: 11). Thus a sense of social commitment can be described as the fundamental personality-characteristic of the model Soviet personality. It comprises a valuing of the interests of the collective over those of the self – or of individuals generally. This is made clear by the definition of the nature of a Soviet conscience, which goes thus: 'The essence of conscience is the self-regulation of behaviour on the basis of inner self-evaluation, comparing one's behaviour with the demands of social morality, social duty and the moral ideal.' (*Osnovy*: 213.) The Soviet individual's conscience is thus to suppress his own desires if they clash with those of the collective. It is held that, in fact, the ultimate interests of the individual will not be at variance with those of society. If, however, a situation arose where the person involved were to feel some conflict, then he must opt for the good of society and not for his own personal gain. Soviet theory, therefore, is opposed to views such as those of Talcott Parsons, which see individualistic action as a powerful motor for the advancement of modern industrial society.

*Discipline*

Discipline is the much praised virtue which helps the individual subordinate any selfish desires to the common good. The *Great Soviet Encyclopaedia* defines discipline as:

an essential condition for the normal existence of society; thanks to discipline, society takes on an ordered character which facilitates collective activity and the functioning of social organizations. . .In the contemporary stage of socialist and communist construction, the more complex organization of society and the scientific-technical revolution present heightened demands on the discipline, efficiency, responsibility and awareness of every member of society. (*BSE* 1972: Col. 942.)

This makes it quite clear that discipline is not regarded officially by the Soviets as part of an out-dated bourgeois Protestant ethic. On the contrary, its role is now even stronger. The Soviet authorities regard it as fundamental to a contemporary secular morality. It is not surprising, perhaps, to find that discipline is a characteristic encouraged by a society in which life is presented more as a striving to achieve long-term aims than as a drive to enjoy the pleasures of the moment; it is accordingly one of the major qualities desired for the New Soviet Man.

Ideally, self-discipline should present no problems. 'To a revolutionary Marxist there can be no contradiction between personal morality and the interests of the Party, since the Party embodies in its consciousness the very highest tasks and aims of mankind.' (Trotsky 1966:38.) The Soviet authorities reiterate that it is essential that a sense of discipline be internalised but, just in case, they insure against its non-emergence in individuals by a series of controls and punishments for undisciplined behaviour. Submission to controls is learnt in the classroom as preparation for submitting to social controls of a not dissimilar nature in adult life.

It is indispensable for the Soviet citizen's peace of mind that he either internalises a sense of self-discipline or else learns to subordinate himself without objection to the various forms of social control, because the Soviet state considers it necessary to regulate its citizens throughout a considerably wider range of activity than is deemed appropriate for state control in most Western democracies. Marcuse makes this very important point in *Soviet Marxism*:

Soviet ethics regard as *immoral* all actions and positions which run counter to or retard the alleged historical necessity. Many areas of human existence, which, in the Western tradition, are morally 'neutral', thus become subject to moral evaluation, for example, the area of scientific and artistic pursuits. . .Moreover the new historical basis of Soviet ethics also necessitates the application of moral judgements to 'neutral' areas in the private sphere – again through the medium of politics. A love relationship with a 'class enemy' is morally condemnable because it is politically wrong. (Marcuse 1971: 180.)

Just, indeed, are the *Great Soviet Encyclopaedia*'s claims that the Soviet citizen now needs a heightened sense of discipline – official demands on his life concern more spheres of his behaviour than ever before.

It should be noted here that the stress clearly remains mainly on right action and behaviour rather than on intellectual comprehension of the reasons making the behaviour necessary. It is clearly more desirable that one should discipline oneself because of a profoundly internalised understanding of the need for discipline but, as long as one is disciplined, it is not stressed as a matter of concern if this is mainly out of fear of the various state methods of social control.

## Love of work

The next Soviet virtue which must be considered is love of work. Dedication to the long-term Soviet goals which require the 'transformation of nature' necessarily implies, as a fundamental tenet of Communist morality, a reverence for labour. Hard and devoted work will be necessary to achieve Soviet Communist goals; it is through work for the community, therefore, no matter how unskilled this work may be, that a person proves his commitment to society and is thereby himself ennobled. Work is not only a glorious duty, it is also a joy. The Communist loves his work for, through it, he himself can play a part in the struggle to create the future Good Society. He also respects the work of all other citizens, having an equal regard for that of the labourer and of the professional man, both of which are indispensable. The Komsomol handbook on morality opens its chapter entitled 'A Conscientious Attitude to Labour' with a paean to the place of work in morality:

As A. S. Makarenko justly remarked, labour in Soviet society has stopped being simply an economic concept. Soviet people connect their ideas about the moral nature of any individual with his attitude to work. From a man's relationship with his work conclusions can be drawn about the degree of his moral maturity. This simple truth has become an inalienable feature of the Soviet person's perception of life. (*Osnovy*: 109.)

A man's attitude to his work thus assumes a central position in official Soviet morality. It occupies the place filled by humility for the Franciscan or by fighting prowess for a primitive tribesman – it is by this that a man is ultimately judged.

Respect for work is not, of course, a value unique to Soviet society. It is traditional to Western society. The Bible teaches that every man shall be rewarded according to his work. In *The Protestant Ethic and the Spirit of Capitalism*, Max Weber discusses the importance attached to labour in Protestant morality and attributes to it the development of capitalist society in the West (Weber 1971). But Soviet theorists claim that in their society work occupies a distinctive position. Marx argued that work in capitalist societies had become, for the masses, 'alienated' – it had become so heavy and specialised that it could bring no joy to the worker, while the profits it made did not go to the worker and his family but to an exploiting factory-owner. Soviet Marxism claims to have abolished alienated labour in that it has rid Soviet society of exploiting factory-owners. The profits from a man's labour are reaped by the state and are used for the good of the collective, of which, of course, all workers are benefiting members. Work, it is argued, too, is no longer alienated in Soviet conditions because of the liberation which man now experiences in his leisure time. He has now, increasingly, both the time and the opportunities to develop a wide range of interests and talents outside working hours. In these ways, the Soviet state maintains that the nature of work in its society is distinct from work in all non-socialist societies.[2] Soviet morality raises work even higher: work made men from apes and is the sovereign remedy for psychological and moral ills – indeed, it is central in all character-forming processes. Thus, in the Soviet presentation, the reverence for work in the Protestant ethic is merely a useful tool of the exploiting classes, whereas Soviet respect for work is based on equality and a mutual love within the collective. Nonetheless, the place of work in these two moralities does have a similarly important position. Just as Weber found love of labour fundamental to the Protestant ethic, so Marcuse sees Soviet morality as primarily a 'work-morale' (Marcuse 1971:19).

## Patriotism

The place of work is certainly basic to the theoretical framework of Soviet morality. In practice, however, it seems that patriotism is the virtue around which all the others revolve; this interpretation will be discussed in more depth when the actual content of Soviet writing for children is examined.

Patriotism in Soviet moral theory is treated as the ultimate form of collectivism, rather than a simple love for one's native heath.

Of foremost importance in a sense of patriotism is one's relationship with one's nation, one's awareness of one's own profound links with

[2] See *Osnovy kommunisticheskoy morali*, pp. 109–36, for a fuller discussion of the theoretical place of work in Soviet society.

it and a feeling for its concerns. Deeply mistaken is the man who considers that patriotism is only love for the place where one was born and grew up or who thinks that anyone can be a patriot if he loves his native town, and the settlement or village where he spent some treasured years. (*Osnovy*: 59.)

Once again, the social element is foremost. It is one's sense of being part of a mighty collective that is important, rather than a comparatively self-centred fondness for one's childhood haunts. Patriotism thus becomes a far broader concept in Soviet Russia. It certainly includes an exultation in the USSR's size and variety but it includes also the major political dimension of a firm belief in the Soviet people as the protagonists of the most progressive state in the world, pioneering the creation of a classless, un-exploitative and just society. Official Soviet patriotism thus at the same time stresses the legitimacy of the Communist Party's role as the only possible guiding force capable of leading society to the attainment of its goals. The Komsomol handbook on morality declares:

For over fifty years now, the Soviet land has traversed a path, the like of which the history of mankind has never before seen. A country of simple ploughs and firewood, where the majority of the population was oppressed by almost total illiteracy, has, in a brief historical span, turned into a leading industrial power. We are proud that it is our country which has become the powerful bastion of peace and progress, that there is no power in the world today which does not meet its match in our country. Pride in our socialist Mother-land inspires each Soviet citizen to do more and more for her future successes and to fulfil the tasks for this set by the 24th Congress of the Communist Party of the Soviet Union. (*Osnovy*: 64–5.)

In view of this crucial political and social aspect of patriotism in the USSR, the concept is usually qualified in Soviet sources by the adjective 'Soviet'. For example, the chapter on this theme in the Komsomol handbook is headed 'Soviet Patriotism and Socialist Internationalism' (*Osnovy*: 57–78; the sister concept of socialist internationalism is the next Soviet virtue discussed below). Constantly using the expression 'Soviet patriotism', as opposed to unqualified 'patriotism', serves to highlight the distinction which Soviet writers make between their form of patriotism – which is a virtue – and other versions of it – which can often be vices.

Genuinely patriotic traditions are distinct from the traditions of false patriotism of a nationalist character which try in all kinds of ways to fan and exploit the reactionary forces of imperialism. The former serve the cause of the construction of the most progressive social system in the world and of the defence of the revolutionary triumphs of those who labour. (*Osnovy*: 67.)

The Soviet concept of patriotism demands far more of its citizens than does patriotism in, say, Britain or the United States. Indeed, Soviet requirements can be likened to the demands on patriotism made in most states only in wartime conditions in that the emphasis is on the requirements of the state rather than the rights of the individual. The Soviet concept of patriotism demands no mere passive love of country or even of its government from its citizens but an active and dedicated involvement in the furthering of its political strength.

It is significant that the chapter on patriotism in the Komsomol morality handbook contains no reference to Marx or Engels whereas those on all the other virtues attempt to show at least some evidence for a Marxian authority. This is because Marx clearly saw patriotism as a dying characteristic – he saw class bonds as far more significant than national ones. The Soviet extolling of patriotism diverges sharply from the teaching of Marx who never believed in the possibility of 'Socialism in One Country' and therefore never wrote of the feeling appropriate to a citizen of a 'Socialist Motherland'. Moreover Lenin rarely mentions 'patriotism' or 'nationalism' without qualifying it with some derogatory adjective like 'loathsome' or 'petty-bourgeois', for example: 'Acknowledgement of internationalism in words but substituting it in practice, through propaganda, agitational and practical work, by petty-minded nationalism and pacifism is a very common phenomenon even not infrequently among those who now call themselves communists.' (Lenin 1963: Vol. 41, p. 165.) Soviet patriotism is, in fact, far closer to the view of the French sociologist Durkheim who wrote on moral education and who similarly saw patriotic feeling as potentially a noble expression of collectivist feeling. He considered that the form which patriotism was to take was the significant problem.

Everything depends, after all, on the way in which patriotism is conceived; it can take two very different forms. Insofar as it is centrifugal, so to speak, it points national activity outside its boundaries and prompts nations to encroach upon one another, *to stress their incompatibilities* [my italics]. Then they are put in a situation of conflict with commitments to mankind. Or conversely, the sentiment of patriotism may be altogether internally oriented, fixing upon the tasks of the internal improvement of society. In this case, it prompts all nations that have achieved comparable moral development to collaborate toward the same end. The first way is aggressive, military; the second is scientific, artistic, and, in a word, basically pacific. (Durkheim 1973:77.)

Unlike Marx, Durkheim foresaw only a limited disappearance of nationalist sentiment:

Doubtless, the specific national characters that currently obtain will die away. They will be replaced by others, probably greater ones. But however vast they may be, so far as we now can see, there will always be a plurality of states, whose collaboration will be required to realize the goals of mankind. (Durkheim 1973:78.)

This seems very much in accordance with the current official Soviet line on patriotism. This theory, with its notable political dimension, could in practice develop into either the centrifugal or the internally oriented patriotism described by Durkheim and, in looking at the content of writing for children, we shall discover which path it does in fact follow.

*Internationalism*

While Marx and Engels dismissed nationalist feeling, they stood for the development of a new spirit of proletarian internationalism. This would provide strength through the unity, not of a nation, but of a class common to all modern nations – the proletariat. In Soviet theory, such a spirit is held to be perfectly compatible with Soviet patriotic feeling. Indeed, as has been noted, the Komsomol handbook on morality discusses them both in the same chapter (*Osnovy*: 57–78). That the authorities are not insensible of the fact that some might find a certain contradiction between these two virtues is shown by the opening of the section on internationalism: 'Is love for one's people and one's Motherland compatible with respect and love for other people's?' (*Osnovy*: 69.) The answer given is like that of Durkheim in that it is all said to depend on the nature of the patriotic feeling, on whether it is a 'chauvinist mask of social oppression' or whether it is inspired by humanist ideals.

Nevertheless, lest there be any further confusion, firm limits are set on the nature of internationalism. Its foremost role is simply to support patriotism by re-approaching it from the angle that proper patriotism is not Russian or Ukrainian, say, but Soviet. 'The Soviet patriot, loving the one multi-national Soviet people, cannot permit the opposition of any one nation or nationality to another people under whatever flag it may manifest itself.' (*Osnovy*: 70.) Internationalism in this primary aspect (the patriotism of the multi-national Soviet state) is thus but another name for Soviet patriotism.

It does, however, also extend beyond the Soviet borders in order to defend the socialist cause elsewhere. 'The duty of the Soviet patriot consists also of giving all possible aid to workers of the capitalist world who are struggling against imperialism and to fighters in national liberation movements.' (*Osnovy*: 71.) Internationalism, in the Soviet context, is an exclusively political concept. Its interest in other countries depends wholly on their political situation. In this sense also, internationalism is subordinate to Soviet patriotism, for only if a foreign movement or nation acknowledges state socialist goals and the leading role of the USSR is it considered worthy of internationalist sympathy. Any other form of internationalist feeling is termed 'bourgeois cosmopolitanism' and is decried:

Cosmopolitanism is one further aspect of bourgeois ideology in the sphere of nationalist relations. Externally it seems in opposition to petty nationalism;[3] it totally scorns the national characteristics of this or that people, and strives to destroy any particular nationalist features of culture and to end any nationalist distinctions in state life, etc. However, behind these demands, which seem at first glance to be opposed to nationalism, is in fact hidden the disguised nationalism of the strongest nation, whose ruling clique, demanding from others the rejection of anything national, strives under this flag to impose its own customs and *mores* on to other peoples, thereby

[3] Throughout this passage the word 'nationalism' is used. This is pejorative – whereas 'patriotism' is reserved for laudable love for one's socialist Motherland, as discussed above.

seizing for itself the most important position among the nations. (*Osnovy*: 74.)[4]

Proletarian, or socialist, internationalism is held to be completely reconcilable with Soviet patriotism. They are reconciled by explaining socialist internationalism in a way which makes it little more than a broadening of the concept of Soviet patriotism (and clearly subordinate to it, were conflict ever to arise).

Durkheim, as we have seen, defends an internally oriented patriotism, but he attaches a much more profound importance to the question of a possible contradiction between the qualities of internationalism and patriotism than Soviet writings are prepared to countenance:

The problem of whether humanity ought to be subordinate to the state, cosmopolitanism to nationalism, is. . .one of those that arouses the greatest controversy today. There could not be a graver issue, since the orientation of moral activity will be altogether different and moral education understood in almost contrary fashion, depending on the group to which priority is accorded. (Durkheim 1973:75.)

Durkheim's own solution is that, in the ideal situation, cosmopolitan and nationalist goals will not clash. They will both be the goals of humanity:

Under these conditions, one must no longer ask whether the national ideal should be sacrificed for the ideals of mankind, since the two merge. Moreover, this fusion does not by any means imply that the particular national character is doomed to disappear. For each can have its own particular way of conceiving this ideal in accord with its own character, temperament and history. (Durkheim 1973:77–8.)

Soviet theory, as we have seen, certainly contends that the goals of Soviet patriotism and socialist internationalism have merged. But it is only through analysis of specific writing for children that we shall be able to gain an impression of whether the goals have merged into those of humanity or those of the Soviet state. The above discussion of the theory of Soviet patriotism and socialist internationalism would suggest that, just as internationalism is subordinated to patriotism in theory, so

---

[4] Ironically, this passage with the substitution of 'proletarian internationalism' for 'cosmopolitanism' and 'Soviet' for 'bourgeois' could be read as a neat summary of the views of a hostile Western political scientist on the pretensions of the Soviet 'ruling clique' *vis-à-vis its* client states.

humanity will be subordinated to the state in practice – but the evidence for and against this view will be examined in later chapters.

It must however be noted that proletarian internationalism cannot be dispensed with as a Soviet value. It must be upheld (in words at least) as part of the regime's apparatus of legitimation of itself as the heir of Marx, Lenin and the October Revolution for, unlike patriotism, this was an important value for the early Communists.

## Atheism

An important feature of Soviet morality is a scientific atheist world-view. From their materialist standpoint, Marxists, of course, reject religion for its idealist nature, its statement that 'In the beginning was the Word'. Religions are created by men, not God, and they arise and endure as a result of the productive relations obtaining in society at the time. Marx wrote in *Capital*:

The religious world is but the reflex of the real world. And for a society based upon the production of commodities, in which the producers in general enter into social relations with one another by treating their products as commodities and values whereby they reduce their individual private labour to the standard of homogeneous human labour – for such a society, Christianity with its *cultus* of abstract man, more especially in its bourgeois developments, Protestantism, Deism, etc., is the most fitting form of religion. (Quoted in *K. Marx and F. Engels on Religion* 1955:134.)

For historical as well as philosophical reasons, the early Bolshevik party was opposed to religion. In tsarist Russia, the Orthodox Church had become almost fully identified with the autocracy and the ruling classes who, through it, managed to preserve the *status quo*. Peasants and workers passively accepted suffering and exploitation largely because of a faith in God and an eventual heavenly respite.[5] Religion was the power-reinforcing myth for the exploiting class and the comforting illusion for the exploited and alienated.

Soviet atheism keeps close to the original Marxist approach to atheism – and Marx made his position very clear on this one

[5] For a non-Marxist historian's statement of this, see Florinsky, *Russia*, Vol. 2, pp. 798–9, New York, 1966.

particular aspect of morality: the Soviet collection of extracts from which we quoted above, *K. Marx and F. Engels on Religion*, comprises 343 pages on the subject. In view of this, it is perhaps surprising that the Komsomol handbook on morality does not devote a whole chapter to the specific question of the Soviet need for an atheist world-view. On the other hand, it can perhaps be explained by the not insubstantial survival of religious belief in the USSR after over half a century of Soviet power. An application of Marx's interpretation of religion's comfort for suffering people to the contemporary situation might raise questions unacceptable for public discussion in the eyes of the leadership. This may provide an important reason why religion is mainly referred to indirectly in the Komsomol handbook. Religious teaching in the West, for example, is dismissed as merely a colourful cloak of fine phrases about goodness, justice and love hiding a reality based solely on self-interest. In general, the approach to atheism in the Komsomol handbook is to start from the Soviet interpretations of society and history and, in passing, to note that these do not permit of the existence of God; it does not seem to feel the need to set out arguments specifically to 'prove' atheism. In other words, it starts from an affirmation, not a negation. Of particular relevance to the discussion of religion and atheism is a chapter in the Komsomol handbook, entitled 'The Purpose of Life and Happiness for the Soviet Citizen'. The Soviet authors here reject religious answers to the question of life's purpose and give secular alternatives. They dismiss any metaphysical after-life but say that future perfection on *this* earth – in the shape of Communist society – is the true inspiration for the dedicated life and the happiness of the Soviet citizen (*Osnovy*: 177–82.)

Atheism, like all the other virtues discussed above, lends support to this Communist purpose – indeed, they are all legitimated as official virtues simply because they do so. Suppression of 'negative' personal inclinations through self-discipline is justified as furthering the goal of Communism. Similarly, dedication to the collective and love of work are all shown as helping the cause. Patriotism and internationalism likewise do not refer as much to adherence to places and peoples as to the Soviet system of government and political thought. Atheism is an affirmation of Marxist faith in science and progress and is a rejection of the other major ways of

interpreting the world which prevail in potentially hostile countries. Thus all the Soviet virtues depend for their legitimation on
the Soviet purpose.


## Some conclusions

The personal qualities exalted are, in fact, those which, if possessed
by the citizens of a society, make them much more amenable to
control from above. The worker who feels that he must work
diligently and must love his Motherland and who believes he
should practise self-sacrifice and self-discipline will be far less
trouble to the authorities than one who has been brought up in an
atmosphere of always being on guard lest his 'rights' are being
infringed. The former citizens will be far more likely to aid the
speedy economic progress of their society than the latter – but they
also can be more easily abused by those in authority if the use of
power is not subject to effective political control from below or
scrupulously guided by the genuine devotion of the political
leaders themselves to Communist goals.

The concept of legitimation here seems very relevant in that it
has already become clear that the effective inculcation of Soviet
morality both depends upon and reinforces the Soviet legitimation
system. In other words, it offers a rationale for the system as it
stands and, more importantly, encourages the development of that
unanimous active involvement in the social and political system
which constitutes a central part of the regime's claim to a unique
legitimacy.

Such an approach results in a set of values that are far from
those normally associated with people who claim to be revolutionary. In Eysenck's politics-and-personality questionnaire, it is
termed 'conservative' to believe that 'I stand by my country
right or wrong' is a saying which expresses a fundamentally
desirable attitude and 'radical' to consider that occupation by a
foreign power is better than war. Tolerance towards criminals,
rejection of authority from above and sexual permissiveness,
those are the characteristics which Eysenck finds in the West,
correlate with left-wing political attitudes (Eysenck 1958:304–7).
Using this scaling of values, the official Soviet 'ideal man' is

conservative rather than radical – for he is encouraged to be intolerant towards the rebellious, to accept the authorities' rulings unquestioningly, to use self-discipline in sexual and other social behaviour, and to commit himself to his country right or wrong. The values stressed clearly support conservation rather than revolutionary innovation.

Writing as a Communist in the Germany of the 1930s, Wilhelm Reich suggested various means of making young people politically aware. Some of his methods are used in the Soviet Union today. 'The disposition to become attached to a leader or ideas which one finds among young people' is clearly exploited; so also are the urge to dance and the love of sport and military parades which, Reich felt, could be used by skilful political groups and certainly are used both by the Soviet school and the Komsomol in their leisure organising activities (Reich 1933:28–31). Significantly, however, one of his major methods – ensuring lack of inhibition in the sex life of young people – is not used. Reich felt that early toilet-training, prohibition of masturbation and a puritanical sexual life in general were advantageous to the Right, encouraging obedience rather than lively spontaneity (Reich 1933:41–2). As might be expected, and will be confirmed later, the official contemporary Soviet approach to sex is puritanical rather than Reichian. Whether one accepts Reich's logic or not, this serves to highlight the fact that the Soviet value-system stresses obedience rather than 'lively spontaneity'.

There is, indeed, little in the Soviet set of values, beyond the atheist viewpoint, which would have shocked a Victorian public schoolmaster or would shock the contemporary teacher at Andover or Exeter in the US. In many respects, the Soviet virtues resemble the Protestant ones. But the fact must not be ignored that these values, despite their connections with traditional Western thought, do have particular Soviet expressions and applications which are worthy of study. These often involve significant shifts in emphasis – we have already noted, for example, how 'patriotism' in modern Russian implies a rather different concept from contemporary English 'patriotism'. Many more distinctions will become evident on examining the teaching of Soviet values in practice. It is therefore important to stress their similarity in broad outline, rather than in detail, to the components of Western value-systems. Their similarity in broad outline to such 'philosophies of life' as the Protestant ethic can be summed up in the phrase, 'subordination of pleasure to duty'. The self-controlling virtues stressed are broadly the same, whether legitimated by a heavenly after-life or a future Communist world. And, if successfully inculcated, their effects are much the same – the creation of citizens who are comparatively easily controllable by authority.

## Soviet theory of socialisation

Soviet socialisation theory follows from a vision of man as being ultimately significant in group situations. The Soviet authorities clearly hope to control moral behaviour by means of the power which the opinions of the child's fellows exercise over him rather than by any exploration of his *id*.

The use of this method is made explicit in a Soviet consideration of the part played by shame in character-education:

In my opinion, the feeling of shame becomes a young person. From their earliest childhood, long before their first acquaintance with the multiplication table, little girls and boys learn the significance of the word 'ashamed'. 'Why aren't you ashamed of yourself?' This rhetorical question is frequently asked of a person who has not yet learnt to walk or talk. Everything that is condemned by people is shameful: breaking toys, insulting a weak person, telling tales, going around in a slovenly way. A developed sense of shame obviously implies that its owner treasures public opinion, takes it into account and is interested in the reaction of those around him to his actions and words. . .Shame does not allow us to slip up morally; it protects us from incorrect deeds. (Indursky *et al.* 1972:100.)

This statement seems very idealistic in its assertion that acting in accordance to others' opinions always leads to moral behaviour; however, it does demonstrate Soviet adherence to the concept that our characters are moulded by the attitudes, approving or disapproving, of those around us. In other words, moral behaviour is, like all other behaviour, conditioned, and the conditioning mechanism is often the approval or disapproval of one's parents or peers. Soviet methods of child-rearing certainly owe much to Pavlov. He is acknowledged in a textbook called *Child Psychology* written for students at pedagogical institutes:

Continuing the working out of problems on which first steps were made brilliantly by J. Larnarque and C. Darwin, the Russian physiologists I. M. Sechenov, A. A. Ukhtomsky, N. E. Vvedensky and, most especially, I. P. Pavlov discovered the laws of adaptation, the laws of the higher nervous system. This research gave a genuinely materialist and scientific explanation of the reflex (psychic) behaviour of animals and its specific characteristics in mankind. (Lyublinskaya 1971:63–4.)

The textbook which follows is indeed based on Pavlovian work on conditioning.

The following Soviet definition of socialisation rests on the idea of children being gradually conditioned by adults. This extract is cited at length for the interest of its comments on 'bourgeois sociology's' definition of socialisation:

The essence of socialisation...is expressed in the well-known statement of R. E. Park: 'Man is not born man but becomes one in the process of education.' The child immediately after birth is a biological being which turns into a person, or a reasoning being able to work and create, only through adults influencing him through training him and 'introducing' him to systems of values and patterns of behaviour. Thus socialisation must above all be considered as the process of becoming a social being...

In bourgeois sociology, socialisation is often understood in a one-sided way – as the passive acceptance into his own behaviour system by the individual of a group of sanctioned routines. Whereas in reality, man does not only accept and make his own certain patterns of behaviour, he also actively works on them, either confirming and consolidating them or else rejecting them. In this he shows himself not only as an individual but also as a socially active being. In class society socialisation inevitably has a class character. Along with assimilating a number of general cultural values and norms of behaviour, the individual learns the values and norms of specific classes.

Socialisation is thus the process of inclusion of the growing generation into the system of social roles determined by the socio-economic structure of a given society by means of the active assimilation and development of the existing system of values and norms of behaviour. (Turchenko 1973:17–18.)

The author's criticism that 'bourgeois' writers do not take account of the class content of socialisation can certainly be levelled at Freud and many other theorists in the West but, true to pluralist diversity, there *are* theorists currently being published in the West who approach the topic from a class angle.[6]

Since Soviet child psychology rests on Pavlovian theory, it is no surprise that in Soviet children's literature no naughty behaviour is ever allowed to bring any pleasant results to its practitioners and that it is always followed by some appropriate form of punishment – at very least, by an uneasy conscience. It is hoped that naughty behaviour will thus be vicariously conditioned out of the young readers. Similarly, good behaviour – that felt to be appropriate to the future Builder of Communism – is consistently shown to be a source of personal contentment, bringing joy through the approval of parents, classmates, Pioneer leaders and, more abstractly, Lenin and the Motherland themselves.

There is no room in Soviet theory for Freud and the psychoanalysts. They are too inward-looking to be reconcilable with Pavlov or social group theory. The *Great Soviet Encyclopedia* in fact condemns Freud's work thus: 'The biologisation of man's demands, the interpretation of all sorts of human activity as instinctual phenomena, led to Freud's teaching becoming not only one-sided but also anti-scientific.' (*BSE* 1957: Vol. 45, p. 583.) Thus we can expect to find no children's stories suggestive in any way of the conflicts central to Freudian psychology. Indeed, there is very little room in Soviet children's literature for any form of conflict at all, as we shall see. The one 'correct' way of behaviour is clear, leaving nothing at all to be said in favour of any other approach.

The fact that the major part of the socialisation process in a monistic society like the USSR is purposive rather than largely fortuitous, as in pluralistic societies, means that Soviet theory also has to be purposive and usable to further the desired goal. Thus it is that only those theories which tie in together and somehow fit the overall world-view can be accepted in a monistic society. Of course, Soviet theorists in all fields debate and disagree – but within a narrower framework. The one official Soviet theory on any fundamental matter is, in public at least, unquestionably accepted, leaving room for lively argument only over questions of application and practical detail. As regards children's literature, this means that, whereas Western pluralist theorists disagree about

6 See, for example, Wilhelm Reich's works.

basic issues – should writing for children be didactic or not? should children be allowed to read about violence? and so on – Soviet scholars, on the other hand, tend to take as read the approved answer to these questions – literature must be didactic, etc. – but to discuss more specific questions of methodology – how can fiction teach most effectively? is X's method of describing violence as educative as Y's? Sometimes, of course, argument over questions of detail concerning methods can be little more than a disguised form of conflict over more basic issues concerning ultimate goals. Thus debates over the best ways of depicting Lenin to Little Octobrists can, at their deeper level, be an expression of differing attitudes to the more fundamental questions of deliberate myth-formation.

One important point on this theme of socialisation in pluralistic and monistic societies relates to the degree of conflict in values and norms demanded by the various deliberately socialising agents in each type of society. In a pluralistic society, the demands made on a child are both fewer in number and more various. One set of values is taught to him in school, another at home, another on television, another at Scout meetings, another in his comics, and these different sets of values are often, at least in part, contradictory. The situation is often even more complex – for all is not unified even within a given agency of socialisation. Individual teachers at one school, for example, may present quite different views of the world; the child at the comprehensive may find the values he learns there completely in conflict with those of his sister at the convent. The point has already been made that the demands which socialisation makes on the Soviet child in his monistic society are as unified as possible. The values and norms fostered by schools, television, Pioneer meetings and children's magazines are the same. It is hoped that those taught at home also coincide. Of course, in reality all differences cannot be eradicated. Despite the strict controls on teachers, some of their own individual views must occasionally emerge. Family values are even harder to shape from above and there is no doubt that some children encounter at home values and norms that are different from, sometimes also alien to, those officially prescribed for the Builder of Communism. Nevertheless, the degree of conflict amongst the various socialising agents in a monistic society is remarkably slight and the values to be found in the children's literature examined in ensuing chapters are remarkably consistent with those promoted by other officially guided agents of socialisation.

In the Soviet Union, as has been seen, official concern for character-education is strong; it is accordingly centrally controlled and planned to the greatest possible extent, thus reflecting the nature of Soviet society as a whole. Every attempt is made to guide the socialising agencies of school, home, peer group and mass media in the same desired direction. The fact that this is done so systematically and thoroughly from above makes it possible to generalise meaningfully about deliberate socialisation in the USSR in a way that would be impossible for the more diverse societies of Britain or the USA – and in a way that is especially remarkable when one considers the geographical and cultural variety of the country.

# Part II

## SOVIET CHILDREN'S LITERATURE

# 3

# Production and dissemination

The importance of the children's press has long been acknowledged in Russia. The nineteenth-century radical critic, V. G. Belinsky (1811–48), wrote: 'Children's books are written in order to educate character, and character-education is of great importance; it decides a person's destiny.' (Belinsky 1948:19.) The revolutionary democrats, N. G. Chernyshevsky (1828–89) and N. A. Dobrolyubov (1838–61) were also important critics in the Belinsky tradition: like him, they looked on children's literature as providing textbooks for life (Chernyavskaya 1971:16–21). It was not the left wing alone in nineteenth-century Russia that attached a large educative significance to children's books. The tsarist censorship saw to it that works were published for young people which would instruct them in the correct attitudes to autocracy and Orthodoxy. E. Dymman, for example, wrote a book called *The Science of Life or How the Young Person should Live in Society*, which maintained that 'one must bow low and show the greatest respect' to the man of means (Chernyavskaya 1971:17). The great nineteenth-century Russian literary masters also had a respect for children's literature and did not consider it beneath their dignity to write for children – Pushkin, Chekhov and Tolstoy, among others, all produced delightful works for youngsters.

The Soviet regime, therefore, inherited a respect for children's literature and a faith in its educative role. Krupskaya reiterated this approach, fashioning it to the new context: 'The children's book is one of the most powerful weapons of the socialist character-education of the growing generation. Through children's books must be laid the foundation of the materialist world-view of the growing generation. This is a great and important task and a task that can be fulfilled.' (Krupskaya 1956:249–50.)

The aim of the present chapter is to examine how the children's press and publishing in the Soviet Union today is organised to fulfil its socialising tasks. It concludes by examining the writing of children's literature in the light of the state of writing for adults in the Soviet Union today.

## Publishing houses

The importance of the children's press was officially recognised by the Party as early as 1919 when it established an Institute of Children's Reading. In the 1920s, Soviet writing for children was marked by its variety; theory in this field 'was characterised by a large number of small groups, engaging in polemics among themselves on the pages of numerous literary journals' (Chernyavskaya 1971:29). Centralisation throughout Soviet society at the end of the decade affected children's literature too. In 1928, the Party issued a resolution on 'Measures for the Improvement of the Press for Young People and Children' (*O partiynoy* 1954:377–9), which sought to increase and improve publishing for children.

Despite this resolution, the Party leadership was still dissatisfied with the state of children's literature five years later and in 1933 decided that some drastic reorganisation was necessary. There were then about sixty organisations producing books for children in a still somewhat uncoordinated way. Maxim Gor'ky and Samuel Marshak, a children's writer and translator of Shakespeare and Burns, prepared plans for the creation of one large-scale publishing house. Accordingly, in September 1933, the Central Committee of the Party authorised the establishment of such a children's publishing house to be called *Detgiz*.

At the First Congress of the Writers' Union, only a year later, Gor'ky was to speak with pride of the greater attention which was now being paid to writing for children. The prestige of the field increased in the 1930s, and the children's press suffered less than other areas from paper shortages. Even during the Second World War, the Leningrad children's magazine *Koster*, for example, missed only one issue – and even that went out over the radio.

In 1963, *Detgiz* was renamed *Detskaya literatura* ('Children's Literature') and it is still the main publishing house for children –

although altogether approximately 150 organisations publish books, periodicals or newspapers for children. *Detskaya literatura* has a Council of Editors which consists of writers, educationalists and scholars whose purpose is to supervise the production of books of suitable instructional and entertainment value. There is also a Council of Artists which is concerned with illustrative material and with the format of books. *Detskaya literatura* has won international recognition for its work; in 1958, for example, it was awarded a gold medal at an international book exhibition in Brussels. *Molodaya Gvardiya* is a sister publishing house aiming at older children and adolescents. *Uchpedgiz* is a third institution publishing for young people. Its output is educational and thus largely aimed at schoolchildren.

## Writers

Writing for children is officially highly respected since its educative role is recognised as being essential for the character-education of the New Soviet Man. I. A. Kairov, a previous Minister of Education of the Russian Soviet Federated Socialist Republic (RSFSR), was confirming the official prestige attached to the profession of children's author when he said:

We men and women of the pedagogical sciences, along with the teachers, consider the writer of children's books our faithful ally. We all have the task of educating a generation that is sound and sane both physically and morally, a generation that is bold, honest and truthful, has integrity of character, a strong will, a firm spirit and a zest for work. (*Sovetskaya detskaya literatura* 1952.)

Out of 7270 members of the Union of Writers of the USSR in May 1971, 206 were classified as children's writers (*Pyaty s''ezd* 1972:186). The Union[1] has, since 1959, had its own Committee on Children's and Young People's Literature. The Committee consists of thirty-one members; its present chairmen are S. Mikhalkov and V. Luks.

Valdis Luks has been one of the chairmen since the Committee

---

[1] For a detailed discussion of the structure of the Union of Writers, see the doctoral thesis of John Murray, *The Union of Soviet Writers*, Birmingham, 1973.

was formed. He is a Latvian poet and writer for children who was born in 1905 and originally trained in law at Riga University. The other, perhaps more famous, chairman of the Committee is Sergey Mikhalkov, a Russian writer, poet and dramatist. His background is more consistently literary. Born in Moscow in 1913, he studied at the Gor'ky Institute of World Literature. Like many children's writers he has direct links with the educational world. He has been a corresponding member of the Academy of Pedagogical Sciences since 1965.

It is, in fact, instructive to look at the backgrounds of some of the most widely published contemporary Soviet children's writers. Lev Kassil', Natalya Zabila and Valentina Oseyeva, for example, have all either had teaching experience or are members of the Academy of Pedagogical Sciences; these career features can, of course, represent very different backgrounds but both suggest a primary concern with education. A delegate from the Children's Book Centre in Moscow (an institution to be discussed below) declared at the Second World Conference on Soviet Children's Literature in 1970 that the children's writer is not only an artist but also a pedagogue; this quite frequently seems literally to be the case. Some other notable writers have had training in other branches of the arts and humanities. Nikolay Nosov studied first at the Kiev Art Institute and then at the State Institute of Cinematography in Moscow. Agniya Barto was a student at the Moscow Theatrical School. Korney Chukovsky was a Doctor of Philological Sciences (he was also awarded a D.Litt. from Oxford in 1962).

There is constant official emphasis on the educative role of children's literature. One could therefore assume that the greatest care went into checking the ideological content of what was published for children, and into ensuring that only the most committed Communists were permitted to write for young people. This is not, in fact, the whole story. There is no doubt that the most widely published material for children − I have school readers and youth magazines especially in mind − contains only work that is officially accepted as morally sound. Nevertheless, there is evidence that children's writers enjoy a surprisingly greater freedom from control than do adult writers. Laurens van der Post noted this point when he met a children's writer on his journeys in Russia giving this relative freedom as the explanation why many notable Soviet authors choose to let their fantasies loose on writing fairy-tales for children (van der Post 1964:276).

Evidence that more can find its way into a child's than an adult's book is occasionally found in the content of individual works if not in school readers. A young boy's wretchedness at a summer camp peopled largely by bullies, snobs and unattainable girls is vividly described by one children's novel which succeeded in being printed in an edition of a hundred thousand in 1971 (Artomonov 1971).

Some of the relative lack of control that there is over a children's writer stems from the very nature of his genre. Fantasy is so much a permitted feature of his style that he has easy scope for allegory. Korney Chukovsky, for example, wrote a long and amusing poem for children called *Mukha-Tsokotukha* which is generally accepted as having a deeper level of social and political comment. It tells of an ordinary fly who is attacked by a malicious old spider (commonly taken as Stalin). All the fly's comrades hide in dark corners as they are too afraid to help (Chukovsky 1967).

Throughout the Soviet period, writing for children has provided work for authors who felt too restricted by the less flexible demands of writing for adults. A number of experimental writers who were involved in a 'left art' movement called 'oberiu' in Leningrad in the late 1920s, earned a basic living by writing for children. Only in that genre was their inventiveness and originality of approach acceptable (Milner-Gulland 1970:65–75).

The most significant reason for the comparative freedom extended to children's writers is clearly the greater need to amuse which there is felt to be when writing for children. In part, this reflects a simple non-machiavellian love of children which is, in my opinion, encouraged by the Soviet atheist philosophy. In a sense, Soviet children are God. Soviet man does not labour for the sake of divine recognition but to bring about a better life for his children. Already today, Soviet children are a very privileged group in society; in terms of facilities or attention, nothing is too good for them. As children obviously like amusing stories, let them have them occasionally. The Soviet adult does not require such pampering. But there is also, probably, a certain sugaring-of-the-pill idea in the minds of the authorities. The amused, happy child is certainly the most amenable one and the one most likely to accept the patriotic and collectivist messages in his stories. The necessary balance between the educative and the entertaining was summed up by Agniya Barto in a speech to the Third Congress of Writers of the RSFSR:

Gor'ky considered that one must talk 'amusingly' with children. Amusingly and seriously? Does not one contradict the other? Not in any way! Serious in thought and content but amusing and diverting in form. Then – and only then – will even the most complex philosophical thought become accessible to the young reader. (Aksenova 1971:5.)

This is a refreshing statement of the Soviet position.

Whether the amusing content of a particular children's author's work is predominantly inspired by the desire to make a child laugh or by the aim of educating him effectively, the fact remains that the less stern controls on writing for children have permitted the publication of some delightful works with a freedom of expression wider than that possible in adult literature. Many of the most notable of Soviet writers have in their time with evident enjoyment produced works for children – for example, Tvardovsky, Paustovsky, Sholokhov, Katayev, Mayakovsky and Tikhonov. Other writers, such as Chukovsky and Marshak, who are remembered primarily for their works for children, have written for children with a vitality and originality that equal only the very best of the works of socialist realist writers for adults.

Having raised this very important point with regard to Soviet children's authors of which we shall be reminded frequently in the following chapters, let us now return to a more detailed discussion of the work of the Committee for Children's and Young People's Literature attached to the Soviet Union of Writers.

When the Committee was formed, it was explicitly intended to work in close collaboration with the appropriate departments of the Komsomol, the Ministries of Education in the republics, the Ministry of Culture of the USSR, the creative artists' unions, publishing houses and the editorial boards of periodicals and newspapers (*Pyaty s"ezd* 1972:186). One of the very first tasks given it in 1959 and 1960 was to discuss the problems of producing new books which would help the Party in the character-education of the Builder of Communism (*Literaturnaya gazeta*, 17 March 1960).

Its work is now extensive. In his report to the Fifth Congress of the Union of Writers in 1971, Mikhalkov told of yet more discussion of the question of Communist character-education through children's literature – quite explicitly seen as a matter of fundamental importance to the Soviet Union. The Committee had devoted much time in preparation for the Lenin Jubilee to the subject of books about Lenin. It had recommended, in particular, that the Union of Writers in the republics should set up commissions to work on books about Lenin. The fact that the appearance of books on Lenin is thus planned, rather than being a spontaneous expression of admiration for a historical leader, of course implies a deliberate attempt to manipulate the way children look on Lenin. When the content of writing for children is later considered, it will be necessary to observe the treatment of Lenin in particular in order to assess whether it does not in fact contain elements of the Platonic technique of myth-making. The Committee, too, had studied both books for the pre-school age group and the work of children's writers for cinema, theatre, television and radio. Seminars had been held on children's drama, the hero in contemporary children's literature, the translation of fiction, and the artistic presentation of the children's books (*Pyaty s"ezd* 1972:186–7). Its work consists solely of debates and report writing. In conjunction with the Press Committee (attached to the USSR Council of Ministers), it was responsible for setting up a children's book pavilion at an International Book Exhibition held to mark the Lenin centenary. Every year in April it organises a Children's Book Week when there are exhibitions, readings and the publication of appropriate press articles throughout the Soviet Union. The Committee has constantly to take on new forms of work. In 1971, Mikhalkov reported that letters had been sent to the editorial boards of all the leading magazines and newspapers in the republics requesting that discussion should be stimulated on the subject of children's literature and, moreover, that all material printed by them on the subject in the last two years should be sent to the Committee for analysis. The Committee helps in the critical work done on textbook drafts as well as on literary productions. In 1971 it was in the process of setting up two-month courses for authors specialising in writing for children and young people (*Pyaty s"ezd* 1972:188). John Murray points out that though its bureaucratic controls can be destructive to creativity, the Union does provide facilities and privileges for writers and its influence must certainly not be dismissed as wholly negative (Murray 1973). To sum up, the work of the Committee is extensive and thorough, demonstrating the seriousness with which children's literature is treated in the Soviet Union.

## Children's libraries

Many Soviet children's writers will become known to children largely through libraries. The total number of libraries has declined in the period 1960–70. This is because there is a trend towards larger libraries run by the Ministry of Culture and away from separate smaller libraries in schools. The total holdings – in the case of both independent and institutional libraries – has, however, increased dramatically over this period.

Like writers, libraries have received official accolades for their role in the process of character-education. A resolution of the Central Committee of the CPSU of 22 September 1958 declared that the most important function of Soviet libraries was 'the active aid which they can give the Party and state in educating, in heightening the communist consciousness and in raising the cultural and technical level of the Soviet people' (Frumin 1969:5). The resolution continued by setting the following task: 'to accomplish the transformation of libraries into real centres for the mass propaganda of political, general educational, scientific, technical, agricultural and professional knowledge, into resolute agencies in the party-minded organisation for the Communist character-education of the people' (Frumin 1969:5).

Each library is advised by a council. The size of the council may vary from nine to forty-five members, each of whom is encouraged to take part in the daily work of the library. In the case of children's libraries, the council is elected at a meeting of parents and other interested citizens. Its members are teachers, librarians, Pioneer leaders and members of the Komsomol *aktiv* or of the local school or Pioneer council. The council thus has close links, both through its membership and through frequent meetings, with the school and Pioneer systems. In the Soviet Union, libraries can now be awarded the honorific appellation 'Library of Excellence'; library workers and readers are urged to try to win this title for their own library. To merit it, a library is expected to show 'daily Marxist–Leninist help' to readers in raising their Communist consciousness and their cultural and technical level (Frumin 1969:85).

Librarians are trained on four-year courses at higher-educational-level Institutes and lower-level Technicums. At both of these, there are special faculties of children's librarianship in which the students study literature, pedagogics and child psychology as well as library work and cataloguing.

The above has dealt either with injunctions about *what should be*, or with *what is* only at the level of simple quantitative data. What in practice is a Soviet children's library really like? In August 1971, the writer paid a visit to a children's library of sixty thousand books in the Lermontov *raion* (district/ward) of Moscow. A thousand younger (pre-school and primary school) and a thousand older children (i.e. pupils older than ten) were registered. The librarian's welcome was warm and she willingly – even enthusiastically – answered all questions put to her.

The section of the library for the youngest children was very colourful. This area was for the pre-school age group and for pupils of the first four classes. The books were divided according to the year group for which they were held to be suitable though this did not mean that children were not allowed to choose from outside 'their own year'. Within each year, the books were subdivided by theme – for example: 'About the Part of Our Native Land', 'For Soviet Power', 'Youngsters' Achievements', 'Fairy-tales', 'About Machines and Things'. Most children usually chose books from several categories and were encouraged to do so. Among the youngest children the fairy-tales category was the most popular, but little boys soon developed a taste for war stories. Girls read stories about nature and animals more eagerly than did boys. The librarian made these assertions about reading preferences according to sex as if they were a matter of innately different tastes.[2]

---

[2] In an examination below of the content of children's reading books, it will be seen, however, that the sexual stereotypes presented in them actually

Also in this section of the library for youngest readers were three special exhibitions. One was about Lenin, entitled 'The Most Human Human'. A scrapbook about Lenin made by the children themselves was displayed. It was mainly about the childhood of 'Volodya' (the diminutive form of Lenin's given name). Also exhibited was a model made by the young readers of the grass hut in Razliv, over the Finnish border, where Lenin hid just before the October Revolution. The second exhibition was called 'The Pioneer's Summer'; it displayed mainly stories of camps in the country. The third was headed 'Check What You Believe'; it was a collection of anti-religious books. Such exhibitions are changed every two or three weeks. They are used to direct the children's attention to books which the librarian or some higher official considers that they are not reading sufficiently of their own accord. The youngest children apparently read about Lenin willingly themselves but older ones needed some encouragement. 'Alas,' said the librarian, 'what children like to read and what they need to read is not always the same!'

For children older than ten, the library is laid out like an adult library. Fiction is arranged alphabetically by author. The child is now allowed much more independence of choice of book; the librarian only offers help if the child is looking lost. There are special catalogues for the children to use themselves. These consist of gaily coloured cards decorated with an appropriate picture and a brief account of the book concerned. Bibliographies for the use of children are also provided.

Children may keep a book for ten days. A list is kept of what each registered reader has borrowed, his comments on each book and whether he chose the book himself. If he doesn't visit the library for a spell, postcards will be sent to him or his parents, or he will be telephoned at home to urge him to use the library again. A careful check is thus kept on each borrower's habits. The information may be used by teachers and Pioneer leaders, as well as the librarian, if they wish to investigate their charges' leisure reading. Readers are often encouraged to write reviews of what they have read or to draw appropriate pictures. This is done in particular in connection with the books in the special exhibi-

encourage socialisation to a sexual division of labour along the lines represented by these reading tastes.

tions. Librarians also keep in touch with the children's opinions through discussing books with them. Such talks take place on both an individual and a group basis. Frequently there are meetings on some particular theme (e.g. 'The First of May' or the work of one particular author); there will then be readings and an informal discussion on the theme.

Links with the school are close. In their first year, pupils are taken on a school excursion to their local library. Librarians are supposed to visit neighbourhood schools regularly and talk to the pupils about new books and about their reading tastes. Each class teacher is expected to provide a list of recommended out-of-school reading for her class; a copy of each list (which is compiled by the individual teacher who is guided by many official publications) is supposed to be given to the librarian. The books recommended must be listed by categories. The librarian has to check that each child is choosing from a sufficiently wide range of categories; if, for example, someone is reading only adventure stories, then he will be guided into a broader selection.

The librarian at the library visited learned about new children's books from the pages of the periodical called *Detskaya literatura* and also from the children's magazines and newspapers.

If a child spoils a book, the library usually makes him replace it. Such 'disrespect for state property' was common, grumbled the librarian. Children nowadays, she complained, had grown accustomed to being given so much that they did not appreciate it. They were unaware of what life could be like and had been like only twenty-five years before, during the war, when even basic food and clothing had been unobtainable; 'not realising how fortunate they were', they acted 'like hooligans' and tore and scribbled in books. No evidence of this was witnessed while at the library, however; the borrowers who were seen came carrying their books neatly wrapped in newspaper.

The overall impression obtained of this library was of a light, cheerful place which was busy with far more activities than just the lending of books. A genuine concern for the young readers seemed to motivate the librarian, who gave the impression of taking a systematic interest in each of them as individuals.

The writer also paid a visit in February 1974 to another children's library, this time in Leningrad. The director of the library was, again, most welcoming and explained the administration of her library with charm and warmth. The library was that of the Dzerzhinsky region of the city which has a child population of eleven to twelve thousand, of whom eight-and-a-half thousand were members of the library visited. The region also had sixteen school libraries – one for each school (three of these schools were 'special schools' with additional training in a foreign language or mathematics).

In each school library there were 'one-and-a-half' workers. Thirteen people worked in this regional library, however, and eleven of these were trained librarians. Those who had not yet completed their training had paid day-release leave once a week for study; these were teachers who had decided to retrain as librarians. Also helping in the library were students from the librarianship faculty of the Leningrad Institute of Culture. In their third and fourth years, they were required to do practical work in such a library as this. Occasionally pensioners would also help with a couple of hours' work a week on, say, the cataloguing of new accessions.

An important feature of this library was that it was the methods centre for all the children's libraries of the Dzerzhinsky ward. Once a week, all the chief librarians from the region assembled there to discuss the progress of the Plan and the various problems encountered. The Soviet State Plan is not limited to the control of economic affairs but embraces also the work of social and cultural institutions including libraries; it covers not only financial aspects of library administration but also provides norms of how often the average reader should visit the library and how many books he should read. Each reader, according to the Plan of 1974, should visit the library at least ten times a year and should borrow at least twenty books. Thus part of the work of the methods meeting was to ascertain whether such norms were being fulfilled and, if not, how this could be remedied. Work on the catalogues, on acquisitions (seven thousand volumes a year; the library's stock was ninety-eight thousand volumes) and various types of work with the children beyond the mere provision of books were also included in the Plan.

As well as regularly meeting librarians from within the Dzerzhinsky region, the director once or twice a month met the other Leningrad librarians from libraries run by the Ministry of Culture (as opposed to those attached to schools – which come under the Ministry of Education), of which there are about fifty in the city. There was considerable competition amongst these librarians to show that their individual library was encouraging the most extensive and varied reading habits and that it provided the most wide-ranging activities for the children.

The staff of the library also engaged in research from time to time. For example, in the late 1960s, they had conducted a survey on readers and their various sources of information about books (teachers, librarians, bibliographic apparatus, parents and friends). Of these, they had found parents to be the least satisfactory. To combat this, they had intensified the campaign for work among parents. They had laid on a course of eight lectures for parents on various aspects of reading for children. Initially, forty-five to fifty parents had attended but the numbers had quickly dwindled. As an experiment, only fathers had been invited to one evening; most of those invited had come.

Co-operation with schools enabled the library to establish stronger links with parents – a large number of parents were reached through talks delivered at schools' parents' meetings. In the library, three shelves were devoted to books solely for parents – these covered all areas of care for children from character-education to diet, from health to clothes to make at home.

Further links between the schools and Ministry of Culture libraries are established by the lessons on bibliographic techniques which take place within the school. The directors of Leningrad libraries produced a reading list for literature teachers; the latter are expected to give pupils in each form four hours a year on the subject of bibliography (Lebedeva 1971). The four lessons of the first year covered 'How to Read a Book', 'Take Care of Your Books', 'Your First Magazine' and 'Illustrations in Books' and progressed to work in the eighth year on 'Reading Critical Literature and Working with It', 'An Independent and Aware Choice of Books' and 'Methods of Independent Work with Books' (taking notes, making references etc.).

This visit to the Dzerzhinsky ward children's library in Leningrad made very apparent the Soviet librarian's involvement with other agencies of socialisation as well as confirming that the work done with the children followed much the same pattern of discussions, exhibitions and quizzes as that found in the Lermontov ward library in Moscow.

Judging by clues in the press, these particular libraries must be fairly typical for, in many children's libraries, lively, wide-ranging activities do seem to take place. Reports such as one from a librarian in Vilnius about a fairy-tales room, decorated with motifs from Lithuanian folklore, where puppet shows very successfully re-enact favourite stories, are not at all uncommon (*Uchitel'skaya gazeta*, 24 October 1970). A library in Yaroslavl' has organised a 'Club of Jolly Whyers' whose aim is to help children to be able to find the answers to questions by referring to books. The club was started in 1968 for pupils of the first to fourth classes, though the youngest ones soon dropped out as they were not yet ready for such work. The group meets weekly and is led by the librarian. Each member asks a question and, if no one can answer it directly, the group itself works out how to find the answer (*Bibliotekar'* 1972: No. 1, pp. 29–32). Another librarian suggests a game to introduce first-year pupils to the library. The library is called *Chitai-gorod* (meaning 'Reading town'),[3] and all first-year children are sent an invitation to visit the town. The librarian, who calls herself *Murzilka* (after the little bear who is the symbol of the children's magazine of that name), gives the children a guided tour of the town explaining its streets and its laws. Older pupils from the fourth to sixth classes will also be drawn in to help by giving readings and acting scenes. This is recommended not only as an entertaining introduction to the library for young readers but also as good training in collective activity for the older pupils (*Bibliotekar'* 1972: No. 3, pp. 30–4). Thus it would seem that many children's libraries in the Soviet Union are lively, imaginative places where much is done to stimulate the child's interest and to develop his reading tastes along lines approved by the Party and state.

### Dissemination of information about children's books

How is the librarian, parent or teacher, to keep up-to-date in his knowledge of what new titles are available and of what their

[3] A pun on *Kitai-gorod* (meaning 'China town'), an old district of Moscow.

content consists? Information about new books does, in fact, reach adults concerned with children's literature through several channels. The main ones are bookshop consultants; Children's Book Centres; the Lenin Library Children's Bibliography Department; the Children's Literature Sections of various institutes (e.g. that of the Gor'ky Institute of Literature); specialised journals; and non-specialist periodicals and newspapers. Taken together these channels provide the concerned adult with regular material on what new books have been published and whether they are likely to be suitable and interesting for his or her children.

In this field, very important work is done by consultants who work for the main bookshops of each district. In Leningrad, for example, there are two such consultants; they are based at the central Book Centre[4] on Nevsky Prospekt. It will be useful to look in some detail at the work of one of these consultants who was interviewed by the writer. Her name was E. G. Dedova and her official title 'Senior Consultant to the Leningrad Collector[5] for Children's and Young People's Libraries'. She receives new books and has the job of preparing criticisms of them and making recommendations to both libraries and schools; these recommendations are all presented orally. Dedova lectures regularly both in a large lecture hall in the bookshop on the Nevsky and in schools – where parents are invited as well as teachers. At her talks, she advises on 'books for the personal library',[6] emphasising new works that will be unfamiliar to the parents' generation. She also broadcasts monthly with criticisms of children's books.

Her reviews are not based solely on her own adult opinions. A special room in the Nevsky bookshop is used for reading to children. She has many discussions with them there about works which they have just heard read and about books which they have read themselves; children also frequently send written comments on books to her (when she has read these, she passes the letters on

4 *Dom Knigi* – this is not only a bookshop but also the centre for many other services connected with books, for example, lecture courses and bibliographic advice.

5 The *Kollektor* is the person responsible for the equipment of libraries with books and technical aids.

6 The phrase 'personal library' ('*lichnaya biblioteka*') is frequently used in Russia today. It has no connotations of bourgeois acquisitiveness – indeed, individuals are officially encouraged to build up their own private collections of books.

for more systematic analysis to the appropriate publishing house or author). An additional aspect of Dedova's work is to inform publishing houses of the requests of librarians: for example, she will not infrequently pass on pleas for works on some practical subject, information on which happens to have come to her notice as being in demand.

In the interview, Dedova spoke about her aims and the criteria she applies to her criticisms. Her main aim, she feels, is to guide children to reading tastes that are as broad as possible, steering boys away from reading, say, just adventure stories or works on some favoured branch of technology. She believes that character-education is the chief goal of children's literature – but that books must also entertain while they are educating. Thus, animal tales – describing, for example, how creatures help one another – are often useful for educating in an amusing way. As an especially important quality to foster in young people, she singled out 'love of the Motherland'. Naturally, she wished to encourage children to read as much as possible; she saw attractive, well-illustrated books for the youngest children as of fundamental significance here. Another popular method of encouraging children to read which she described was by organising various literary games, arranging quizzes and puzzles about the stories they had read. Through such 'character-education in play', children could learn to look on books as a source of enjoyment and pleasure.

All in all, such work as Dedova's is clearly very significant in the dissemination of information about children's literature. Hers is a job which has no parallel in US or British society although many librarians and primary school teachers would certainly welcome the services which she provides.

A second highly important institution in this field is the Children's Book Centres, of which there are three in the Soviet Union. Two were visited: one on Gor'ky Street in Moscow and another on Kutuzov Quay in Leningrad. The third is in Tbilisi. The first of these, the Moscow one, was opened in 1950. It consists of a lecture hall, an exhibition room, a library and a correspondence department. The exhibition is, by and large, devoted to the most popular works for children. It is displayed under various themes – such as stories about Lenin and other revolutionary figures, translations, technical books, fairy-tales, books for the very young and books about soldiers. Each section has an appropriate quotation as its rubric. A placard above the display of technical books cites Lenin: 'It is impossible to build communism without a store of knowledge, of technology, of culture.'

The library contains some 21 500 titles. It includes not only examples of children's literature but also works on the theory of writing for children; within it, there is a substantial collection of pre-revolutionary material. The cataloguing system is very thorough: there are separate catalogues of titles, authors, illustrators, translators, literature of the republics, foreign books and adult books about children's literature. The library is said to be used extensively by teachers, writers, illustrators, journalists and students.

The correspondence department is a fascinating place, dealing with letters from children – letters complaining about illustrations in one book, praising the foreword to another, and so on. One letter from Bukhara was addressed to Winnie the Pooh at the Children's Book Centre. In 1970, the three people who work in this section received 35 250 letters; in the first six months of 1971, they had already had 19 293. All these letters, it was said, were scrupulously answered. Short lists of books in commonly requested categories like adventure stories or folk-tales have been prepared and are sent out to children who express interest in these genres. Usually the letters come from children who have written independently – although occasionally schools organise letter-writing sessions where each pupil writes about some favourite or some disliked book. Adults also occasionally write to the department if they feel especially strongly about a book. The letters, once answered, are arranged and catalogued according to the book to which each refers; authors, journalists and students come frequently to study these bulky files. For less purposive scholars, a bulletin of some of the more interesting letters is produced.

The Children's Book Centre is clearly an invaluable institution for those who provide, those who distribute and those who study children's literature. The library, the exhibition room and the correspondence department all play their part in providing teachers and librarians – not to mention the children themselves – with ready access to information about new books and, indeed, about anything connected with children's literature. Again, this service is, by its centralised nature, uniquely Soviet. It is certainly extremely useful.

The Lenin Library in Moscow is the main library of the USSR with important central functions for both adult and children's libraries. Part of its role is to co-ordinate specialised work in library science at the national level. For example, it attempts to avoid duplication in research in the field by drawing up a general plan for the whole country. Interested research groups (in appropriate institutes or libraries) will then select a topic from the plan. Attempts will be made to assign projects which are not spontaneously chosen to researchers who are considered suitable. Once a topic has been arrived at, the research, especially that done by subordinate libraries, will usually be carried out by a team – for example, the main children's library in Moldavia chose as its focus of interest the theme 'How Libraries can Help Children Assimilate Material from the Syllabus'. In this project the library staff aimed to combine research work with their practical duties – the acquisitions and bibliographical staffs selected relevant material, while the servicing staff checked the selections through work with the readers and also strove to determine the best methods of encouraging reading. Even when a project is due to take several years to complete, annual reports have to be presented to the Lenin Library central planners (Medvedeva 1972:207–8).

The Lenin Library Children's Department has an important bibliography section which furnishes teachers and librarians with information about children's books. It publishes lists of suggested out-of-school reading for schools and libraries. The schools then recommend to pupils the books which they have available. These official lists are frequently revised though not at any set intervals.

The Gor'ky Institute of Literature in Moscow is the central Soviet institute of literature. It is one of the institutes of the Academy of Sciences and has a special Children's Literature Section in which many famous figures in the world of Soviet children's literature – including Kassil, Chukovsky and Marshak – have worked. The present chief of the Children's Literature Section is Sergey Mikhalkov (who, as has been seen, is also one of the chairmen of the Union of Soviet Writers' Committee of Children's Literature). The post is certainly not an honorary one.

It involves co-ordinating the research, the teaching and the reviewing work of the department.

As well as concerning itself with theoretical research problems the Gor'ky Institute examines the content of specific works and produces reviews of new books. These are made available to teachers and librarians, who are usually said to find them of considerable use. There are, however, occasional suggestions that the work of the Children's Literature Departments in this and in local republican institutes of culture is inadequate. There are those who feel that the country needs a whole institute devoted to children's reading alone (*Uchitel'skaya gazeta*, 3 February 1972).

Soviet teachers, librarians and parents do not learn about new trends in children's literature solely through the lectures, broadsheets and bibliographies produced by the institutions mentioned above. There is also a specialist journal which has an even more far-reaching influence, in that it can be easily subscribed to by anyone, in no matter how farflung a corner of the Soviet Union. This periodical, *Detskaya literatura*, was first published in January 1966 and appears monthly. It describes itself as a 'literary-critical and bibliographic monthly of the Unions of Writers of the USSR and RSFSR and of the Committees on the Affairs of the Press attached to the Councils of Ministers of the USSR and RSFSR'. The present editorial board of twelve includes such illustrious names as Barto and, again, Mikhalkov. The journal is intended to keep teachers, parents, librarians, writers, illustrators and any other interested adults up-to-date with developments in all aspects of the field of children's literature. Clearly the main function of the journal is to review new books and to pass on information about them in the form of articles on more general topics – e.g. 'Let's Talk about the Library of War Adventures' (N. Toman, *Detskaya literatura* 1972: No. 2, p. 17). A large proportion of each issue is devoted to this; ten to twelve pages out of eighty are filled solely with reviews and there are also several articles informing the reader about new books either exclusively or else in part – by, say, describing the *oeuvre* of one particular author who has recently written a new book. Despite this primary function, the journal shows a consistent preoccupation with theoretical and historical questions concerned with children's literature; in 1972, articles were published on such themes as 'Our Goal is Spiritual Maturity' (S. V. Mikhalkov: No. 7, p. 2) and 'The First Story for Children' (F. Setin: No. 7, p. 43). The magazine is clearly concerned not only with writing for children but also with the illustrative side of book production. No less than fifty-two articles were published in 1972 issues on illustrating books for children. A very substantial part of the journal's pages is given over to literature from the Union republics. Foreign countries also have considerable space devoted to their publications. To sum up, *Detskaya literatura* is a specialist journal which takes a scholarly interest in all aspects of writing for children, although its basic concern is with current Soviet work.

Similar information is provided on a much smaller scale by some other periodicals and newspapers, for example, *Sem'ya i shkola* (*The Family and the School*). This monthly magazine has in each issue a section headed 'Books' which usually includes several articles of a general nature as well as a list of newly published relevant books. The August 1971 issue, for example, had one article on books intended to inspire the child with the desire to become a defender of his country, another about the work of a particular writer of fairy tales and a third on a new sports encyclopaedia for children. The bibliography of a dozen new books included both some titles for children and some for adults on aspects of character-education. This journal, as its title indicates, is directed particularly at parents. So also is *Doshkol'noe vospitanie* (*Pre-School Character-Education*) which has a similar section of bibliography and criticism of the relevant literature. The teacher's specialist paper *Uchitel'skaya gazeta* (*Teacher's Gazette*), issued three times a week, also prints frequent reviews of new children's books and advice for the teacher on how to encourage pupils to read in their spare time. Finally, a brief mention must be made of general-interest newspapers which, while not regularly dealing with the subject in any detail, do publish fairly regular exhortations to parents and teachers on the necessity of training children to love reading and to read wisely. Parents, for example, are told in *Izvestiya* that they must not sit back on the laurels of having full bookcases at home; they must actively stimulate and guide their children's choice.

Thus the field is given considerable attention throughout the press which is probably the main means whereby most interested adults get information about new works and trends in writing for children. All in all, as we have seen, the problem of information dissemination is treated with a thoroughness appropriate to the importance explicitly attached to children's literature in Soviet society.

## The children's periodical press

Children themselves receive information transmitted by the services discussed above only after (and if) it has been processed by teacher, parent, Pioneer leader or librarian. They are also, however, approached directly by the authorities through the children's periodical press. This is a characteristic aspect of Soviet publishing for children which has today no counterpart in approach or scale in the West. Children in the USSR are provided with a range of 'serious' magazines and newspapers which bear no real resemblance to Western comics. These are published by the Pioneer organisation; it issues, in all, twenty-eight newspapers and forty journals. An interview obtained in 1971 with the editor-in-chief of one children's magazine, *Koster*, proved useful in providing a fuller insight into the scope and aims of the children's periodical press.

*Koster* is a Leningrad monthly aimed at children aged twelve to fourteen. In 1977 it was published in an edition of 570 000. It was founded in 1936; the first editor was the renowned Samuel Marshak. Korney Chukovsky, Mikhail Zoshchenko (the adult satirist who also wrote stories for children about Lenin and was persecuted in the purges), Sergey Mikhalkov and Agniya Barto are among the other famous literary figures who have in their time worked for *Koster*.

Twenty people are on the editorial board; each is responsible for some aspect of the magazine's work – e.g. poetry, sport and so on. Most of them trained at institutes of journalism where about half specialised in children's journalism. Most of the editors are themselves children's authors who, said the editor-in-chief, often hanker after writing rather than editing but nevertheless make good editors. He himself had worked previously as a poet writing especially for children. One editor, the head of the 'Life of the Sea' section (important because Leningrad is a port), was formerly a sailor. These editors are all members of the Union of Journalists (Children's Section).

The magazine prints primarily fiction. Nothing published in *Koster* may have been previously published – except for some translated works which are felt not to have been adequately translated before (in 1971, for example, a serialised version of *Alice Through the Looking Glass* was printed). It keeps in close contact, it was said, with sister magazines in the national languages of the Union republics and translates the best items from them. It has only limited space and must be selective in what it prints. The editor-in-chief saw as his main problem obtaining stories of the highest quality. Usually writers would send him their work but occasionally he would approach an author whom he considered a potential source of good stories. Most of the stories are short and published complete in one issue, although the occasional serialised book is also included. In 1970, an interesting experiment was carried out in that a book in which each chapter was written by a different author was serialised. The editorial board would like to publish more science fiction but cannot find work of a suitable calibre. Comic-strips are rarely published; if they are, they must not be purely adventure stories but must provoke the child to thought. The editor deplored particularly the lack of humour in Western comics' stories for children. *Koster* sometimes publishes stories written by children.

The magazine does not, however, consist solely of fiction. It has, for example, a section on sport and another on nature. Moreover, it publishes and answers letters from children asking advice on school and family problems as well as factual questions. Like *Pionerskaya pravda* and the other children's magazines and newspapers, it also publishes reviews of new books and suggests works that the children should enjoy.

The editor-in-chief saw his main goal as being to unite the functions of entertaining and educating in the most interesting way possible. He wants to make what children like to read and what they need to read synonymous. Above all, he wants to be instrumental in the educating of Men, with a capital M. By this he meant 'playing a part in forming Builders of Communism', in accordance with the Party's Moral Code. Thus *Koster* provides children both with new stories and with *information* about them in the form of reviews and is thus typical of a number of Soviet children's periodicals.

# 4

# The primary school reader

'To maintain and transmit a value-system, human beings are punched, bullied, sent to jail, thrown into concentration camps, cajoled, bribed, made into heroes, encouraged to read newspapers, even taught sociology.' (Barrington Moore 1967:486.) These words of an American sociologist seem strong but examples supporting his statement are easily found from the persecution of Christians in ancient Rome through the Spanish Inquisition and Mary's imposition of Catholicism on England to the more recent oppressions of Stalin and Hitler. In their time, every one of these methods has been used in the name of Soviet power – but here the concern is with the less violent but much more widespread means of transmitting a value-system, namely children's reading books. In this chapter the focus is on the anthologies of stories used as primary school readers. These are of particular interest both because they are read by every Soviet schoolchild and also because they comprise the works of a wide range of authors, thus representing a striking variety of the type of material read by modern Soviet children. Moreover Soviet school textbooks are clearly the central written means for the character-education of Soviet youth. As school syllabuses are standardised throughout the USSR, it is certain that the greatest attention will be paid to the compiling of the textbooks employed. After all, schoolchildren are a captive audience at a very important period in the formation of attitudes and opinions. School reading books therefore have a particularly significant role to play. The Soviet educational authorities are explicit about their intention of making use of school readers as a means for the character-education of youth. The teachers' notes in the programme for primary classes read:

The content of the reading contributes to the ideological and political, the moral and aesthetic education of children. Reading articles and stories about the Motherland, about nature and people helps educate pupils in the spirit of collectivism, of love for their Mother-country and of friendship between the workers of all lands. (*Programma vos'miletnoy* 1971:5.)

Thus it is of great interest to look in detail at the standard Soviet school readers. The first-year book is called *Zvezdochka* (*Little Star*), the second-year reader is *Flazhok* (*Little Flag*) and the third-year text is *Nasha Rodina* (*Our Motherland*).[1] Each is arranged into sections on particular themes – for example 'Life before the Revolution', 'Our Native Army' or 'Summer'. Table 1 lists all the categories used in the three books and shows the number of lessons which the teacher is supposed to devote to each topic.

TABLE I    *The primary school reading programme: number of lessons spent on particular themes*

| Theme | First year (126 lessons) | Second year (175 lessons)[a] | Third year (175 lessons)[a] |
| --- | --- | --- | --- |
| Octobrists and Pioneers | 6 | 6 | 6 |
| Winter | 25 | 20 | – |
| The Family | 6 | – | – |
| Our Native Army | 6 | 7 | 9 |
| Folk-tales | 12 | 12 | 16 |
| Good and Bad | 10 | 15 | – |
| Spring | 26 | 8 | 20 |
| Lenin | 8 | 6 | 10 |
| First of May | 3 | 6 | – |
| Summer | 13 | 6 | 15 |
| Our Native Land | 8 | 10 | 9 |
| Seventh of November | – | 7 | 7 |
| Life before the Revolution | – | – | 12 |
| Soviets Build a New Life | – | – | 8 |
| International Workers' Friendship | – | – | 6 |
| Autumn | – | 16 | – |
| Eighth of March | 3 | 5 | 8 |

[a] The extra lessons included in the totals are accounted for by lessons on out-of-school reading.

The majority of the categories listed clearly have direct socio-political or moral content. The content of the stories within the

[1] Henceforward referred to in references as *Zv*, *Fl* and *NR* respectively.

categories has not been analysed statistically because this approach would not add anything to the indisputable conclusions that can be drawn from a systematic and thorough reading of the texts. Lenin, for example, is mentioned so frequently that one would not learn anything more by simply adding up the number of times his name occurs – it is more telling to describe and discuss the particular contexts in which he is mentioned. If the points to be made were more contentious or less striking, a statistical content analysis might give weight to arguments that others might dispute. But this is certainly not necessary here.

It is only in the sections dedicated to the seasons that elements of character-education in the content are not immediately made explicit by the title. These constitute only four out of seventeen sections but they do account for 173 out of 392 teaching periods (forty-four per cent). Does this mean that, in fact, the overall character-education content of the primary school readers is not so very high? To answer, it is necessary to look at the nature of the stories and poems in these sections.

Here character-education is much less concentrated than it is in the sections headed, say, 'Octobrists and Pioneers' or 'Our Native Land'; it is present, but in a diluted, less overt form. The *intentions* of the section on 'Spring' for instance, are, according to the teacher's companion to the syllabus, to 'draw pictures of the Russian spring, to create a poetic image of spring and to investigate the relationship of man to nature' (Vasil'eva 1971:128). In practice, this would seem to include elements of the patriotic (Russia is specifically referred to) and of the social (nature is important mainly because of man's relationship to it) as well as of the purely aesthetic (a poetic image of spring is conveyed). How far are these expressed intentions implemented in the actual content of the material on the seasons? They do communicate a delight in the countryside, a fascination for the wonders of nature – a zest for life in general. Each season is shown to have its own charms and interests; one soon feels rather like the child at the end of *Zvezdochka* who thinks each season is his favourite while it is there – and then the next one arrives and that is even better (*Zv*: 213). The content of the seasons' chapters, therefore, by showing the Motherland to be worthy of love and a source of joy, backs up the exhortations to love her and to have a positive and active attitude towards life, found in less subtle forms elsewhere in the readers.

Much attention is paid to presenting nature not simply as a source of passive enjoyment but rather as a stimulus to action. Pupils are, for example, asked to check by their own observations the validity of various folk-sayings on the weather ($Zv$: 46). Children's activities at different times of the year are stressed; the joys of Pioneer camp, for example, are especially emphasised in the summer section. At one camp, small boys are playing at being medieval knights. One asks the other if he would really like to be a knight. The latter replies that he would rather be a modern one 'with a Star and a Mauser like Dzerzhinsky' ($Fl$: 284). Dzerzhinsky was the first head of the Cheka, the Bolshevik secret police. (This is, by the way, one of the rare references to any revolutionary leader other than Lenin.) Nature at various times of the year is used as a background in many passages designed to introduce different types of work fitted to each season. Thus the nature headings in the readers cover passages with the clear moral themes of patriotism and love of work. The importance of character-education in the readers is apparent; it emerges from the sections on the seasons and is even more explicit in the other sections.

The aim of this chapter is to examine the nature of Soviet character-education as presented in the school readers. The emphasis is first on topics which have a specifically Soviet flavour in order to analyse the substance of the character-forming messages that they were intended to convey. Attention will then be drawn to the presence of certain behaviour patterns and moral values inculcated in all modern industrial societies. From focusing on the content of the messages, we next shall turn to the methods used to present the content, dealing firstly with contextual and secondly with linguistic methods. The conclusions will summarise the implications of the values inculcated and the methods used for the Soviet character-education system.

## Themes

### Patriotism

In *Democracy in America*, de Tocqueville foresaw modern industrial man reacting to the mass nature of his society by withdrawing into his family and losing any sense of belonging to a particular country (de Tocqueville 1961: Vol. 2, Bk 4, Chap. 6). The Soviet authorities are taking every precaution against this happening in the USSR, for the main central virtue expounded in all the readers is patriotism.

The young child is urged: 'Be proud of your red star, Little Octobrist, grow, study, be brave and skilful and above all else on earth, love your Soviet Motherland.'[2] (*Fl*: 24.)

Every other quality hinges on patriotism. The native land is an inspiration for the child's good behaviour:

> Thus we want to live and study,
> Thus we want to serve you, our country,
> That not only should we be proud of our country
> But our country should also be proud of us. (*NR*: 13.)

Work is joyful because it is to the greater glory of the Motherland. The biggest and most celebrated of all collectives is the Motherland. Often the Motherland is invoked with a religious fervour:

> Live, study and be proud, my son,
> That you are a Soviet citizen,
> And having chosen your path in life,
> Everywhere: in battle and labour,
> Always: in happiness and sorrow,
> Be true to your Fatherland. (*NR*: 120.)

Elsewhere the treatment looks somewhat chauvinistic:

> We live brightly and justly
> In the best country on earth. (*NR*: 3.)

However in considering the place of patriotism in Soviet theory in chapter two, it was noted that it is held not to be merely a love for the geography of the country, but, above all, a love for the social and political system of the country. Brzezinski and Huntington point out that the USA and the USSR were the first two countries to define themselves in political rather than geographical terms; they quote C. J. Friedrich: 'To be an American

---

[2] The Russian word translated throughout by 'Motherland' is *rodina*. This is a highly emotive word compared to the impersonal word for 'country', *strana*. It has, moreover, very different connotations from the military and 'masculine' one of *otechestvo* ('Fatherland' – from the root *otets*, 'father'). Its root is *rod* ('birth') and it implies the gentle 'female' characteristics of caring and tenderness.

is an ideal; while to be a Frenchman is a fact.' (Brzezinski and Huntington 1964:34.) Being a Soviet citizen is likewise presented to the child as being an ideal; it implies loyalty and a willing duty to all the central institutions of Soviet life.

These basic Soviet institutions are all introduced to the pupils in these early readers. What a local Soviet is, for example, is explained to the children in a neat article. Who works in those buildings with red flags flying above them? asks the article. It goes on to explain that, on the days when there are red flags flying all over the town, adults hold an election and choose reliable, honest and authoritative representatives. These could be any people who have earned the trust and respect of the community. When you have a problem, the article says, addressing the child, you seek advice from a friend or parent. The Soviet serves this purpose on a bigger scale. What the Soviet decides is done. How else could it be? For you yourselves chose it. It deals with such questions as the building of houses and the beautifying of cities. Decisions must even be made as to where the most comfortable park benches should be placed, for example – for comfort and beauty are significant concerns of the Soviet (*NR*: 134–7). In describing the Soviet's work, the article has carefully chosen aspects of its duties which will be meaningful to a young child. Forgetting about rational education, it gives the paragraph on keeping towns beautiful a personal relevance to each pupil by introducing the topic in this way: 'We know that your town is the most beautiful of all.' (*NR*: 136.) The passage ends with a brief reference to Soviets at higher levels. This is a thoughtfully constructed and obviously carefully planned article giving the child an idealised view of the work of his own local Soviet. None of the less comforting duties of the Soviet (those concerned with aspects of social control, for example) are discussed. Nor is there any suggestion at this stage that the elections are controlled by the Party.

The Party is, of course, the other main institution with which the children must be familiarised from the very beginning. It is always introduced in patriotic terms along the following lines. The Motherland is a big family of peoples, all of whom are co-operating to build a bright new life. In this they are led by the Party, 'the leading detachment of the working class' (*NR*: 4). In one poem, Octobrists are asked, 'What is the PARTY?' The PARTY, which appears in capital letters throughout, is seen in a number of metaphors. It is a force against enemies, it is a hero, a good friend, a scout, and itself a family headed by dear Lenin (*NR*: 14–17). It is presented, in rather vague sentimental terms, as a general Spirit of Good.

Socialism itself is likewise mentioned in vague terms rather than specifics and, again, it is usually linked to the patriotic motif. One passage states: 'We are proud of our Motherland because she is the first country in which capitalism was annihilated. In her, the first socialist system was established. Our Motherland has shown the path to freedom and happiness to all peoples.' (*Fl*: 251.) In another article, a teacher is heard to tell her pupils: 'How wonderful life will be under communism.' (*Fl*: 264.) The Revolution itself is described in similar apocalyptic language: 'It was and is the beginning of all beginnings' and 'On that day the erstwhile slave/Became forever more the master of the earth.' (*NR*: 98.) Stirring expressions – and the time when some of these young pupils may start to question the nature of their citizenship is still many years and many textbooks ahead.

Soviet patriotism involves, in addition, admiration for the figure of Lenin. As the examples throughout this chapter demonstrate, Lenin is a constant figure in the poems and stories of every section of such of the readers. Every virtue is given some foundation from his example; it is as if the Soviet authorities agree that there can be no morality without a Saviour; Lenin's heroic qualities are examined in more depth below. Marx, on the other hand, is rarely mentioned although, when he is, to him is attributed the significance of being the first man to envisage a completely new form of society. The injustice of life in the past (and in other countries still today) tormented most humane men, but Marx alone in his time saw that the old unjust order could be changed if all workers united (*NR*: 77). But he is given only a cursory glance by the youngest Soviet schoolchildren.

Loyalty to the Soviet institutions, ideals and figures mentioned above is thus shown to be an important facet of Soviet patriotism for all these institutions embody Good and Justice and Beauty.

Western liberals today tend to consider patriotism a dangerous emotion prone to lead to the abuses of imperialism or fascism.

Durkheim has, however, shown that it can also be a positive quality – all depends on whether essentially it is centrifugal or internally oriented. In order to determine which is the case *vis-à-vis* the contemporary Soviet Union, it is helpful to turn to the treatment in the readers of the themes of war and peace. If the stories relating to this topic are examined in some detail, it can be seen that the intensely patriotic flavour of so many of these texts tends towards the formation of centrifugal attitudes.

### Peace

Soviet ideologists affirm that the Soviet people is a peace-loving nation whose patriotism contains no chauvinism. There is evidence to support such a claim in the readers despite the fact that there is a sizeable section on 'Our Native Army'[3] in each of the books. The titles of these sections ('The Soviet Army Protects the Motherland', 'The Motherland must be Protected' and 'In the Defence of the Motherland') certainly stress the defensive role of the army.

The first piece on the army in the first-year school reader is a poem defining the purpose of the contemporary Soviet soldier[4] in the following way:

> The border guard on the frontier
> Protects our land,
> So that the whole people peacefully
> May work and study. (*Zv*: 88.)

In other words, the Soviet forces exist 'so that there should be no war'. Another anti-war song goes: 'We are the children of a free and a peaceful country./Our great people does not want war.' (*Fl*: 176.) The song longs for war to disappear from the planet for ever because it is of no use to either adults or children. Also, in the prominent final position of this section of *Nasha Rodina* is a poem praising peace, happiness and freedom, all of which are protected by the Soviet army. The army is afraid of nothing and

[3] *Rodnaya*, here translated as 'native', has strong emotional connotations and could best, if clumsily, be translated perhaps as 'native and beloved'. Its root, *rod*, is the same as that of *rodina* ('Motherland') and suggests 'birth' and things dear to us because we are innately bound together.
[4] The border guards are actually from the Ministry of Internal Affairs rather than army troops.

urges the child: 'Study. Work. Your young years/Are cradled and protected by your country.' (*NR*: 289.)

The fundamentally peace-loving nature of the Soviet soldier is also suggested by a number of stories which illustrate how, even in wartime, he is not vindictive. In *Zvezdochka*, there is an account (by Lev Kassil') of how, when the Soviet troops entered Berlin at the end of the Second World War, a Russian soldier went out of his way to protect a little lost German girl (*Zv*: 99–100). (This incident is also commemorated in the huge monument to the Soviet soldier erected in Berlin: in one hand the stone warrior holds a sword, in the other he is carrying a child.) In the second-year reader, there is a similar tale of a Russian soldier giving a German child food because he looks so frail. The soldier tells the child's mother to make sure that her son and his will never fight (*Fl*: 168). The implication is that, if they did, the war would certainly be started by Germany.

In the treatment given to the Civil War, it is stressed that the workers and the peasants did not want to fight. They only wanted what they themselves earned. But the former owners hankered after the old life and, aided by foreign capitalists, started a cruel civil war. The workers knew that 'death was better than the previous life' and so fought back heroically (*NR*: 265).

In other sections, too, a love of peace is fostered. *Nasha Rodina* has a whole subsection headed 'For Peace and Friendship'. This has as its epigraph: 'Children of different peoples/We all live with a dream of peace.' (*NR*: 356.) Children and peace are frequently linked motifs in the Soviet context. Some passages highlight the pointlessness of war – or at least of imperialist wars. One tells of a small boy in the First World War asking where his father is. He is too young for his mother to explain to him that the capitalists have compelled him to go to war to fight for them and that, on both sides, the soldiers are merely the tools of the wealthy. The passage is dramatically, if journalistically, written: 'Trenches, trenches, trenches. Mountains of slain men. More and still more orphans in the world.' (*NR*: 357.) There is much use of pathos and the child's father despairs, convinced he will never see his son again. Then there is a sudden change in mood: 'In Petersburg, power to the workers. Peace, Peace, Peace. To all peoples and lands – peace! And so Soviet power made the famous decree on peace.' Thus the story ends with this first and dynamic action of Soviet power which it contrasts significantly with the other governments of the time. The questions at the end of the passage generalise about war: 'Who gains from war? Who is brought grief and ruin by war?' The message of all this is backed up by a Mikhalkov poem on the differences between the forces of peace and war, of which this is a typical verse:

> They send dollars in exchange
> For giving weapons to murderers.
> But we, on the other hand, give our roubles
> That schools and hospitals may be built. (*NR*: 357.)

One can, of course, imagine an American poem claiming the converse. The poem ends with much use of antithesis:

> They go back – the path of darkness,
> But we go forward – the path to light.
> In the whole world now there is They and We.
> And we are the stronger! There's no doubt of that!
> (*NR*: 358.)

The message of this poem is not 'peace at any price' but rather 'our cause is just; we shall prevail!'

A more masterly poem on the same theme is Marshak's 'A Lesson in the Mother Tongue'. This is highly relevant to our primary theme as it tells how Soviet children are deliberately taught moral qualities (in this case, hatred of war) through the ordinary school lesson. Throughout the Soviet Union, children are learning to write by copying down that war is unnecessary:

> Distinct in the morning light,
> Each letter is clear.
> Soviet children are writing
> 'Peace to all peoples on earth.
> We need no
>         War!'
> Peace to all peoples on earth.
> There is space for all on the globe.
> The world is rich and great.
> In this way our Soviet children
> Study their native language. (*NR*: 360.)

Soviet children are shown as feeling instinctive bonds with the children of other nationalities: for example, in the account of

Juan's visit to the Pioneer palace with his friend Vanya. (Symbolically, they have been given Spanish and Russian versions of a single name.) Juan is overwhelmed by all the opportunities which are open to Soviet children; the final surprise comes when he learns that there is actually a palace from which children are not chased (*NR*: 358–9). Another story tells of a girl in a remote Siberian village who makes a hazardous journey in order to meet some North Korean children who, she knows, will be passing through on their way to the October celebrations in Moscow. Many other Siberian children also travel from afar to meet them and, although there is no common language, there is much laughter and gaiety and exchanging of presents (*NR*: 268–372). Youth is seen to be on the side of peace – or, at least, of friendship with allies. This is vividly summed up by a poem on the power of the international friendship of youth:

> For peace, youth!
> You will find happiness
> If you raise the banner of friendship.
> . . .
> We do not beg, do not beg for
> Peace and happiness.
> We ourselves shall win it. (*NR*: 373.)

This is no passive prayer but a determined call for action.

Not just youth, however, but Soviet adults are seen to uphold peace and international friendship. One story tells of a sinking ship belonging to a capitalist country. The people on board know they'll be saved when they see approaching a ship with a hammer and sickle emblem. When they read about the incident in the papers next day, all poor people are overjoyed that the passengers were saved but rich people's only reaction is to regret the loss of the ship (*NR*: 360–4). (It could, of course, be argued that the main aim of this story is not to demonstrate how Soviet people love peace but to encourage a hatred for capitalists.)

All these stories, then, suggest that there are, firstly, healthy, progressive forces in the world which accept the leading role of the USSR and, secondly, despicable enemies who oppose the progressive Soviet line. Occasionally also there is a third more troublesome category which includes unstable and vacillating elements. Towards the third category, attitudes are fluctuating and complex but towards the first two they are invariably firm: international friendship is felt for the first, intolerance for the second. There is no question of humanitarian feelings rising above political systems in the school readers – although, very occasionally, enlightened pre-revolutionary Russian aristocratic children transcend class barriers.

## The military

Within the limits outlined, it can be seen that peace and international friendship are qualities much praised to the Soviet child. Although peace is highly valued there is no attempt to turn children against war in general by depictions of its brutality and futility. Rather, the glamorous and romantic aspects of army life are highlighted. One such passage in *Zvezdochka* describes Soviet soldiers marching and it singles out the drums, the singing and the gay colours of the standard (*Zv*: 89). Similarly, the stories of war are romantic ones full of heroism and glory.

The Soviet army loves peace and is not without pity, especially towards children, but it is to be honoured for its merciless hatred of enemy armies. Zoya Kosmodem'yanskaya, the famous young heroine of the Second World War, is heard to reply boldly when asked by her Nazi interrogators before being hanged what the aim of her partisan activity was: 'To annihilate you.' (*NR*: 276.) Similarly, Kutuzov's task 'to eliminate Napoleon's army' is shown as a glorious one (*NR*: 263–5).

The reasons which are put forward justifying Russian participation in wars are always defensive ones. The chief goal is to protect the Motherland, which the Russian has dedicatedly and successfully, though in the face of great odds, defended from attack in the past. When these readers deal with the past, even the corrupt Russian tsarist system is preferred to more enlightened foreign domination. Many proverbs are quoted to show native Russians' love for their country and to advocate death before rule by any foreign power. Thus Suvorov and Kutuzov are both presented as heroic saviour generals. Both are also shown as modest men who acknowledge that the true glory and thanks are due first to the ordinary Russian soldier (e.g. *NR*: 259–63).

At this point, it must be remembered that the readers are not just for Russians but for Soviet children of all nationalities. While it is easy to give contemporary patriotism an emphasis on its Soviet flavour, problems arise when attempts are made to show that patriotism is part of a noble tradition, as do the previous stories. Patriotism for the ancestors of the Uzbek or Estonian or Belorussian child often meant antagonism towards Russia. Stories of historical patriots never allude to this – patriotism in the past is always shown in reference to Russia alone.

In the name of Mother Russia, the soldier, and the civilian too, are capable of amazing heroism. An adaptation of Polevoy's *Povest' a nastoyashchem cheloveke (Story of a Real Man)* is one of the most striking examples of this. It tells of a pilot who, though he is wounded and has to have both legs amputated, manages to fly his plane again (*Zv*: 97). There are many tales of heroism in *Nasha Rodina*. An old man, whom the Germans dare to try to bribe, tricks a large group of fascists into an ambush though this involves his own death too (*NR*: 267–73). Children also are able to do glorious deeds for the Motherland. Fifteen-year-old Lyonka is awarded the title 'Hero of the Soviet Union' for his courageous saving of an injured comrade and his widespread partisan activity. He dies for his country too (*NR*: 281–6). Heroism is shown also by young nurses at the front (*NR*: 277–81). Age and sex are seen as no barriers to bravery and effective action. Thus the modern Soviet child is encouraged to identify with war heroes at least as much as he is taught to revere peace.

The army's peacetime presence is validated in the following ways. Firstly, the army exists to protect the Soviet borders against attackers. A poem in *Flazhok* is written as if by a border guard; it expresses the pride he feels in protecting all the familiar things of Russian life – swallows and Russian stoves, for example (*Fl*: 257). The protection of children is similarly much stressed. The Soviet army nowadays is shown to stand 'night and day in defence of peaceful life so that you and all children in the world need fear no one, can live bravely, sleep peacefully and read all sorts of books' (*Fl*: 162). This is taken from a passage called 'Your Defenders' and the word 'your' is, significantly, in the intimate form. The passage opens: 'Our Motherland has many friends in different countries. But it has also evil enemies – those who have grown accustomed to living off others and to stealing others' rights. They hate our peaceful, working country. But the Soviet Army firmly guards the Motherland.' (*Fl*: 161.)

It is shown that there are wicked forces in the world today which would do children and the future world great harm were it not for the deterrence of the Soviet army, ever ready to defend the Good. Occasionally, it is called upon to act today rather than just to be a passive deterrent. One story tells of a young soldier who has a medal although he was born after the end of the Second World War. He shot down an enemy plane which was flying over the Soviet Union and photographing military secrets.

To sum up, in the military sections of the readers, the children are presented with justifications for a contemporary army. They are given a picture of a military force following in a glorious and heroic Russian tradition. Peace is highly treasured but not to the extent of tolerating hostile action by any country potentially antagonistic to the Soviet Union. The readers do not advocate world revolution nor do they glorify fighting in the blood-and-thunder style of some Western children's literature. But, on the other hand, neither do they protest peace without qualifications. A love for peace is a desirable quality but it must always be subordinated to one's love for the Motherland and her political system.

If viewed in the light of Durkheim's centrifugal–internally oriented continuum, the above material demonstrates that the contemporary USSR is closer to the centrifugal than the other extreme – for its patriotic sentiments can be seen as being 'in a situation of conflict with commitments to mankind'. It certainly does not go to any extreme of aggressiveness but its emphasis on the military (even if it is continually stressed that this is only for defensive purposes) means that the patriotic interests promoted are not just scientific and artistic ones. Above all, Soviet attitudes to other countries are delimited by political considerations which are concerned not so much with the state of justice or equality obtaining in a particular country as with that country's attitude to the Soviet Union. When presented in those terms, patriotism cannot be seen as an altogether creative force unless one is convinced that the Soviet Union really is a society one stage in advance of other societies.

*Collectivism and the family*

Patriotism emerges from a study such as this as the central contemporary Soviet virtue, on which all the others depend. Durkheim felt that the nobler but more abstract concept of collectivism could be instilled in the child through the sentiments of patriotism. In Soviet practice, on the other hand, collectivism (which can certainly claim greater authority than patriotism as a virtue from the writings of Marx and Lenin themselves) is used above all to provide a rationale for, and legitimation of, patriotism. The Motherland is the noblest collective of them all.

Collectivism, as was seen in chapter two, is an essential component of Soviet moral theory and, as such, is introduced to the child at an early age. This is done so by a story in which the meaning of the word 'collective' is explained to a child who has not heard it before. To do this, the teacher indicates a group of children helping with the school garden plot, saying 'All are helping for the general good.' (*Fl*: 33.) This inspires the child in the story to suggest that his class helps one of their number who is in trouble. The questions at the end of the passage ask the pupils what collectives they can think of and in which they themselves participate. Even in the first-year book, the lesson that devotion to the collective may demand some sacrifice is taught in terms relevant to the child's situation. One story tells of a class of twenty-five children which has twenty-four beautiful new cups and one ugly and old cracked one. The monitress takes the cracked one for herself in order to avert disharmony within the group (*Zv*: 14–15).

As frequently occurs, the moral theme is reinforced by an illustration from the life of Lenin. The following story is intended to show the basic significance of the collective in the new Soviet life. Some peasants bring Lenin a problem. He listens with interest to their somewhat incoherent story. They have some bricks and wish to build a church but they are worried lest the Soviet authorities will take their bricks away from them. Lenin reassures but gently tries to persuade them that it would be better to build a school than a church. However, he insists that: 'As your community decides, so it must be.' (*NR*: 124.) A school is built. This story is a significant one in that it stresses the importance of collective decision but none the less shows the collective needing guidance from a wiser authority.

In connection with the same story, it is noted in passing that, after the school was built, it was found that 'the more literates there were in the village, the fewer believers there were'. Eventually the old church in the village is closed and a House of Culture is built in its place and named after one of the peasants who originally asked Lenin's advice. This is one of the very few passages in these modern school readers which deals in any way with the Church or religion; it is worthy of note that the believers are reasoned with and not mocked (*NR*: 123–4).

It has been seen that the family is viewed in Soviet theory primarily as one of society's collective units, important for the healthy functioning of the bigger collective, the state or Motherland. As this is also the approach to the theme of the family as presented to children, this is examined in some detail here.

A question at the end of 'The Friendly Family' sums up the concept of the family which the Soviet child is given. It asks: 'Why can the family be called a collective?' (*Zv*: 86.) Basically, then, the family is seen as a small collective in which each member contributes to the general good. Much importance is attached to the helpful role which the child himself can play. One story tells of a family which goes fishing to make a fish soup. Young Yura catches only a small fish but is happy because in the big family soup there is his little fish as well (*Zv*: 78–9). Clearly, the message is that, though the child's role is small, it is still important.

A poem by Mikhalkov illustrates that, although young and inexperienced, the child can perform many useful duties around the house.

### Our Jobs

– In the morning I rise earliest of all
And I myself make my bed.
– And every morning I clean my shoes
For my brother and myself.
– At home I also as much as possible
Help my mother in the kitchen.
– I refuse to sit idle –
I can use an iron too.
. . .
There's plenty for children to do

In the deep forest, in the broad field,
On the collective farm, at home, out of doors,
But above all – behind a school desk. ($Zv$: 77–8.)

The last line of the poem is the one which is most emphasised by the questions at the end; a few pages later follows a story further stressing the point that the main aspect of a child's social role is his schoolwork. This is a humorous account of a small boy who decides he need not go to school anymore as he has already learnt his three Rs. He says he will become a doctor like his mother – who thereupon asks him to write a prescription for a patient with flu. He decides he doesn't like this work after all and will do the same as his father who works in a car factory. So his father asks him to correct a design for a new car. He is, naturally unable to do this and realises he has much more to learn before he can be a useful member of society ($Zv$: 79–82). This story also clearly suggests that parents should guide their children to their right conclusions rather than simply dictate their behaviour.

Because the family is a collective, in it one must occasionally discipline one's individual desires. A poem in $Zvezdochka$ tells of a child who longs to do all sorts of noisy things but restrains himself because his mother is tired and asleep ($Zv:$ 106). In the same book is a story of a little girl sewing a purse for her sister. She keeps getting weary and wants to abandon the half-completed project. But her grandmother makes her first rest and then finish the job. When it has been done, the girl experiences much pleasure at having created something ($Zv$: 83–4). It is interesting to note that the pleasure is seen to be in the creating rather than the giving: this story illustrates not only the benefits of discipline but also the joy to be derived from work.

By being treated as a collective, the family is given a wider social significance. It is not supposed to be so much a haven for the individual from the vicissitudes of the outside world but rather a microcosm of that outside world in which the child prepares himself for future civic participation. In other words, as a collective, the family is subject to rules in the same way as other collectives.

The grandparents and their role in the upbringing of children form another significant element in the discussion of the family in these readers. There is, for example, in $Zvezdochka$ an affectionate poem about a grandfather who can answer all a child's questions. It ends:

> I ask him
> All sorts of questions.
> – Where?
> – When?
> – Soon?
> – How much?
> – What for?
> To everything my grandfather
> Can give me an answer.
> My grandfather
> Isn't at all old
> Although he's a hundred. (*Zv*: 77.)

A grandmother also has a poem dedicated to her. She is not the prototypical grandmother. She doesn't have a stick or spectacles or grey hair. In fact, she works as an engineer on a building site. Yet, like all good grandmothers, she loves to sing and play with her grandchildren (*Zv*: 110).

At this point, it is of interest and relevance to our theme to consider the portrayal of women in the school readers in an attempt to assess the nature of any stereotypes found. The depiction of a mother in the readers is similar to that of the grandmother. Her only characteristic that is purely traditional is her love for her children. The mothers in the stories drive tractors and work in factories. They are certainly not primarily associated with the kitchen.

Mother's work may be as tough as father's – but the child's attitudes to her are particularly sentimental. A poem about 'Mummy' in *Flazhok* sees her as a good friend and a shoulder to weep on. She is occasionally angry but her love is constant:

> And simply because
> She is our Mummy,
> We deeply and tenderly
> Love her. (*Fl*: 177.)

Lenin's mother is used to illustrate the mother theme by means of an extract from Voskresenskaya's story, 'A Mother's Heart'. This tells how Lenin loved his mother even when he was adult. From prison, he wrote to his brothers and sisters reminding them always to remember their mother and not to leave her on her own (*Zv*: 107). He always referred to her as *mamochka*, a double diminutive in Russian, expressing especial tenderness.

The mother and family theme is broadened in the second-year reader to include more general discussion of women. There is reference to their life in the past. 'Before the victory of the working class', they were not respected enough to have a day in their honour (8 March: International Women's Day). Neither did they have equal opportunities before the Revolution. This is again illustrated by pointing to the Ul'yanov family. Lenin's sister Anya was a talented poet. 'She sought a path in literature in order to be useful to society.' But the result of this was exile. Ol'ga Ul'yanova was likewise very clever, leaving school with a gold medal, but she could go no further because she was a girl and the tsar had excluded women from higher education. She day-dreams of earning money to go and study abroad but is laughed at for the sheer ridiculousness of the idea (*Fl*: 181–2). Thus women are shown as an especially deprived group before the Revolution.

A point which is repeatedly emphasised is that, although a woman is traditionally weaker than a man, her deeds can be equally heroic. Krupskaya, for example, braves and outwits the tsarist police by carrying on the secret correspondence linking Lenin's émigré paper, *Iskra*, with Russia (*Fl*: 182–4). Similarly, there are frequent war stories featuring courageous heroines. Finally, attention is drawn to feminine heroism today with a passage adapted from an article by Valentina Tereshkova, the woman cosmonaut (*Fl*: 189–91).

The stories do reflect aspects of a Soviet woman's life which strike the Western reader as characteristic – for instance, the wide range of jobs open to women, the norm of working mothers and the important upbringing role played by grandmothers. Basically, however, the view of women presented to Soviet children is only a modified version, rather than a radically different one, of that in Western children's literature. Although Soviet woman is accepted as a surgeon or a tram driver, her husband is not expected to unburden her of any of the traditional child-care and home-maintenance functions. It is not that the kitchen is now shared between husband and wife but rather that the wife has important duties both in the kitchen and on the factory floor. To put it in terms of Talcott Parsons' distinction between instrumental and expressive roles within marriage, women now help men with their traditional, instrumental functions (earning to provide for the family, etc.) but the expressive functions (such as caring for the health and comfort of the family) are still overwhelmingly the prerogative of the female in Soviet children's literature. In no contemporary story is the child urged to help daddy as well as mummy with the housework and it is always the standard female caring figure to whom he takes his tears.

## Urban industrial behaviour patterns

From the basic themes of patriotism and collectivism, which are not values predominant in all modern societies, certain aspects of character-education must now be considered which will be found to some extent in the children's books of any modern industrial society – even though they may certainly be given a specifically Soviet flavour. It is not, for example, exclusively Soviet publicists who sing the praises of human labour. It is obviously to any modern society's interest to foster feelings of satisfaction in work. This is especially necessary because a contemporary economy's success depends so much on an industrial production now so specialised and de-personalised that an individual's commitment to it may well not arise spontaneously.

Work morale is considered by Marcuse to be the fundamental attitude present to some degree in any modern industrial society. Society morality he terms a 'competitive work-morality proclaimed with a rigidity surpassing that of bourgeois morality' (Marcuse 1971:191). This study suggests that Soviet morality is, in fact, primarily a patriotic morality; work, however, is certainly repeatedly stressed as a joyful way of proving one's love for the Motherland. The modern worker often may not even see the results of his own work. In one story an old man finds joy in planting a cherry tree because of the pleasure which it will eventually bring to others (*Fl*: 74–5); actual contemporary work, however, is more likely to be industrial. A Marshak poem, 'War with the Dnepr' (its title makes characteristic Soviet use of military metaphor), discusses the benefits which building a new dam will bring (*NR*: 130–1). A story by Gaidar portrays some Siberian boys who learn that a factory is to be built in their peaceful home area. They are excited at the prospect of a new life beginning and certainly express no regrets at the destruction of the still of the forest (*NR*: 131–4). Such stories would not be out of place in a modern American or German reader.

It can be claimed that the encouragement of a love of work is not uniquely Soviet but, like the other virtues described above, it is given a specifically Soviet flavour, both by the thoroughness and by the orientation of its approach. The dignity of toil is one of the implications of Marxist thought and it is, therefore, unsurprising to find that, in *Zvezdochka*, the people of the Soviet Union are summed up as all those who work – rather than just live – there (*Zv*: 183). Similarly a passage in *Nasha Rodina* describes the exciting life ahead for Soviet children not in terms of, say, where they may travel or how they may have children of their own, but purely in relation to the kind of work they will be able to do (*Zv*: 193). The Soviet attitude to work is also very highly idealised. In one passage pupils are dreaming about what they will do when they leave school: all their dreams are shown as coming true (*Fl*: 26–8). A further characteristic feature of the Soviet view of work is that it is stressed that all jobs are equally worthy. A Mayakovsky poem, 'What Will You Be', ends:

> All jobs are good.
> Choose
> According to taste. (*NR*: 163.)

At the same time, children are even more frequently urged to study hard at school; this is in order to be 'better' qualified to be able to contribute 'more' to society (implying inequality of contributions, at least).

The Soviet presentation of the theme of work has thus both positive and negative aspects. On the one hand, it is a humane concept, proclaiming that all kinds of work are of equal value and that work ennobles man. On the other hand, this attractive concept once accepted, it could make it easier for many people to be manipulated to secure a few people's goals.

A second common element of the mass consciousness of any industrial society is that it is not a reflective one, setting great store on the meditative ideal. It measures worth by tangible achievement – and hence a standard tenet of such a society is that actions speak louder than words. This is a recurrent theme of the Soviet school readers. A story in *Flazhok* describes a group of children on the way to school telling of all the heroic deeds they would like to do. Sema alone is quiet, saying nothing: he, however, is the one who sees the need to build a bridge over a river which, even though frozen, is not safe. Moreover, he himself builds the bridge (*Fl*: 70–2). On similar lines, a Marshak poem warns children that they must not just be proud of their fathers, they must also act well themselves (*Fl*: 70). Another story tells of two boys who look after a dog when its leg is broken. When it recovers, they quarrel about who is the dog's master. The dog is then set upon by two larger dogs. Vanya just cries for help but Kolya attacks the big dogs with a stick and drives them off (*Zv*: 128). One is reminded of the way Solomon determined the baby's true mother – although the moral here is not only that caring means caring more for the beloved than for oneself but also that a person must be judged by his deeds, not his words.

A third virtue which is a part of most ideologies is that of comradeliness. This is advocated, albeit on different grounds, by Christianity and Marxism alike. It is exemplified in the readers by an Octobrist variation on the Good Samaritan theme. This tells of a small boy who has lost his midday sandwich. Two of his friends merely sympathise, asking where he thinks he may have left it and so on. The third simply gives him half of his own lunch. The questions at the end of the passage ask the pupils who behaved in a truly comradely manner – and further emphasise the lesson by asking them to act the story out themselves as a little play (*Zv*: 10–11). Throughout the books, the need to behave in a do-as-you-would-be-done-by way is stressed, as it is in children's literature universally. Again, however, there is a difference of emphasis. The Christian must love his enemies, but the Soviet Marxist is told that it is morally rotten to be kind to enemies. In one story, the reader is directly told that Petya was 'right' to hit a little boy who was mocking him (*Fl*: 68). The social relationships are, of course, crucial here; Petya is a poor pre-revolutionary boy being mocked by a spoilt wealthy child.

Schoolroom discipline is another concern common to school teachers everywhere. Some in the West call for the deschooling of

society but actual experimenters are rare. In any modern industrial society, where classes tend to be large and diverse and where
the teacher has no longer an inevitable dominie's charisma, one of
education's basic preoccupations is maintaining classroom order.
It is not surprising that there are stories in the Soviet readers
which illustrate what is good behaviour for the pupil in school.
One of these, for instance, tells of a little girl who spends her
arithmetic lesson drawing. She is indignant to find that she is
given a low mark for her day's work although her drawing was a
good one (*Fl*: 85–6). In another tale, a child's conscience prevents
her from enjoying sunshine and birdsong because she is playing
truant (*Fl*: 28–9).

Politeness and keeping one's word are two other norms which
need to be considered here. There are plenty in the West who
consider that these are overstressed as virtues; it is worth noting
that they have not been discarded in the contemporary Soviet
Union, despite the cult of the direct in the early revolutionary
years. One story, 'The Magic Word', is about a mysterious old
man telling a boy about a word which has enchanted powers. The
word turns out to be 'please' (*Fl*: 91–5). Keeping one's word is
given a Soviet gloss in a story about Lenin to illustrate its seriousness. It relates how the young Lenin wouldn't steal even one
cherry and wouldn't allow his friend to do so either because he
had given his word of honour and that must be quite simply final
(*Zv*: 16–18).

To sum up, Soviet schoolchildren are presented in their reading
books both with values that are specifically Soviet and with others
which are common to all urban industrial societies, though often
with a distinctive Soviet gloss. But what are the methods used to
present these values?

## *Methods of presentation*

These school readers are remarkable for the variety in style and
in approach that they display but there are certain methods of
presentation which are used to a noteworthy extent. Some of them
will have become apparent, at least in part, from the examples
already quoted; it is, however, worth analysing the most significant of them explicitly.

*Creation of heroes*

It has already been noted that the creation of positive heroes is seen as one of the major ways of fulfilling the general educational requirements of socialist realism. The depiction of heroes is perhaps the chief means of character-education of the young used in the readers.

Lenin is the hero *par excellence*. Current Soviet society attaches a lonely prominence to him – no contemporary politicians, for example, are ever mentioned: Krupskaya, Sverdlov, Kirov, Dzerzhinsky and Kalinin are the only other Bolsheviks who are named even in passing (they are among the few whose reputations have survived both Stalin and de-Stalinisation). Hence it is important to look in some detail at the way in which Lenin is represented to the children. In what way are the historical facts selected and simplified for the young reader?

Lenin appears in most of the sections of the school readers but each reader also has a section specifically devoted to him. In *Zvezdochka*, it is titled 'Lenin's Birthday'; in both the other readers, it is called 'Lenin Is With Us', suggesting that the treatment he receives is not going to be simply historical.

Lenin's greatness is stressed, as the heading 'Lenin Is With Us' implies, in almost biblical terms. There is a poem, for instance, on how 'he brought light and joy to the whole country'. This refers, at one level, to his electrification schemes but it also is clearly meant to have a second-level figurative significance (*Zv*: 165–6). Several poems point out the 'appropriateness' of the fact that his birthday is in the spring, a time of freshness and promise (*Zv*: 156). His greatness is felt especially in the mausoleum. On Red Square, many different languages can be heard, 'but all pronounce with love and pride the name of Lenin'. Everyone approaches the mausoleum in an intense, moved way: 'Each of them understands that for everything that is bright and happy in life he is indebted to Lenin. Indeed, the very mausoleum has the inspirational powers of a temple: 'When something joyful happens to a person or when he has to think something important in life, he makes straight for Red Square.' The scene was symbolic in the Second World War as it was here that the nation took an oath to protect the country from Hitler's troops. Nowadays the cosmonauts leave from here. 'It is as if they receive here good wishes from Lenin for their arduous and distant journey. They carry with them to the stars Lenin's banner, Lenin's glory.' (*Fl*: 219–21.) Thus, although he died long before the Second World War or Soviet cosmonautic successes, Lenin is at the centre of these two events, which, more than anything else, are presented as sources of inspiration of patriotic feelings.

All that is best in the Soviet Union is seen to bear the name of Lenin because 'for each Soviet person, be he a hardened soldier or a Little Octobrist, the name of Lenin is the nearest and dearest thing to him' (*Fl*: 235). He is appreciated not only by Russians. For his funeral, factories and trains throughout the world stopped. He thus serves to unite people of different nationalities. One writer in *Nasha Rodina* declares that, near the mausoleum, he experiences an especially intense feeling of love and brotherhood towards the African and the Indian who are also waiting to see Lenin (*NR*: 249–50).

It can be seen that there is a strong religious element in the treatment of Lenin in these readers. One poem, 'In the Lenin Museum', says that every relic there is to be revered because it was once familiar to Lenin:

> How dear to us is every object
> Preserved under the glass!
> Every object which was warmed
> By the heat of his hands!
>
> A pen. He took it in his hands
> To sign a decree.
> A clock. By it he knew
> When to go to the Soviet. (*NR*: 327.)

On a somewhat less trite but equally religious level is a poem which depicts him as an inspiration both in war and peace. In war,

> Il'yich went with us invisibly
> through the endless fire and gloom.

Nowadays in peacetime,

> Still now we
> on each step of the way

> carefully check
>      against his dream.
> So as to carry on
> the torch,
>      which Lenin lit,
> towards Communism. (*NR*: 351.)

Thus he is a solace in wartime and an ideal in peace. He is even a modern prophet.

> He saw the people's path
> With its clear fate –
> He saw everything that today
> You and I can see. (*NR*: 355.)

Apart from his great past and his living present, he lights the way to the future.

> Our path is wondrous and bright,
> Our faith in happiness burns.
> The wise rays of Il'yich
> Send out their light to all peoples on the globe. (*Fl*: 236.)

Lenin is constantly portrayed as being loved by his contemporaries. When he lectured to workers in pre-revolutionary times, for example, they knew he would be patient enough to explain any point and they always felt he was one of them. A story in *Flazhok* tells how a young guard on duty outside the Smol'ny once stopped Lenin, not realising who he was. Far from being angry at being detained in the cold, Lenin takes pity on the guards and arranges for them to be better clad, even giving this particular soldier his own pair of mittens (*Fl*: 227–32). The affection of the peasants for him is illustrated by a letter which a group of peasants send to him: 'First of all a thank-you for the forest and the meadows.' (*Fl*: 323.) The 'you' is the intimate *ty* rather than the formal *vy*. They send him a bag of rye and, though Lenin thanks them, he tells them not to forget the workers. In fact, he gives the grain to the workers – and the peasants give them many more sacks 'from Lenin'. As well as demonstrating Lenin's popularity in his own times, this story sets out to show both his considerateness and the force of his example.

Lenin is also presented as a hero undergoing all sorts of adventures for the sake of the cause. He has, for example, to hide at

Razliv from 'the spies of the bourgeois Provisional government, whose policies were harmful to the people' (*NR*: 337). The children are told of the hardships of his life there. He builds his own hut and has to live on very little food – but he doesn't bother about this as he is capable of enduring many difficulties (*NR*: 337–40). The taking of the Winter Palace is presented as an exciting adventure story (*NR*: 340–3), as is the assassination attempt on Lenin (*NR*: 343–5). Another dimension of the heroic stature of his character is the way he devotes his whole self to the cause. After the Revolution, he even gives up his own great love, music, because 'it affects me too much'. He is advised that he is killing himself by his unstinting work but his reply is 'Is our cause not worth it?' (*NR*: 346–7.)

A considerable part of these stories deals with Lenin's connections with children and childhood – obviously a likely way of capturing the pupils' interest. There are stories about his own childhood and youth. Even then, he was dreaming of a life in Russia where man would live by his own labour and there would be no exploitation. There is an extract from his sister's book, *The Childhood and School Years of Il'yich*, which shows his home mainly as a very ordinary one (*NR*: 328–30). Every effort is made to help the readers to identify with young 'Volodya Ul'yanov'. For example, they are told how he used to break toys and to chase his sister. He is even shown to have a big fault – he is hot-tempered. However, the patient example of his elder brother, Sasha, whom he profoundly admires, has a good influence on him. He is conscious of his own failing and deliberately sets out to overcome it, which he does successfully (*NR*: 330). Thus he is not just an ordinary child; he has qualities of fortitude and determination which every child should emulate.

There are stories, too, about the adult Lenin's relationships with children. When he was in exile in Finland, he was very friendly with the children of the family with which he was staying, even though they had no language in common (*Zv*: 161). His love of children is shown in another story of his exile, in which he shows children how to construct a skating rink and then persuades the uncle of one little boy to allow the delighted child to go out shooting with the two of them (*Fl*: 223–4).

A final aspect of the Lenin and children motif is the attitude of contemporary children to him. One passage in *Zvezdochka* tells of a small boy gradually getting to know the name of Lenin. At first, he thinks of him as his grandfather; he is sure he is alive because everyone speaks of him as if he were. Gradually he realises that *everybody* speaks of him as if he were one of their own relatives and that he is loved by young and old alike. Then he learns of his revolutionary role and finds out that he is now dead: 'But all the same Lenin remained for me a living and beloved person.' (*Zv*: 165.) The Soviet child of the 1970s feels he can identify with Lenin. *Nasha Rodina* contains a passage purportedly by a child from Vorkuta, a new town in the Arctic Circle, expressing his love for his native town and his thrill at visiting Moscow. In Lenin's study in the Kremlin he feels that Lenin had had a vision of Vorkuta and that he would be pleased with the city could he see it (*NR*: 351–4). Moreover he is an inspiration to today's young Leninists:

> We swear to live on earth
> As our great leader lived,
> And to serve our Motherland
> As Lenin served her.
>
> We swear there is no better path
> Than Lenin's path.
> Behind our wise and dear leaders,
> Behind the Party we shall go. (*NR*: 327–8.)

Thus Lenin is presented as a number of types of hero, all attractive in different ways. He is an epic hero in the romantic revolutionary tradition begun by the medieval folk ballads (*byliny*) of ancient Russia; he is a Christ-like figure providing both inspiration and comfort; he is an ordinary child who, by self-discipline and determination, raises himself to the pinnacle of humanity; he is a kindly father to all small children. Such are the Lenins presented to children – there is little suggestion of what his actual political achievements, let alone his failures were.

Aspects of his personality are highlighted to the point of distortion or even invented in order to make him into the prototype of the Builder of Communism whom all children are urged to emulate; in him are embodied all the virtues of patriotism,[5]

[5] N. B. Lenin's own attitude to patriotism noted above.

discipline and comradeliness which the pupil is throughout exhorted to revere and to practise. The use of hero figures has long been used to such didactic ends – Plato discussed which qualities of the gods should be portrayed in stories for children, saying that there must be nowhere any suggestion that they could be capable of evil (Plato 1973:116).

Certainly, most young people seem to find themselves some hero who greatly influences their childhood and adolescent aspirations. The Soviet authorities are not going to let this psychological phenomenon pass unexploited. Heroes are ready-made and presented to schoolchildren from an early age so that they are steered away from selecting some random popular singer or footballer as their primary pattern for living. In the thirties and forties Stalin was the major Soviet hero. After Khrushchev's secret speech to the Twentieth Party Congress in 1956, the cult of personality was officially condemned; the authorities are still aware of its psychological appeal and, although living individuals are now carefully avoided in the school readers, the role of the personality of Lenin has grown ever stronger (as will be shown further in the next chapter).

Lenin is not the only heroic figure of the readers but he is by far the most important one. Few other real people are mentioned by name; the late Yury Gagarin is the only other actual person who is to any extent presented as a contemporary folk-hero (see below). Yakov Sverdlov, the first Soviet President, gets a brief but significant treatment as a child from a poor home who had had only four years formal teaching but had continued his studies on his own. Even when in prison, he occupied himself with reading and with contriving clever ways of teaching the other, very grateful, prisoners. Thus two favourite virtues – loving learning and never wasting time – are emphasised here by holding up to the child a revolutionary hero model.

In addition to the few real-life heroes, there is in the readers an abundance of fictional ones, especially in the tales of wartime adventure and those illustrating good, comradely behaviour. It is worth noting the comparative lack of stories about naughty children in the readers. These are a regular part of English children's literature – from Hilaire Belloc to Enid Blyton – but in these Soviet school readers there are very few stories of this type.

The stories, rather, give the pupils examples of perfect behaviour so that the characters in them can serve as models for their readers' own conduct. On the infrequent occasions when a naughty child *is* depicted he is shown to have reformed (or, at least, repented) by the end of the story. This seems to be part of the general Soviet practice of screening citizens from alternative patterns of thought or behaviour. It is the children's equivalent of not permitting adults to read newspapers or books that may not fully agree with the official viewpoint – just in case they get 'wrong' ideas from them; children are presented only with positive heroes, just in case they find themselves attracted by the alternative (rebellious) viewpoint of the naughty child. The approach is slightly less rigid in children's writing outside the school readers but the latter are scrupulously careful in protecting their young readers from potentially harmful examples. The presentation of positive heroes of fact and fiction is the major method used to educate the characters of their readers.

### Linking stories to child's daily life

A second common feature of the character-education contained in the readers is that its impact is frequently strengthened by expressing its message in terms of the child's daily life. Thus comradeliness is not described as a vague and pompous ideal but it is exemplified through some everyday incident relating to the child's range of probable experience at home or school. In one story, for instance, the virtue of comradeliness is given a concrete form for the reader with the familiar elements of classroom, teacher, dogs and daddy. It describes a little boy who is ashamed to sit beside a girl who is scared of dogs, geese and many other trifles. By telling him how his own father encouraged her when she was a little girl, his teacher inspires him to be a true comrade to his classmate. Strengthened by his friendship the girl loses all her fears (*Fl*: 81–3).

Similarly, love of the Motherland is expressed in metaphors related to aspects of daily life: 'Our republics are like sisters and our peoples like brothers. All have as their great mother our Soviet Motherland.' (*Fl*: 259.) A poem describes the Soviet Union:

> She is like a big
> Many-storeyed house.

And everyone is friendly
And happy inside. (*Fl*: 259.)

A similar family metaphor – borrowed (unacknowledged) from Stalin's victory speech – describes the Russian republic as an older sister helping her younger sisters develop properly (*Fl*: 260–1).

Not only are the familiar environments of home and school used to give the virtues more meaning for the child, but the appeal of the natural world is also used to illustrate moral values in a way that will interest the reader. In one story, a starling migrates to find on his return that the authorities have built him a new nesting box (*Zv*: 194). The Party does not just see a sparrow fall, it prevents him from falling.

Sometimes animals are the protagonists in a story; in one they are bears – two cubs are told by their mother not to venture far from the den but they disobey her in order to save a badger from being molested by wolves. The mother is angry until she hears their explanation (*Zv*: 122–3). Rules, then, can be disobeyed if there is a good reason. This is an unusual story, involving a complication which one does not expect in a Soviet first-year reader where the stress is usually on hearkening to authority.

Stories in which animals are anthropomorphised are limited to the first-year book (except for fables and folk-tales). There are, however, frequent stories in which nature is used to illustrate the virtue of comradeliness in which it can, as part of the setting, provide an extra stimulus to the child's interest. For example, at a time of great danger, Lenin is shown as remembering to pick some wild flowers for his wife (*NR*: 142–3).

## Setting a framework of tradition and universality

One method of helping a child to identify with the values inculcated in his country is to encourage him to feel part of a long tradition. Below it will be seen that highlighting contrasts between the miserable past and the happy present is a means frequently used to teach admiration for the present. It is not altogether contradictory that the converse method – stressing a certain continuity with the good in the past – is also used. Each serves to strengthen the other: inspiring with a sense of tradition less often occurs than striking an awesome contrast but a certain continuity

is seen as having an important role to play – perhaps because it is
assumed that most children will have acquired at home some of
the American's longing to search out his roots or perhaps because
it is an inescapable part of nation-state patriotism. A dramatic
example of this device is a story about the Revolution as seen
through the eyes of a small boy of a southern town. He longs for
the Revolution and pictures heroic Russian warriors (*bogatyri*)
saving his beloved town. When the Revolution comes, these
'knights' turn out to be his own uncle and grandfather (*Fl*: 65–6).
Indeed, the frequent stories about the Revolution – which usually
have young heroes with whom the readers can identify – are all-
important to this method of creating a sense of revolutionary
tradition. The Revolution is always treated in a romantic way
which both emphasises historical continuity and presents its
*dramatis personae* as heroes in the same continuum as those of
the romantic medieval epics – the use of the medieval word
*bogatyr* in connection with 1917 is a striking case in point.

Analogous with this device is that of stressing not only diachronic but also synchronic bonds with 'good' people. We have
seen how children are encouraged to feel ties with their 'heroic
forebears'; they are likewise encouraged to feel bonds with contemporary workers in other countries and with their children.
These latter feelings are certainly less fostered than the more
patriotic historical ones – but, though a minor theme, this is yet
another means whereby children are given a specific sense of
identity, of being part of something universal and significant. An
example is to be found in the third-year book's account of the
Civil War, in which children are told about international working-class support for the Reds. In the interventionist countries,
workers refuse to loan equipment for troops; many also refuse to
take part in the fighting (*NR*: 266). It is noticeable, however,
that the Soviet Union's allies in the Second World War are never
given a mention. Feelings of internationalism are to have definite
limits; it would seem that these limits preclude any encouragement of feelings of unity with the governments of non-Warsaw
Pact countries – especially, of course, over a war so recent and
about which the Russians have such intensely patriotic feelings.
As Soviet victory in the Second World War is often used to imply
proof of the superiority of the socialist system, it is not convenient

to stress that the USSR had capitalist allies who shared in the victory.

## Use of the excitement of space

A theme which is much used as an aid in character-education is the exploration of space. It has clearly captured the imagination of most modern children to an exceptional degree and is seen by the authorities as having great potential for conveying moral instruction.

In the textbooks, it is used primarily to further the patriotic motif. Journeys to the moon are not so much achievements of human science as of the Motherland. That a Soviet man was the first in space serves as a bond linking all the Soviet peoples, for the conquest of space is presented as the outcome of the whole nation's working together. A poem on these lines ends:

> To the glory of the people
> To the glory of the Country!
> Working men
> And men of science
> Are strong through peaceful and comradely labour.
>
> (*NR*: 143.)

Although success is shown as being chiefly that of the collective, there is still praise given to the hero who went first into space. After Lenin, Gagarin is, as already mentioned, the most frequently presented major real-life hero; indeed, with Tereshkova, he is the only figure of recent times to be mentioned by name. The presentation of Gagarin as a heroic figure is well exemplified by the following poem:

> Glory, O Motherland.
> The world will always remember
> that spring morning.
> Into space
> from Lenin's Motherland
> flew one man.
> He carried over the distance
> our song of labour
> and all our towns took this song
> to their hearts.
> And all looked dreaming

at the lofty sky.
Glory, O Motherland of the eagle,
glory, flier-hero. (*Zv*: 196.)

From this poem alone it is evident how neatly the subject of the
cosmos links the favourite themes – work, Motherland and Lenin.

Gagarin's endearing public personality and latter-day folk-hero
stature are exploited by including an address from him to the
young readers. He tells of the tradition, now an established one, of
starting off on a space journey at the Lenin mausoleum. In this
way even this most scientific of Soviet achievements is incorporated
into the Lenin myth. Gagarin dedicates his flight to the people of
Communism, the social formation into which the Soviet people is
soon to enter and which, one day, all peoples will enter. He relates
how a foreign correspondent once asked if he was not tired of all
the publicity he received. He replied – perhaps with diplomatic
obliqueness – that it is a duty and an honour for all Soviet citizens
to work and to be an example to others (*NR*: 147). Gagarin is
made to exemplify the type of commitment to the Soviet cause
which every child should emulate; a hero naturally by reason of
his bravery and charm, he dutifully accepts the ascribed role of
political hero as well.

Above all, Gagarin is presented not as a distant figure on a
pedestal: he admits to being a little scared before the flight. The
child can identify with him, too, because he claims that, in the
hour before he took off, he was thinking mainly of the day when
he was given his Pioneer tie (*NR*: 146). Another of the articles on
cosmonauts ends in a way certain to appeal to the schoolchild:
'And I believe that some one of today's young readers will one
day add his own heroic page to the country's starry calendar.'
(*Fl*: 266.)

*Contrasting the old-and-rotten and the new-and-good*

In teaching or in literature a fundamental method of driving a
point home is by drawing a striking contrast; this method is frequently used in the Soviet school readers.

The central virtue of loyalty to the Soviet system is fostered
mainly by pointing up the contrasts between life before and life
after October 1917. One passage, for example, is entitled 'How
Workers Lived before the Soviet Power'. Its main character is a

young boy living in a damp basement which never sees the sun. His mother is a washerwoman and their home always smells of wet clothes. His father returns from work only late at night and soon he dies. The death is directly blamed on the owner of the factory where he worked who 'didn't care about the workers. He was only out for profits'. The child's mother goes to see the owner to beg for help for the children's sake but she is dismissed abruptly with fifteen roubles and told to look after her children herself. The pathos is spread thickly in this story and its points are forcibly, if unsubtly, made through contrasts both implicitly and directly stated (*Fl*: 56–7). It has a sequel called 'How Peasants Lived before the Soviet Power'. Here the mother persuades her brother to take the child to live with him in the country. The boy learns to love nature but food is scarce and bad, the peasants have to work cruel hours, and they live in a hut that is crowded and dark. By way of contrast with all this, he sees rich children living care-free, well-fed lives. The poor children trespass and pick some raspberries in the landlord's wood; they are discovered and scolded, the fruit is taken from them and they are sent home with empty baskets. They vow revenge on this greedy cruelty – there is no Christian suggestion of turning the other cheek here. In this text, the word 'landlord' (*pomeshchik*) occurs; it is explained in a footnote that it is 'an obsolete word' meaning 'a landlord – one of the gentry (an oppressor)' (*Fl*: 58–9). The questions on this passage emphasise the harshness and the injustice of the poor people's way of life in the past by asking the pupils to compare the lives of the nobility and the masses. The sharp contrasts of pre-revolutionary life are also brought out in a passage entitled 'Vladimir Il'yich Lenin' written by his wife, Krupskaya. In this, a father describes to his son the severity of his life as a factory worker before 1917 when he and his friends were saved by Lenin. Lenin is shown as having worked himself to death for the cause, earning the devotion of the whole Soviet people, who have found him a profound inspiration for the future. 'We try to do everything as he advised.' (*Fl*: 60–1.)

Another passage is ostensibly a comparison of school-life then and now. Previously, it says, only the children of rich parents could go to school, such children as Kirill, Pavel, Natal'ya and Modest. It is significant that these names are given in their formal form and one at least of them has a foreign and alien ring, whereas the working-class boy in the story is called Petya, an altogether Russian name, given in the intimate form so that the children can more easily identify with him (*Fl*: 67–8). His mother is, again, a washerwoman and has to work till her hands bleed – and all for such spoilt children as Kirill and Modest. Then comes 1917 and a new school is opened which all the poor children attend. All the Kirills and Natal'yas have disappeared (it is not explained how). Petya's dream of going to school has come true and the passage ends with a lyrical climax: 'In throngs the children are all going to the new school, the free school, the Soviet school.' (*Fl*: 68.)

Contrast is again the main device in a whole section entitled 'The Life of Peasants and Workers before the Great October Socialist Revolution and their Struggle against Oppressors'. The epigraph, a little verse stressing how different Russia's present is from its tsarist past, sets the tone of the whole section (*NR*: 55). It begins in the distant past with an extract from a poem 'Our Ancient Capital'. This is a purely descriptive poem about people gradually building a settlement on the site of Moscow. This theme brings out a measure of continuity with the past (*NR*: 55–6). The next passages, on the other hand, adduce as many as possible of the unfamiliar features of that past. They tell of the life of a child of the nobility who is taken to Moscow against his will because the tsar has ordered it. The aspects of his life which would seem strange to a twentieth-century Soviet child are given particular prominence. For example, his nanny takes him to see his princess mother before he leaves and he prays in front of the ikon for a blessing on his journey. These features of past life are recounted in a factual and non-emotive way. The story has a sequel about the noble child's peasant friend without whom he refuses to go to Moscow – which conveys the feeling that, even in the past, children were to some extent outside class distinctions. It is interesting that, although the old system is presented as rotten, not all those in elite positions then are themselves necessarily rotten. Comradely feelings could transcend the class prejudice of masters even then. Again, great use is made of the device of contrast; in this case, that between the lives of the peasant boy and the aristocratic child. It is significant that, although the peasants' lot is much harsher, it is the peasant mother who weeps and is distraught because her child is being taken from her: there is much more love, if not wealth, in the people's way of life (*NR*: 56–62).

Having touched on the rural life of the past, the section moves on to deal with conditions for urban workers. The first story, again, plays on contrast. First, it depicts a factory-owner's home flooded with sunlight. In the very next sentence, the children are shown a woman worker's gloomy and dark basement. Owner and worker each have a daughter and an ikon – but only the worker really believes that God can help. Both of the daughters fall ill. The rich girl is treated by famous doctors who are paid well and soon cure her. But all the worker can afford is to pray for her daughter. She cannot pay for treatment and is not even able to stay at home to tend her as she has to go to work in the factory. In spite of her prayers, the child dies. What for us seems a startling amount of detail is given here about the corpse which lies 'like a withered yellow leaf' on the death bed. The reader is told that the rich girl grows up and blossoms but that the poor girl decays in the grave (*NR*: 66–7). There is no sparing of the young reader's sensibilities and one is left in no doubt as to the message of the story.

The next tale paints in equally thick colour the cruelty of life before the Revolution. This is a Chekhov story called 'Van′ka'; it takes the form of an orphan writing a letter to his grandfather one Christmas Eve. He is apprenticed to a shoemaker and writes about the dreadful inhumanity of his master. He cannot stand it any longer and begs his grandfather to come and take him away. The final touch of pathos comes at the end: he addresses his letter simply to 'grandpa's village' (*NR*: 68–72). These examples demonstrate how vividly the device of contrast is used in these Soviet school readers.

*Use of symbols*

A method of furthering character-education which the Soviet publicists use, for both old and young, is the provision of symbols of the system to which the citizen can attach his loyalty and through which he can feel at one with all others who recognise and respond to the same symbol. This is a method used universally to some degree; it is that of the totem pole, the cross and the crescent, the national flag, the school motto and the club tie.

From his first years at school – as these readers plainly demonstrate – the Soviet child is instructed in the significance and
mystique of his system's symbols.

The child himself has his own set of symbols – those which
relate to the Pioneer organisation. The very titles of the first two
readers are Pioneer symbols: *Zvezdochka*, which means 'little
star', refers both to the badge of the movement and to its basic
unit (the 'patrol'); *Flazhok* ('little flag') is also an Octobrist
symbol. These symbols are frequently discussed in the stories and
poems in the books. Along with the Pioneer scarf (the personal
symbol of membership), they are presented as objects reminding
members that they belong to a noble movement and so the objects
are to be highly valued. The child who wears an Octobrist star
has a duty and an honour to behave as a model Young Leninist,
strictly obeying the organisation's rules. This theme is illustrated
repeatedly by such stories as one in *Zvezdochka* about Vovka who
swept the floor at home one day. His friend could also have swept
his floor but he didn't. Vovka, however, had no choice because
he was an Octobrist – and yet to him this was a pleasure because
of his great pride and happiness in having the right to wear the
little red star (*Zv*: 9–10). Thus, rather than simply telling the
children that they must be proud of their badges, the message is
neatly communicated by example in a concrete little story, easily
intelligible to the young child.

*Flazhok* enlarges on the significance of the red star: it is a
symbol not just of the Octobrists but of all Soviet society (*Fl*: 23).
One passage is exclusively devoted to the red star; it opens: 'All
people who live under the red star are friends and comrades.'
When people are fighting for freedom this little star seems to give
them strength and courage. There is also a suggestion that it has
certain magic-charm qualities – it always leads to peace. The red
star links not just people in the Soviet Union but also workers
throughout the world. 'Working people of the whole world love
our army because under the red star it defends Labour and
Freedom.' (*Fl*: 23–4.) *Flazhok* also contains articles about
Octobrists in Bulgaria, Hungary and Poland; the child is thus
linked through his Octobrist badge to a movement that extends
beyond national boundaries. In the third-year book, the symbol
emphasised is the Pioneer scarf; children are urged to treasure it

because of its historical significance: their grandfathers and fathers built the Revolution for the sake of all that the three-cornered scarf represents (*NR*: 4–5). Thus the child is first taught to revere symbols for their relevance to his own everyday life and later for their wider significance.

Symbols are used not only to reinforce loyalty to the Octobrists and Pioneers or to the political system but also to deepen patriotism. The birch tree, for example, is eulogised as the most Russian of trees. The Volga, similarly, is shown to have highly emotive associations for all Soviet people. Moscow has a special significance for all – for this, says a passage in *Zvezdochka*, is where the Soviet government and the Party Central Committee works: that is why it deserves the name of capital. It adds grandly: 'The voice of Moscow is the voice of peace and friendship and it is listened to by the whole terrestrial globe.' (*Zv*: 187.)

There is also an interesting account exploring the folk etymology of the word 'red' in Russia, where it 'has always been a significant colour' suggesting distinction and honour. The ancient chroniclers used to make the first letter of each paragraph red; according to folk tradition, guests were always put in what was called the 'red corner' (i.e. the best part) of the house. Now Red Square[6] 'is the most respected place in our huge house' (*Fl*: 253).

Other symbols unifying the nation are the national flag and coat of arms. The Soviet Union did not choose to put any predatory animal on its coat of arms[7] because

> We do not threaten other nations.
> We prefer to keep a spacious house
> Where there is a place under its vaulted sky
> For all who live by their labour. (*Fl*: 258.)

In this way, a whole series of symbols is in part exploited and in part created as a further facet of Soviet myth-making. There can be no doubt of the role which symbols can play in relating the individual to an idea or an institution. They can even come to assume more importance than the referent itself – as when, for

---

[6] The name is not a Soviet rechristening, but exemplifies the old use of 'red' (*krasny*) to indicate beauty or distinction; the usage emerges most clearly in the still used word *prekrasny* – 'lovely', 'superb', 'wonderful' (literally 'extremely red').

[7] This claim cannot be made by Poland or Albania.

example, theologians argued about the 'correct' way to cross one-self or when schoolboys are sent home because they are wearing the wrong tie. As well as facilitating assimilation of a concept, a symbol may also serve to ritualise that concept, deprive it of its living substance and permit the replacement of realistic by schematic thought. There is nowadays some concern in the USSR at the fact that symbols (initially useful in the formation of identity) can become ritualised and eventually meaningless if over-used. I. S. Kon writes: 'High ideals and symbols should not turn into daily change, which becomes effaced from too frequent usage and assumes the character of cliches.' (Kon 1973:150.) It is not, of course, desired that symbols and slogans should become hackneyed to the extent that they no longer arouse the desired feeling in their users.

### Habituating to ceremony and ritual

Ceremony is but an extended form of a symbol with the same inherent social advantages (providing foci for the individual's identification with the group) and, for the individual, if not always for the authorities, the same snags (discouraging realistic thought). Again, ceremony is a method of character training favoured by the Soviet system. It plays a part in the school readers in that the major Soviet ceremonies are frequently described and explained in colourful and romantic terms. The ritual-laden occasions of May Day, the anniversary of the October Revolution and Women's Day even have whole sections devoted to them.

The section on October deals with the events of the Revolution in dramatic and stirring language, as one might expect. The treatment of May Day is perhaps less obvious. Its significance on two levels is stressed. Firstly, it is a celebration of continuity, linking Soviet workers with the workers of tsarist times, who also marked this day. Secondly, it symbolises synchronic as well as diachronic unity for it is a festival celebrated by workers through-out the world today. By implication those who do so are 'our people', people to whom internationalist feeling can be extended.

To show the bonds with the past, there are several depictions of former May Day demonstrations. In such passages, the contrast with the gaiety of Soviet parades is underlined. One story tells of a small boy going to a secret pre-revolutionary May Day meeting. He is inspired to become a revolutionary, thereby making his father very proud of him. But the police discover the meeting and break it up with whips (*Zv*: 174). This shows the harshness of the old regime – especially when contrasted with a preceding passage about a Soviet parade where the workers are seen to be at one with their government. They cry spontaneously: 'Glory to the Communist Party. Hurrah for the Soviet Government.' (*Zv*: 169.) In another pre-revolutionary tale, a father promises his son a shirt for May Day. The child is thrilled and there is much excited discussion as to what the shirt should be like. Then the father is arrested. The workers, because of their strong natural feelings of solidarity, bring the boy a shirt. He is overjoyed and thanks his father who, he believes, must have sent it to them to give to him. They do not disillusion him for they are not interested in gratitude, only in a child's happiness (*Fl*: 241–4). This rather sentimental story aims to convey a sense of workers' innate feelings of class solidarity.

Even more than stressing unity among workers of all ages, the readers glorify May Day as linking the workers of all nationalities today. A vigorous, proud-sounding poem in *Zvezdochka* is a salute to all Soviet workers, be they metal workers in the Urals, Kuban collective farmers, or dwellers in the Arctic (*Zv*: 170). But it is not, of course, just people within the Soviet Union who are linked by this day; it is on May Day that the Soviet citizen is reminded of such children as Joe. Joe is a coloured boy, living in either England or the USA to judge by the illustration. He longs to go to school but must spend his day cleaning boots because his father was killed in the war and he must help his mother earn enough to live. So, in all weathers, he must stand and beg for custom. The story ends: 'And the black boy beat out a gay little dance with his brush although his heart was very heavy.' (*Zv*: 176.)

There is a similar rather tear-jerking story in *Flazhok* about Nancy, an American Negro girl who lies awake at night listening to the rats under the floorboards. One night, they chew her shoes and destroy them. Her mother gets some advance money to buy her a new pair. By dropping such a 'casual' detail, the story makes us aware of the extent of the family's poverty. Because Nancy is coloured, the shoe-shop assistant will not help her to try on the shoes; her mother has to help her. They are too small but the assistant tells them they must take them because no one will buy them after a Negro has put them on. A white worker, however, saves them by saying they will just fit his daughter. As a worker, he knows what poverty is like (*Fl*: 244–6). Thus by arousing the pupil's feelings of pity for their under-privileged contemporaries, this story aims to stimulate hatred for the capitalist system as well as a belief in the class unity of workers whatever their colour. Nowhere is it suggested that real workers can also have racial prejudices or be anti-Soviet.

The racial equality theme is also singled out in a poem called 'We have Friends Everywhere', illustrated by a page of photographs of beautiful children of different races (*Zv*: 180). A further story on this topic tells of an African boy visiting a Soviet Pioneer camp. The Soviet children are amazed to learn that he does not know when his birthday is. The reason for this is that there are eleven children in his family, which is far too poor to celebrate eleven birthdays. The Soviet children fall silent in wonder at this until one of them suggests that he celebrates his birthday while he is at the Artek camp. They decide his day will be 17 July which, symbolically, is the Day of Peace (*Fl*: 246–9). There is, then, no treatment of coloured children in Little Black Sambo style.

In these passages, children, as well as workers, have been used to illustrate the fundamental bonds between 'peoples'[8] of all times and nationalities. These bonds lead to great strength, as is proclaimed in a poem called 'Together with Everyone' which includes this verse:

> Together with everyone,
> How powerful you are!
> You are almost
> Like a giant.
> Together with everyone
> You can turn over mountains. (*Fl*: 249.)

[8] In such contexts, the Russian word used (*narod*) has a very specific and highly emotive meaning. It does not simply mean the entire population of any country. Ozhegov, in his dictionary (1968 edition), defines it as 'the fundamental, labouring masses of a country (in capitalist states, those who are oppressed by the ruling classes)'. The Soviet *narod* consists of the whole population, of course.

May Day is a ceremony which binds people of different times and nationalities together. But, lest the child get too carried away by the spirit of internationalism engendered by these stories, the song with the following famous refrain is included in the *Zvezdochka* May Day section:

> Great,
> powerful,
> unconquerable,
> my country,
> my Moscow,
> I love you best of all. (*Zv*: 179.)

Most of the symbols which the readers evoke are, as we have seen, not only of national significance but of particular relevance to children. Similarly, the child, through the Pioneer movement, is given his own ceremonies. The intense significance of the moment when the Octobrist 'flies up' into the Pioneers is conveyed in a story about Serezha who undergoes this ceremony. As the teacher knots the Pioneer scarf around his neck, he repeats the oath with pride and loudly, because he wants all to hear. He runs home immediately as he is eager to show his grandfather his scarf. This reminds the old man of an incident in the Second World War when a young girl displayed great heroism. The little boy is jealous and wants his grandfather to think well of him too. He is inspired at once to useful activity (*NR*: 10–12). Elsewhere in *Nasha Rodina*, there is a report of a talk to new Pioneers given by some old Communists. They tell how times have changed since they gave their ceremonial promise. Their fathers were illiterate but 'The Communist Party and great Lenin pointed out to us the path to a bright and happy life and for you it will be still better, still more joyous.' (*NR*: 8.)

The desire for ceremony seems to be innate in many people. It is advantageous to authorities to create a taste for ceremony in those who do not have it 'naturally' for, like symbols, a ceremony can help the growth of a sense of identity but it can also distract attention from too much intensive thought about the implicit meaning of one's actions. It is significant to see how the Soviet leadership, having proscribed religious and tsarist parades and rituals, has replaced them with ceremonies of its own. These are explained to the child at an early age. It must be noted that the ceremonies are primarily presented so as to make the child feel part of a great tradition. Thus symbolic acts are used for the same purposes as symbolic emblems in the Soviet character-education process.

## Repetition and multiple-content presentation of values

Another method that is used again and again is the intertwining in different ways of the various themes so that each one is repeated in many varying forms and one value reinforces other values. Constant repetition is accepted by pedagogues as indispensable to the learning process and this is achieved here by the way in which the fundamental themes – work, the collective, Lenin, the Motherland – are shown to be inter-related. Each time one is the main feature of a story or poem, with the rest often being included in passing. This was noted in the poem 'Glory, O Motherland' about Gagarin. Another example is a wartime adventure. Once there was a little town with a Lenin memorial round which children had planted flowers and birch trees (symbolic of the innate Russian love for peace, nature and the Motherland). War comes and the Germans overrun the town, knocking down the memorial. Before the last Russians have to flee the town, however, they risk their lives to re-erect the statue. Its uprightness is an inspiration for partisans to attack the town, annihilating the Germans there ($Zv$: 92–4). The significance of the Lenin statue – with its connections with children and nature – is considerable: Lenin provides the bond uniting the collective to struggle for the defence of Mother Russia.

The intertwining of themes not only serves to reinforce each of them by the repetition which is afforded but also provides a certain supporting rationale for each value. Work is desirable because it helps develop the Motherland. The Motherland is lent extra glory because Lenin was born in it. Lenin is good because he abolished class rule and established one big collective. The collective is a joy because it is based on work together. And so on.

## Linguistic and stylistic aspects

There are, finally, some points concerning the language used in the readers which should be discussed.

A constant element of the readers' style is that the child is always addressed in an intimate, friendly manner. This is evident from the use of *ty* – the Russian equivalent of the French *tu*. The Russian child is told 'You[*ty*] were born in a country where there are no distinctions between rich and poor.' (*NR*: 77.) Whether he is convinced by this or not, he will feel that he is being personally spoken to by a friend. Likewise, the intimate form of the possessive adjective is used when the Red Army is described as 'your defenders'. Young readers, then are not addressed pompously or *en masse*. They are all individuals, each of whom is cherished by the state, by the Soviet power; this is the implication.

A second point concerning style is that much use is made in the readers of the rich Russian folk tradition. Not only are many folk-tales included, but every section includes a selection of proverbs to illustrate the patriotic and collectivist themes. The significant choice of the proverbs quoted is worth noting: the plentiful folk-sayings advocating indolence (e.g. 'If you do nothing, you make no mistakes'), not to speak of wife-beating ('The more you beat your wife, the tastier the cabbage soup will be') are not present, even for humour's sake. An interesting device is the use of folk models for the construction of Soviet slogans; e.g. 'A red tie upon your chest – ahead of you is all the best.'[9] (*NR*: 19.) The traditional form is given a contemporary content in a way that occasionally seems somewhat contrived.

Even more striking is a whole tale in *Nasha Rodina*. This is a Tadzhik story, 'The Blue Carpet'. It tells of a poor peasant who works hard for a rich man. He has, however, a carpet which brings peace and happiness to his house, despite its poverty. Having long coveted the carpet, the rich man steals it. The distraught peasant goes alone to the mountains where he lives for years far from the troubles of the world. Eventually he returns – to find that all has changed. He hears songs of battles for freedom, of cruel struggles and of an immortal Lenin. He weeps for joy at

[9] *Krasny galstuk na grudi – vse na svete vperedi.*

the new order and for sorrow that he was not there to help in the exciting time of change. This story is a strange mixture of fantasy and reality. There is the fact of Lenin but there is also a conversation between a man and an eagle (*NR*: 217–23). Such odd contrasts may perhaps seem more convincing to the Russian child because the story is set in Central Asia and not the suburbs of Moscow (although, of course, to the many Asian Soviet children, Moscow would seem a more exotic environment!). As a Tadzhik story, this is also a moderately rare illustration in these readers of the expression of non-Russian gratitude to Lenin.

This story and the Soviet proverbs illustrate in a startling way the official cultivation of a Soviet mythology. It seems bizarre that Lenin should be presented in the same way as a fairy princess – but undoubtedly the folk idiom is one which has a powerful appeal to children and is likely to be a successful way of conveying the desired attitudes.

It is not only the folk style which has been borrowed and lent a new Soviet content. The epic style of the old Russian saga *The Lay of Igor's Host* is also used to describe not medieval battles but the Civil War. It is difficult to translate this adequately but the following passage perhaps gives some flavour of the heroic and lyrical contrasts typical of the style: 'At that time the Red Army had driven far and wide the white troops of the accursed bourgeois and it had grown peaceful on those broad fields and those green meadows where the rye grew and the buckwheat flourished.' (*NR*: 112.) The Revolution, it is stylistically implied, is part of the great Russian tradition rather than being a cataclysmic change of course.

Folk and heroic styles are used to notable effect but they are among several styles employed in the readers. Indeed, the books are noteworthy for their variety of style, ranging from the journalistic to the lyrical, from the terse to the flowery. Examples of triteness can be found, but, on the whole, the standard is high. The best children's writers from the past and present are included and the aesthetic aim of teaching the children to appreciate good writing ranks high in the notes for teachers on the syllabus (*Programma vos'miletney*: 4).

The variety in styles gives the books a liveliness which helps to relieve the repetitiveness of their basic themes. Careful thought has clearly been devoted to making the books entertaining as well as instructive. The motive for this is doubtless the sound educational one that children will learn more willingly, and hence more effectively, when they are amused as well as exhorted. As a result, the books produced are certainly ones in which most children will find stories and verse to their taste.

# 5

## *Murzilka*

The children's periodical press in the West tends to provide material that is purely frivolous and often of so poorly written a nature that many teachers and parents will actively try to discourage children from reading it. As might be expected, the situation is not the same in the Soviet Union; there this medium, too, is not neglected as a means of moral and political education. In order to see the extent and the ways in which it is used as such, and to examine another major area of Soviet writing for children, *Murzilka*, the most popular magazine for Little Octobrists (the under-ten age group), is considered in this chapter.

The present work deals essentially with the reading matter of Soviet children of the early 1970s. Without setting out to write a history of Soviet children's literature and its changing role in child socialisation, one is nevertheless obliged to ask some questions which involve at least a brief excursion into the past: are the values and norms we detect in contemporary literature of long standing? Are they unchanging or fluctuating? Have techniques become more sophisticated over time? In this chapter, the *Murzilka* of selected years is examined in order to set contemporary problems in a more meaningful context. The years considered are 1928 (pre-industrialisation), 1938 (purge time) and 1958 (post-Stalin reform); these are compared with more recent (1970–1972) issues.

### Format

The name *Murzilka* is that of a little yellow bear which is the symbol of the magazine. It was, in fact, the title of a pre-revolutionary children's magazine; the Soviet publication using the old name was first produced in 1924. At that time it reached a comparatively small number of children. Table 2 shows how its circulation has steadily and dramatically increased over the Soviet period.

TABLE 2    *The circulation of* Murzilka, *selected years*

| Year | 1928 | 1938 | 1958 | 1971 |
|---|---|---|---|---|
| Average monthly print (thousands) | 135 | 250 | 1000 | 5600 |

One of the questions raised above was whether there has been a rise in the level of sophistication of techniques over time. That is easily answered as far as format is concerned by a glance at issues throughout the period. The first thing that strikes one about *Murzilkas* of 1928 in comparison with more recent issues is the far cruder appearance; colours and drawings are comparatively monotonous and clumsy. Although the pages are smaller, the printing is much larger and one feels the intended audience must have been younger. This is not the case; the average level of education was far lower in 1928 and it is this which is reflected in the appearance of the *Murzilkas*. Both the producers and the readers of the magazine have become more discriminating over the Soviet period. It would seem that this was a fairly rapid process for the layout of 1938 issues is already more adult. There are fewer pages than in 1928 issues but they are larger; the print is no longer babyishly large. The colouring of the illustrations is more varied. Between 1938 and 1958, the physical presentation of *Murzilka* did not change much, apart from the addition of two extra pages. The next main developments in format occurred in the sixties when ten more pages were added (it now regularly has thirty-two), while the issues became in general more artistically imaginative and attractive to look at. There has unquestionably been an improvement in techniques of presentation over the years. Has there been a parallel rise in the level of sophistication of its written content?

*Some comparative issues*

In order to give an overall impression of developments in the nature of the contents of *Murzilka* over time, a brief description of one of the issues of each year examined is presented below. In every case no notable changes of approach can be observed within the year, so that, in each instance, the issue described can be taken as typical. September has been arbitrarily chosen as the issue to be examined for each year. This exercise having provided a general feel of the changing face of *Murzilka*, changes over time in the treatment of particular topics (e.g. naughty children, children of other countries) are examined in more detail.

The Soviet twenties were a time of experiment and variety in many areas of life and this is clearly seen in both the literature and the educational writings of the time. The children's press was no exception. It had freed itself from the bonds of tsarist orthodoxy and was thoroughly enjoying this freedom. The 1928 *Murzilka* shows itself to be almost totally oriented towards pleasure. The burden of its content is stories and verses about animals or games – there is as yet absolutely no hint of the need for a love of work or the Motherland or for a reverence for Lenin. If the stories included at this time could be said to have had any deliberate purpose at all, this could solely have been to cultivate in their readers' imagination, a spirit of inventiveness and originality of thought – all qualities in keeping with the still strong revolutionary ethos of the time. These qualities are encouraged both by the example of fictional children and by features which suggest various games for children to play and toys for them to make themselves. The most revealing social content is perhaps the large numbers of stories and poems about children from children's homes.

The September 1928 issue takes the following form:

*Front cover:* An autumnal picture of children outside a children's home.

*Inside cover:* Advertisement of new titles of children's books and a suggested game.

*Title page:* Picture of children collecting autumn leaves.

*Pages 2–5:* A story about children who are reluctant to return to Moscow after a summer in the country.

*Pages 6–7:* A story of a child and his fright at being lost in a big Moscow shop.

*Page 8:* A poem about the comradeliness of a children's home.

*Page 9:* A poem about birds migrating.

*Pages 10–11:* A humorous tale of a child who is completely hidden by an enormous harmonica.

*Page 11:* A reader's drawing of a cat.

*Page 12:* Some verses about a window-cleaner, a 'dirty uncle'.

*Page 13:* Story of a boy chasing his hat in the wind.

*Pages 14–15:* Story in which some children get lost in a mist.

*Page 16:* Poem about collecting mushrooms.

*Page 17:* Another poem about mushrooms.

*Pages 18–19:* A story about a children's home where one little girl annoys everyone else by her laziness.

*Pages 20–22:* Continuation of a serial about some youths who masquerade as members of the Komsomol and intrude on a Pioneer camp.

*Page 23:* Poem about a hungry crow.

*Page 24:* Poem describing a girl feeding chickens and inviting the other farmyard creatures to come and eat too.

*Page 25:* An article about a camel and how to make a toy one.

*Pages 26–27:* A humorous story about birds.

*Pages 28–29:* A set of illustrations showing what children from a children's home do in the autumn.

*Page 29:* Three letters from readers. Two are about pets but one tells of the new buses in the writer's home town, Berdichev. The cab drivers, angry because they are earning less, have taken to throwing stones at the buses and one person has been injured.

*Pages 30–31:* More letters and a song to autumn.

*Page 32:* Picture puzzles.

*Inside back cover:* Advertisement of new titles of children's books.

*Back cover:* Display of readers' paintings.

*Supplement:* Cardboard train model to make at home.


By 1938 the situation had altered dramatically. The thirties saw rapid change from the variety and spontaneity of social organisations in the period of the twenties to the stringent controls and centralisation of Stalin's rule. The purges were at their height in 1938, when neither the arts nor education were permitted to experiment or to be directed any longer merely towards unproductive pleasure. Originality of thought was certainly no longer an officially desired quality. It is not surprising to find that amusing little stories of children playing inventive games have entirely disappeared from *Murzilka*, giving way to a solid mass of politically educative material. 'From the readers' postbag' in 1938 selects for printing not the previous accounts of pets but praises of Stalin and the Motherland which to such an extent echo the content of the rest of the magazine that one cannot help wondering whether it was really the readers who wrote them. The *Murzilka*s of 1938 are typified by a very heavy weight of character-education content and this is almost exclusively of the directly political – often chauvinist – type using extravagant hyperbole to praise the Soviet system and individual politicians.

The September 1938 issue looks like this:

*Front cover:* Picture of children happily on their way to school.

*Page 2:* Patriotic poem, 'About the Motherland', which first praises the geographical variety and beauty of the country and then claims:

> The country where oppression has been abolished,
> When the strong man does not exploit the weak,
> Where honour is given to labour
> And labour is worthily protected.
>
> Where happiness enters every home,
> Where life wears a golden costume,
> Where the fields are again worthily sown
> With reliable grain.
>
> A noble people lives here,
> Building a happy order,
> And hammering out again the whole world
> So that man can live worthily in it.

Such verses strike the reader as particularly ironic in hindsight.

*Page 3:* A song, 'Learning is Interesting', with the refrain:

> We live in a wonderful country,
> Learning is interesting,
> Very, very, very
> Interesting.

The culminating verse refers to Stalin.

> But there is one leader
> He is better, better than all!
> He is the first friend of children,
> And how glad he will be
> To hear of our success!

*Pages 4–5:* A story by Lev Tolstoy describing a little child's longing to go to school although he is really too young.

*Pages 6–7:* A story about a mischievous pupil who persistently interrupts lessons by showing the other pupils his inventions and pets which the teacher has to confiscate. One day she forgets to return a pet snake. Her husband objects and decides to deal with the boy himself. As he is an engineer, he wins the child's interest and, as a consequence, has to learn some aviation engineering to be able to answer all the boy's questions. The boy henceforth behaves in class. In the story, naughtiness is treated on a humorous level but it is none the less made clear that it is wrong behaviour and that it has to be righted.

*Page 8:* Two lyrical little poems, one about a dandelion and the other about the wind.

*Page 9:* Humorous story in which some children frighten themselves in a make-believe game about a grey wolf.

*Pages 10–11:* Poem about the celebrated Artek Pioneer camp in which the children sing thanks to Molotov for giving them such a beautiful new camp and ending:

> There is nowhere happier in the world
> Than the country where we live!
> We are proud of our country,
> Where man is happy.
> Dear Comrade Molotov,
> Thank you for Artek.

*Pages 12–13:* Poem about children who give some raspberries they have collected to a parachute hero who lands nearby.

*Pages 14–15:* A traditional Russian folk-tale about a boy with a magic stick.

*Pages 16–17:* An extract from the Medieval epic, *Slovo o polku Igoreve* (*The Lay of Igor's Host*), which stresses the wrong both of foreign attackers of Russia and of the native Russian princes who could not stop fighting among themselves.

*Page 18: Murzilka* postbag. This includes a picture from one reader showing 'Mummy voting for Kaganovich', an essay from a ten-year-old girl entitled 'I Try to Study like Lenin' and a poem in which a child aspires never to get anything but top marks.

*Page 19:* Some puzzles and the tune for the song on page 3.

*Page 20:* A picture of Murzilka getting on the train to go home after his country holiday. Many wild animals are sadly saying goodbye to him because he has been considerate and kind to them.

By 1958 social and political conditions had again radically changed. The war had come and gone, Stalin had died and Khrushchev had two years previously made his secret speech to the Twentieth Party Congress revealing some of the 'errors and crimes' of the Stalin era. *Murzilkas* for 1958 show a clear shift from the emphasis on narrowly political education of 1938 towards the pleasure principle which predominated in 1928 but at a far higher level of maturity. There has been no replacement for Stalin. The character-education content is mainly of a mild, not specifically Soviet kind: do your homework diligently, be kind to birds and so on. The September 1958 issue of *Murzilka* is as follows:

*Front cover:* Picture of children returning to school.

*Page 2:* Poem by Marshak about all that the Little Octobrist learns to do in his first year at school.

*Page 3:* A second Marshak poem, supposedly from a little girl thanking the school and the printer of her alphabet for having taught her the joy of reading: 'It is as if a bright magical lantern has been brought into dense darkness.'

*Page 4:* A story about a little boy who is very ashamed of his low marks and covers them up with blots so that his father won't know. A classmate suggests they do their homework together; she explains any difficult points to him, he starts getting good marks and no longer blots his book.

*Page 5:* Story about a girl who gets all her spellings correct except for the one she copies from her neighbour; the teacher says: 'That always happens when a person does not rely on himself.'

*Pages 6–9:* A freshly written story about a Central Asian child from a remote village who goes to visit his brother on his first trip to a town. He is excited by all the novelties (like ice cream) and gets separated from his brother. He is taken to the militia station (labouring under the illusion that he has been arrested) and is very impressed by the treatment he receives there, the sweets and the teasing and the pillows. When his brother eventually collects him, he agrees that militia men are fine people because 'they do important things'. From that day on, the little boy is determined to be a militia man when he grows up.

*Page 10:* A story about three girls arguing about which of them will get the top marks of the class. Each claims this honour for herself on such irrelevant grounds as 'I'll be the best because Mummy has sewn me a new uniform with a white apron'. They go to ask a fourth girl for her casting vote. She is sitting reading her lesson book; suddenly they all understand what is really needed to be the top pupil.

*Page 11:* Poem about an electrical current hurrying to work in all the varied places where he is needed.

*Pages 12–13:* Story about two little boys who observe a nightingale building its nest, taking great care not to disturb it in any way.

*Pages 14–15:* Story about a little boy with an Italian father and a

Russian mother who have all recently come to live in the Soviet Union. He has spoken on the radio about his family's life and, as a result, children from all over the country send him their greetings and good wishes – saying, for example, 'I shan't ask whether you like it or not in the Soviet Union – it is impossible for you not to like it', or 'You say, Sasha, that you love music. When you grow up you can become a famous musician. In our country, everybody can realise his dream.'

*Page 16:* A couple of Pioneer poems: one gay little one urges the star badge to shine for ever; the second is about a garden created by a particular Pioneer detachment.

*Page 17:* Poem about a Little Octobrists' party dedicated to 'Dolls' Day'. At first, the little boys are embarrassed – they would prefer to be playing with boats or spaceships — but soon they all join in too.

*Page 18:* A Russian folk-tale about a boastful hare who is eventually taught his lesson by a crow.

*Page 19:* Full-page picture illustrating the previous tale.

*Pages 20–22:* Story judged one of the best entries in a competition organised by *Murzilka* about a boy's friendship with a horse.

*Back cover:* List of winners of *Murzilka*'s story-competition.

Since 1958 social and political changes have, of course, been less dramatic than the developments in earlier Soviet periods. The comparative relaxation of controls over the arts after Khrushchev's secret speech, reflected in the 1958 *Murzilka*s, has gradually been eroded. The thaw has been followed by another frost, nothing like as hard as in the thirties or forties but still below zero. Once more the state of society is reflected in *Murzilka*. The issues of the early seventies have nothing like the very hard-line political content of 1938 but are much more didactic than those of 1958. There are certainly aspects which have a purely entertainment purpose, an attractive example being the page numbering in one issue (August 1970). Along the bottom of each page stretches a line of mushrooms. A little girl is collecting these mushrooms, but, as the reader progresses through the magazine, the line becomes shorter and the girl's basket becomes fuller until all the mushrooms have been gathered by the last page. Similarly the puzzle pages featured in each issue have a purely entertainment purpose. But the Soviet purpose of moulding the Builder of Communism, the new patriotic, hard-working, Leninist and collectivist man, is never long absent from the pages of *Murzilka*, and one feels that the presence of purely entertaining material may partly be accounted for by a sugar-on-the-pill theory. One feels that those who produce *Murzilka* have in mind the fact that amused children are more likely than bored ones to learn effectively and to be appreciative of Soviet power.

The sugar-on-the-pill theory is supported by the comic-strips which appear occasionally. These nearly always have at least a slight moral. The little yellow Murzilka bear features in a comic-strip on the back cover of many issues. The 'message' in these is always the same: in an amusing sequence, the reader is shown how comradely behaviour and mutual help makes life easier and more enjoyable. For instance, in one issue, Murzilka is seen riding a bicycle when there is a sudden downpour. He is drenched although he can at least ride through puddles without getting his feet wet. He passes a little girl who has an umbrella but is unable to walk across puddles. He offers her a seat on the back of his bicycle and so, with her umbrella over both of them, they ride along and both keep completely dry (July 1970:32). Thus the comic-strips which appear from time to time in *Murzilka*, although depicting humorous events, do contain a certain didactic element, though cast in a very light and appealing vein.

The September 1970 issue is as follows:

*Front cover:* Picture of a little girl at her studies.

*Pages 2–3:* Poem about a girl's first day at school. Her toys are sad to be left at home when the little girls gets up early, checks that she has all her belongings and sets off for school. In class, she doesn't laugh or talk but raises her hand quietly when she knows an answer. Her toys go to look for her at school but are told that they would hinder the lesson and must wait for her at home.

*Pages 4–6:* Story about a seven-year-old's birthday and her first day at school. Her whole village takes a pride in the thought that she is beginning school and many of the villagers give her presents which will be useful to her at school.

*Pages 7–11:* Poem about a circus. Children are very excited at the prospect of the circus, the chief attraction of which is an African lion called Cyril. It is a great disappointment to them when the show is cancelled because Cyril is ill. One of the children creeps round to have a look at the lion which she hears roaring from pain. She wraps a towel round his head and sings to him. Her nursing cures him and the show can take place after all.

*Pages 12–13:* An eight-line nursery rhyme about Shushenskoye, the place where Lenin and Krupskaya spent their Siberian exile. These pages are filled with a reverence for the place, its isolation and its revolutionary associations.

*Pages 18–20:* An article in a series called 'Our Favourite Artists'. This one deals with an illustrator of children's books, Pakhomov, and writes about him with many illustrations from his work.

*Pages 21–22:* A humorous, fantastic poem about a yellow no. 5 tram which sets off into the skies but picks up so many cloud passengers that it becomes overloaded and falls back down to earth again.

*Pages 23–24:* Picture puzzles.

*Pages 25–28:* The first instalment of a serial supposedly written by a scots terrier. In this episode, the dog is wrongly accused of stealing a sausage.

*Page 29:* A game. Some nonsense stories.

*Pages 30–31:* A page of puzzles in Bulgarian to show the readers how easy it is for the Russian-speaker to understand Bulgarian.

*Back cover:* A picture-strip in which Murzilka grows some flowers for a little boy to take to school.

In general, of course, the *Murzilka*s of the early 1970s aim to teach the same virtues as those cultivated by the school readers (or, indeed, those permeating the whole system) but they do so in a more diluted way than the readers.

The general nature of *Murzilka* for these years can be summed up thus: 1928 is full of stories about animals and imaginative games – totally pleasure-oriented; 1938 is full of material with a highly political content eulogising Stalin and the Motherland; 1958 turns back some way towards the pleasure principle with character-education content of the behave-in-the-classroom variety; 1970 has character-education content fostering patriotism, collectivism, love of work and of Lenin but presented in an often attractive and entertaining way.

## Themes

### Naughty children

Mischievous children rarely appear in the school readers. They are, however, present on the pages of *Murzilka*, and their treatment there – in the NEP period and the early seventies – provides support for the varying explanations of the presence of 'pure entertainment' features at different periods.

In the 1928 *Murzilkas*, stories on this theme should certainly be included in the 'pure entertainment' category. There are many stories on this theme and naughtiness is allowed to enjoy itself undetected and unpunished. In one story, for example, Vitya decides to play with his new sledge rather than go to school on time. No criticism is made of his truancy. The reader could as easily be left with the impression that sledging is more fun than school as with the idea that one ought to arrive at class on time (January 1928:6–8). In another story, two children carelessly drop some eggs when they have been sent shopping. The only comment made is that there was scrambled egg on the pavement. Thus the incident is treated as amusing rather than as an illustration of reprehensible behaviour (August 1928:6–7). To those familiar with the *Murzilka* of forty-five years later, such an approach seems startlingly frivolous.

Modern school readers present mainly good children in their stories. In concurrent *Murzilkas*, on the other hand, behaviour that does not live up to the Soviet model of perfection is regularly the subject of some amusing incident in a story or poem. Naughtiness is never glamorised (as it frequently is in Western children's comics which often foster the idea that the child who conforms to teachers' or parents' demands is boring and soft; such terms as 'goody-goody' with undoubted pejorative connotations spring to mind). In *Murzilka*, even if the naughtiness depicted is only some minor mischief, it is never presented as in any way heroic. The author of light-hearted mischief is not harshly punished, though. In one issue, for example, there is a humorous poem by Agniya Barto about a little boy who gets bored with adults always saying how good he is and so determines to behave badly for a change. So he pulls cats' tails – but, once it is dark and no one can see him, he asks their pardon. In the end, he clambers up on to the roof where he cannot hear the adults exclaiming what a 'good soul' he is (February 1972: 10–11). The behaviour described in such passages is often not so much naughtiness as normal boyish[1] high spirits. It is perhaps reassuring to find that it is treated as such, not with heavy-handed seriousness but with a light touch of sympathy. Examples of this

[1] It is notable that the high spirits in such stories are demonstrated by boys rather than girls.

are some stories about a boy called Alyan. He is an ordinary little boy whose behaviour is occasionally tiresome, but only because he does not always stop to think. In one anecdote, he goes to the cinema and is so noisy in his excited involvement in the war film being shown that the other members of the audience demand his removal. He begs to be allowed to stay until all the fascists have been annihilated and is, in fact, so quiet after his lack of consideration has been pointed out to him that the manager gives him permission to stay to watch the second showing. Although at first overjoyed at this, he does not stay because he knows his mother would worry about his lateness. In this way it is made clear that, in spite of occasional lapses, Alyan is at heart a thoughtful and good child (August 1970:3–7).

However, the *Murzilka*s of the seventies also contain stories about what are seen as somewhat more significant misdeeds. Many are set in the classroom and most are concerned with cheating and evasion of homework. One tale describes an ingenious method of cheating at dictation. The girl in the front desk is good at punctuation and so she pulls a string linking her and the pupil in the desk behind her whenever a comma is required. This process is repeated to the back of the room. Unfortunately, the string-pulling cannot be synchronised all the way back and so commas are placed gradually later and later in the passage as one proceeds to the back of the room. It is the humour of this situation rather than its naughtiness which is stressed (May 1970:20). This is true also of a little tale entitled 'The Hypnotiser'. The chief character in this story has not learnt his homework and, in an attempt to prevent being found out, he tries to hypnotise the teacher. His fixed gaze, however, has the opposite effect of attracting her attention to him. Again, there is no direct moralising. The author does not comment on Genka's slackness over his homework. Rather, the reader is allowed simply to laugh at the child's entertaining attempt to mislead his teacher (February 1971:31).

Yet it is significant that, even if the mischievous child is not always openly scolded in the stories, his behaviour is never permitted to escape detection or retribution. The boy who plays with his friends all evening and then blames not having prepared his lessons on his mother's illness tells his fib to a teacher who noticed his mother at the cinema on the evening concerned (December

1970:17). Varya is sent to fetch a newspaper but slips in a puddle and spoils the paper. She tells her mother that a little boy pushed her in the puddle; later, when she wants to go and play with this boy, she is refused permission because he is rough. Although her mother does not here detect the lie, Varya suffers appropriately for her deception (March 1971:20). Pangs of guilty conscience are sometimes felt to be sufficient punishment for wrong behaviour. Pavlik copies his homework off Zina but, in his own copy, he corrects a mistake which he notices in Zina's working. The shame he feels at her startled glance when he gets full marks and she does not is punishment enough for him (February 1972: 29).

Any administered punishment described is always both neatly appropriate and successful. In one issue, there is a poem by Agniya Barto which is written as if in the first person by a boy who is the black sheep of his Little Octobrist group. He is lazy and likes to fool around while the others are conscientiously working. Scoldings no longer have any effect, for he has grown accustomed to them. He is reformed by being excluded one day from the group's work project, which makes him appreciate the value and the pleasure of the collective and of communal work (January 1972:8).

It is important to note that good behaviour is expected and, therefore, does not require reward. The child who clears snow off the house roof and then boasts about how he acted without being asked and how he risked hurting himself does not receive any praise from his mother (January 1971:27).

As the examples show, the stories illustrate natural retribution rather than punishment proper. The child suffers for his bad behaviour not through a beating but either through his conscience or as the consequence of his own action. The punishment always neatly fits the crime; the motive here is clearly not simply to produce an artistically rounded story but also to inculcate the belief that bad behaviour automatically brings unpleasant results (and not only if it is discovered). The writers might well have Pavlov's work on conditioning in mind.

Sometimes an element of fantasy is introduced to enliven passages about mischievous behaviour. A poem reminiscent of a Belloc cautionary tale is one translated from Polish. In it, a boy refuses to eat, despite the pleadings of his grandparents. His grandfather buys him a balloon, but he has grown so thin that he is carried up into the air clinging to the balloon. The only way of bringing him back to earth is to throw him food until he is heavy enough to sink back to the ground (November 1970:12–13). In another poem, a doll is scolded as if it were a child for its grubbiness and its reluctance to help. The refrain is a humorously used reprimand that will be as familiar to the Soviet child as it is to the English one – 'When will you ever grow up?' (August 1970:19).

Naughtiness is, then, a common theme in the *Murzilka*s of 1928 and of the early seventies. At both times, it is treated in a light-hearted and often amusing way. In 1928, that is the end of it. In the early seventies, on the other hand, it is made clear that no naughty behaviour can benefit the child. He will either suffer from the pangs of conscience or from the fear of detection, or he will find that his actions bring consequences that are unpleasant to him personally. This makes clear the point that, whereas in 1928, frivolity and 'pure entertainment' features were welcomed for their own sake and to encourage creativity, in the more recent issues they are subordinated to the main goal of character-education. They are permitted in the *Murzilka*s of the seventies not solely because they are stimulating but because it is considered that they provide a valid and efficient means of character-education in a child's leisure hours.

## Evil

Naughtiness has not yet been discussed in relation to 1938 because the villainy described in the pages of *Murzilka* in 1938 is not the naughtiness of a child cheating over his homework or refusing to eat but the 'wickedness' of certain real political figures. In 1938, we are presented with an evil that is far removed from *Murzilka* of any of the other years examined.

Here one must remember the very real threats which authors and editors personally felt themselves to be under if they showed less than the (escalating) average degree of righteous indignation against the victims of Stalin's twentieth-century demonology. It is difficult not to feel, though, that the element of corruption of the innocent involved in their particular role in the campaigns does not carry with it a certain burden of complicity. The full psychological consequences for the generation of children involved are not yet completely revealed but must still be playing some significant social role.

A dramatic example of the type of material which editors at this time felt themselves obliged to produce for their young readers occurs in an article entitled 'Three Cheers for the Soviet Intelligence Service'. It deals with the purge of the 'Right Opposition': that such a theme should be dealt with at all in a magazine for young children will probably strike the reader as strange, for even wars may make little impression on his children's reading matter. It is not that it is well done, it is that it is done at all. The article itself is astounding for its venom and the un-subtlety of the extreme black-and-white characterisation it uses.

Children! Our glorious intelligence, led by Nikolay Ivanovich Yezhov, People's Commissar of Internal Affairs, has unmasked yet another vipers' nest of enemies of the Soviet people. The fascists, Bukharin, Rykov and Yagoda and others, were called to account before the Supreme Court of the USSR. The bandits who were caught by the intelligence were obliged to admit their crimes in front of the Soviet people. They wanted to sell their native land to the German, Japanese and English fascists. They wanted to make our happy country capitalist again, to give back the factories to the capitalists and land to the landlords. The free life of the Soviet people was hateful to them. As early as 1918, these traitors and brigands were contemplating the murder of our beloved leaders – Lenin, Stalin and Sverdlov.

Many of the accused were convicted of having been servants of the tsarist police. Running-dogs of the tsarist secret police wormed their way in to responsible posts in the Soviet State. They were saboteurs; they destroyed factories and collective farms, they murdered cattle, burnt grain, threw glass and nails into butter.

They hated the Soviet country and tried to weaken its strength in all sorts of ways.

They were spies. They sold state secrets to the German and Japanese fascists and they wanted to give them the Ukraine, Belo-russia, Azerbaidzhan, Armenia, Georgia, the Central Asian republics and the Maritime Region.

The fascists, Bukharin, Rykov and Yagoda, led by the enemy of the people, Trotsky, killed our beloved Sergey Mironovich Kirov. With the help of criminal doctors they caused the deaths of Comrade Menzhinsky, Comrade Kuibyshev and the great Russian writer Maxim Gor'ky and his son.

The fascist Yagoda intended to poison the leader of the Soviet intelligence, Comrade Yezhov – But the firm hand of the intelligence seized the betrayers of the Soviet Motherland. There is no place on Soviet land for the enemies of the people, for Trotskyists, Bukharinites or the hired spies of the fascist secret police.

All the peoples of our great Motherland with one voice demanded: 'Shoot the bandits!'

The State Procurator of the USSR, Comrade Vyshinsky, in his speech for the prosecution, said:

'This time will pass. The graves of the hateful traitors will become overgrown with grass and thistles and covered with the eternal contempt of honest Soviet citizens, of the whole Soviet people.

'But over them, over our happy country, our sun will as before clearly and joyfully shine with its bright rays. We, our people, will, as before, step out along the path, cleaned of the last dirt and filth, led by our beloved leader and teacher – the great Stalin. Forward and forward to Communism!'

The Soviet People is proud of its intelligence men. The whole people helps them in their honourable work.

The people's bard of Kazakhstan, Dzhambul, expressed this feeling of pride in the Soviet intelligence in lines dedicated to Comrade Yezhov:

> Enemies of our life, enemies of millions,
> Trotskyist bands of spies have crept among us,
> Bukharinites, among us, crafty snakes from swamps,
> An evil mob of nationalists,
> They exulted, bringing us fetters,
> But the brutes fell into the traps of Yezhov,
> The devoted friend of great Stalin.
> Yezhov broke up their treacherous circle.
> The snakelike enemy species was uncovered
> By the eyes of Yezhov, by the eyes of the people.
> Yezhov waylaid all the poisonous snakes
> And smoked out the reptiles from their holes and lairs.
> The whole scorpion species was destroyed
> By the hands of Yezhov – by the hands of the people.
>
> (April 1938:2.)

Stalin's aims in encouraging such writing were, perhaps, three-fold: the legitimation of his own rise to power and of the means used to effect it; the creation of a highly emotional and unreal atmosphere in order to divert attention from the real nature of the society for which he was responsible; and the creation of a taut fighting spirit in a populace that would thus be prepared to sacrifice itself to achieve his purpose. In many ways, of course, these aims intertwine.

The means used to help to fulfil these aims in *Murzilka* are basic and powerful. The passage quoted at length is obviously a Stalinist up-dating of an archetypal genre in moral education and literature, the struggle between Good and Evil – Theseus and the Minotaur, Christ and Satan, the Pilgrim and Despond, Henry VII and Richard III, Beauty and the Beast. Everywhere there are variations on this fundamental theme. The Stalinist version is remarkable for its presentation of still-living people in the roles of Good and Evil. In no way, either, is the depiction of Yezhov and Bukharin meant to be allegorical; the account of them and their colleagues is presented as if it were strictly factual. It is the clearest of examples of deliberate mythologising in the attempt to distract citizens from thinking realistically – in this instance from thinking about the real nature of the relationship between Stalin and the 'Right Opposition', and the actual role of the 'intelligence' in Soviet society.

The striking feature of the passage is that it is both infantile in form *and* extraordinarily like similar texts for adults proliferating at the time. One has only to read *Pravda* for the same period to discover that the Soviet adult was credited with no greater sophistication than his children – to him also Bukharin, Rykov and Yagoda are denounced in almost identically childish and unrestrained language. It does not seem wholly absurd to suggest that the trial dramas constructed for the Soviet citizens of the thirties were based on a psychology fitted for children and that the suspension of disbelief which they involved was a forcing of the whole country back into a world of bogeymen and monsters. By creating such an atmosphere, of course, no room is left for reasoned debate about the costs of alternative courses, for that, in those years, was the only arena of battle in which the leadership had no certainty of winning.

In the seventies, Soviet children's literature tends to provide heroes to emulate rather than villains to detest. Even naughty children have usually reformed by the end of the passage so that eventually they emerge good rather than bad characters. There do remain some villains for hating (in the school readers, these are either callous foreign capitalist exploiters or nineteenth-century

Russian landowners displaying similar cruelty towards innocent children) and these villains also have their place in *Murzilka*. But, despite the stress on 'intolerance' remarked on in relation to the Moral Code of the Builder of Communism, 'sacred hatred' has only a minor part to play in the children's literature of the seventies as compared with its pre-eminent role in 1938. Throughout the *Murzilka*s for that year, there is in the creation of detestable villains one among several facets of an ethos of hate. Psychologically, of course, an external enemy can serve to awaken collectivist consciousness. Wars certainly tend to unite otherwise discontented nations and have on occasions been deliberately used to divert civil unrest into 'useful' channels. Consistently throughout Soviet didactic literature, military metaphors are used in an attempt to strengthen patriotic feeling (cf. the production 'front'). Stalin took this method several steps further by actually deliberately creating enemies outside the collective, portraying them as seeking to destroy the collective just as one nation might seek to crush another in wartime. He was thus trying to simulate wartime moral conditions in a peacetime situation in the hope of creating indiscriminate terror and a blind submission and loyalty to the collective led by himself. In such an atmosphere, people police themselves with great scrupulousness. This technique was not confined to the children's press; hatred for the 'enemies of the people' was preached in harangues in all the media for every age group. It is not altogether surprising that, under such a pressure of propaganda, even many of those who had been unjustly arrested did not for many years abandon their idealised view of Stalin the Good, but continued to believe that the major trials were genuine and that there was, indeed, a need to rid society of all-pervasive 'enemies of the people'. And if adults, fully conscious of their personal innocence, could be persuaded to believe in the guilt of all the others, what chance did a child have of resisting the childish melodrama of purge trials and commination meetings? One can only speculate on the nature and extent of the long-term psychological consequences for this generation of living through a spy drama in which the amateur actors (fathers, teachers, childhood heroes) did not get up and wipe off the grease-paint blood when the lights went down. It may seem a slander on humanity to suggest that adults or even children could be fooled by such crude techniques. But how many of us in the West completely resist the persuasions of persistent TV advertising, regularly couched in similarly childish language? There is no doubt that advertisers deliberately use researched psychological techniques; the writers of *Pravda* and *Murzilka* in 1938 either did the same or their or Stalin's flair led them to use similar tactics.

A rather moving impression is given by one Soviet novel which tells a convincing, possibly autobiographical, story of a child of this period who catches the spirit of the messages described in exactly the desired fashion. Vlad longs to please his headmaster by unmasking some 'enemy of the people' in the style epitomised by Pavlik Morozov, a little boy who informed on his own parents (and who is still a hero of contemporary Pioneer songs). His chance comes when a classmate tells him a mildly political joke (unfortunately it doesn't translate well):

> Q. What does USSR stand for?
> A. Herrings cost a hundred roubles.
> (*SSSR – Seledka Stoit Sto Rubley.*)

His teacher is obviously distressed by his informing on his friend. She tells the headmaster that Vlad is becoming a tell-tale – in the pejorative English sense of the word – and herself loses her job (Maksimov 1974:18–23). One wonders, too, what must have happened in such a child's mind when, in 1956, the myths behind such passages as 'Three Cheers for the Soviet Intelligence' were even partially exposed, when the citizen learnt that Yezhov was himself an 'enemy of the people' and later that even Stalin was not worthy of the mausoleum. Did his faith in the rest of the myth crumble? Some of the evidence is examined in chapter nine.

## Children in other countries and internationalism

The mythology-of-hatred element in Soviet society in the Stalinist period again comes to the fore when we examine the theme of 'children in other countries'. It is a particularly valuable one for tracing the development of Soviet social attitudes through children's literature.

In 1928, the theme was still uncommon. One of the rare mentions of foreign children is a story of a Chinese village where a very poor family decides that one of its children will have to go out to work. They go to a factory partly owned by an Englishman. Wages are low but the workers have to take the little they can get. The owners drive a hard bargain. The Englishman gropes all over the children and says the boy will do but not the girl even though she is offered for only two dollars (i.e. four roubles, at a time when *Murzilka* itself costs fifty kopecks). The Chinese co-owner decides to take her as his own servant, because she won't eat any more than his dog (August 1928:22–3). This is certainly a foretaste of a type of writing for children which later became more prevalent, but it is a lone example in a year's issues.

By 1938, this had become a major theme. The main enemy presented as threatening the Soviet collective was foreign fascism. Soviet 'enemies of the people' were said to be in the pay of foreign fascists. A certain conflict can be detected between the two professed virtues of patriotism and internationalism in the seventies but 1938 was almost free of all traces of such a conflict for the practice of internationalism was then, for all practical purposes, suspect rather than praiseworthy. This is, of course, reflected in the *Murzilka*s of the period which contain numerous stories emphasising the injustice of foreign ways. Nearly every issue includes something like the ironic story of Pedro, the little refugee from the Spanish Civil War who is so happy to be in Moscow 'because they don't shoot people there' (November 1938:3), or the tale about a Japanese factory in Shanghai where the young children employed are forbidden to study or even to talk to one another (October 1938:4–5). Children are somehow allowed to remain immune from corruption by the perniciousness of foreign systems; they are regularly used to elicit sympathy and thereby to excite disgust for the societies in which they have had the misfortune to be born.

These stories were a major product of the publicist-made mythology of hatred already mentioned. By 1950, the change is striking. The treatment of foreign life is now sympathetic and generous. Thus, for example, there is a beautifully written story by Paustovsky about Naples – which could certainly have provided material for easy anti-capitalist propaganda, given its piles of refuse in the streets and its big area of slums. But the story is much more subtle. The poverty is not overstressed and even an Italian policeman is shown as being eventually delighted with a Soviet 'guest' who gives a *matreshka* doll to a little girl (August 1958:6–9). For the sake of detente and the thaw, social criticism has actually been moderated. A long article about a Ghanaian boy (April 1958:12–14) and a serial about a young Arab (beginning January 1958:7–11) similarly treat the societies they describe with respect and sympathy.

The liberalness of tone, however, does not last. In more recent issues the amount of sympathy elicited for foreigners depends ultimately on the extent to which they align themselves with the USSR. This does not mean that there has been a return to the Stalinist mythology of hatred; the treatment of foreigners is now much more subtle. In recent *Murzilka*s the theme of international-ism has been developed in a number of ways. It is frequently approached through translations of the works of non-Russian authors, either Soviet or foreign; most issues have at least one story or poem that is translated into Russian from one of the other Soviet languages. A typical example is a two-page feature appear-ing in October 1971 on works by Latvian poets. This is intro-duced as if by a doll who, 'like all Latvian children', speaks both Latvian and Russian. She describes briefly the characteristic features of her republic's geography and claims that 'our children sing and dance beautifully and read poetry well'. This intro-duction links the poems which follow to the lives of the children of Latvia. In the poems themselves, it is as if a child were speak-ing. Two are lullabies. One is a lullaby to a pair of boots which have had their fill of running about, of kicking balls and of trampling through puddles for one day. The second is a lullaby to a book. The sad fairy-tale and the jolly fairy-tale are both urged to fall gently asleep till morning. The final poem tells of a little boy who pretends his cap is a bird and throws it in the air to watch it 'fly'. Unfortunately, like a bird, the cap lands on a tree (October 1971:10–11). These poems, have a charm that is not affected by any national boundaries. They do not use as their appeal the strangeness of the foreign: rather they highlight the fact that what delights Latvian children will also be enjoyed by Russian children. This is usually the case with the material translated from other Soviet languages. If, as occurs occasionally, there are articles on the lives of the young people of different republics, these emphasise the bonds linking all Soviet people rather than the particular characteristics which distinguish the way of life of children in, say, Georgia from that of those in Moscow.

The approach is rather different when dealing with children from other – particularly non-socialist – countries. Certainly, the assumedly instinctive bonds between children of all nations are stressed but background material is given to demonstrate what are presented as the central differences between life in socialist and capitalist countries. Three examples will show how this is done. In the first of these stories, the writer Yuri Karinets recalls his childhood friendship with a little German girl called Gizi who came to live in his block of flats. The political reasons for her being in Russia are carefully explained:

Gizi's father was a communist, an underground one, and he was at that time unemployed. As you know, there are now two Germanies: a socialist one and a capitalist one. But when I was small there was only one Germany, a capitalist one. And the workers there, especially the communists, lived very badly. And so Gizi came to the USSR to be cured of tuberculosis. (February 1971:26.)

The superiority of the Soviet way of life which demonstrates concern about the health even of foreign children is made very clear.

The presentation by a Russian of the situation in an allied country at war occurs in a reportage entitled 'Children of Vietnam'. The reader is left in no doubt as to the correct response to the war in Vietnam: it is not just one of sympathy for the innocently suffering children, it is also one of angry condemnation of the American aggression in that part of the world. The article is introduced in a way meant to demonstrate Soviet youth's spontaneous compassion for the children of Vietnam. The author tells how she received a letter from some seven-year-old Soviet schoolchildren who wanted the address of a Vietnamese school so that they 'could send the children of Vietnam words of good cheer and support'. But, because of the indiscriminate cruelty of American bombing, the comradely intentions of the Soviet children cannot be put into action because the author doesn't know if the school she would have suggested has been destroyed or not. The random nature of attacks is emphasised. Not only bridges and roads, but also homes, hospitals and schools are bombed by the imperialists.

The writer continues by describing her own experiences in Vietnam, thus lending her words first-hand authenticity. A direct appeal to children, too, is provided by quoting from a letter which she says she received from a Vietnamese schoolchild. The bravery shown in the child's letter heightens the reader's sense of the deprivation and adversity of existence for children in Vietnam. He writes:

I am in the third class. Just now my studies are interrupted because the Americans have completely bombed our school. But now our mothers and grandmothers have built a new school. It is simply a bamboo hut. But it's a very good school. When they bombed our school, all of us children were very angry with the Americans and now we are working hard so as to get the very best marks because we know when Vietnam decisively wins, our country will need educated people so that everything can be built anew.

The war is depicted as if it were simply between the USA and Vietnam. The author goes on to describe in some detail the school life of Vietnamese children which is dominated by war conditions. Most of the instruction takes place at night because bombing hardly ever ceases in daytime. But, at night, lighting is a major problem. The electricity mains have been destroyed but, even if they had not been, bright light at night would be dangerous as it would attract enemy planes. So all the pupils can use are tiny kerosene lamps. They are severely handicapped also by the restricted supply of paper. Every child writes in very small letters so as to economise on exercise books.

School conditions are contrasted with those in the Soviet Union. Soviet children do physical exercises, led by their teacher. But, in Vietnam, they have begun to build schools underground where there isn't sufficient fresh air for exercises. So, at night, classes are taken outside in turn for gym practice and singing. Their songs are not filled with fear about the war and bombs; they tell, rather, of the future victory and they glory in their courageous motherland. The children of Vietnam have to grow up at a very young age. Those who would still be going to the kindergarten in the Soviet Union have to work in the fields and to help drive the buffalo. They, though, are likened to flowers as 'the tender growths of the future'.

The pathos of the situation is underlined even more dramatically by describing the case of a little boy with a bandaged head. He was wounded but refused to stay for long in hospital. Despite the pain, he longed to study again because, like the child who wrote the letter, he realised his country's need for literate people. His eyes were painful after his wounds and so his schoolfriends made for him an especially bright light with a palmleaf shade so that his page was well illuminated but his eyes were protected. In the half-dark, his bandage shone white, 'a symbol of courage and determination'. If the Soviet schoolchild could escape experiencing much feeling for the generalised plight of Vietnamese schoolchildren, he would hardly be able not to empathise with so specific and touching a case.

Having thus guided the young Soviet reader to identification and empathy with his Vietnamese brother, the passage ends by directly stating the attitude which he should have: 'All over the world now, all honest people are helping Vietnam to conquer the American bandits. And all – even the very youngest – know and believe: Vietnam will be victorious.' (July 1971:11–12.) Thus the treatment of Vietnam is not limited to sympathising with children growing up under war conditions; it builds on this sympathy in order to legitimate Soviet policies on south-east Asia.

There is a similar distinctly political approach to Italy in the third example, an article on the poet Gianni Rodari. The children are advised to read the work of this writer if they want to experience Italy but haven't the ticket (it is significant that the passage says 'ticket' rather than 'money' or 'visa'!). Rodari will seem to take them by the hand, show them Italy's ancient towns and introduce them to their Italian contemporaries.

At times, sadness and pain sound in the poems. Why? It is because Italy is ruled not by the working people but by the wealthy. They live freely in their seaside palaces. For the worker, life is not like that. Things are good for him if he has work. You, probably, don't even know the word 'unemployment' – for, in our country there is sufficient work for everyone. But the Italian boy will tremble, terrified, when he hears this word. For he knows what will happen to his family if his father is out of work.

The two poems which are chosen as an introduction to the work of Rodari for Soviet children are, it is important to note, not those which emphasise Italy's natural or architectural beauties. They are sad poems on the harsh lives of the working people.

Rodari writes about the bad and the unjust because he wants all honest Italians to fight to put an end to all this and to win a happy life for the people. For Rodari is not simply a poet. He is a communist poet.

Rodari is, of course, a disciple of the school of socialist realism with its stress on the didactic significance of art. The facts that he is a fighter for justice and that he is a Communist are treated as synonymous.

The first poem is a conversation between a postman and a female worker. She asks the postman what has brought him to their road. He has brought a letter to one particular worker from his boss, firing the worker because he is getting old. It is this worker's birthday and it is emphasised that it would never have entered his employer's head to send him a greeting. The woman comrade begs the postman not to deliver the letter. It will kill the worker and his wife and little son with grief. Let them have their gay birthday and find out this sorrow another day. The themes, then, are employers' cruelty, workers' comradeliness and the horror of unemployment. The poem is ironically called 'The Present'.

The second poem is entitled 'Sad Spring'. It tells of spring in a working-class quarter of an Italian city; Spring is personified as being at a loss to know how to make her presence felt there. There are no trees to turn green and no birds to start singing. The poem ends with a rather neat couplet: 'Not only the people/Are unemployed.' (June 1970:22–3.)

These two poems and the introduction to them have a clear political lesson for Soviet children about the capitalist system prevailing in Italy.

These three examples serve to bring out the main elements in *Murzilka*'s treatment of the theme of 'children in other countries' in the seventies. While it stresses links between children of all the Soviet nationalities and the 'instinctive' sympathies between children throughout the world, it also seeks to develop hostility towards capitalism. No representation is given to non-Communist foreign authors except those of fairy-tales.

These examples allow one to discuss more fully the role of internationalism in the Soviet Moral Code. From the amount of space accorded to this theme in the school readers, it is clear that it is not one of the attitudes seen by the authorities as most important to instil in future Soviet citizens. The school readers imply that patriotism is the primary virtue round which all the others revolve, while a more generalised collectivism and a love of work play prominent supporting roles; internationalism is very much in the background with few stories on what could be termed in any way an internationalist theme. This quantitative impression is confirmed qualitatively by the nature of the internationalist material in the *Murzilkas* of the seventies. In them, internationalism is unequivocally subordinated to patriotism in its Soviet highly political sense. Internationalist feeling is certainly encouraged as far as other Soviet republics or socialist countries are concerned, with an emphasis on the bonds of shared experience between the children of the socialist camp.

As far as non-socialist countries are concerned, the message is not a xenophobic one in which most foreigners depicted are fascist spies trying to destroy innocent Soviet children, but gone, too, is the ideological tolerance extended to other systems in 1958; it is rather hard to imagine a kindly Italian policeman in the *Murzilkas* of the seventies. Now the message is that one should experience feelings of spontaneous trust and sympathy for foreign workers and – more especially – children, but hatred for the alien capitalist system.

However, there is no attempt to create a revolutionary spirit; it is not an aggressive internationalism. One is certainly to hate foreign capitalists but the natural extension that all working people ought to set out to destroy their power is nowhere suggested. The tone may not be militantly revolutionary, but is certainly not unmilitary. There is a strong military thread running through contemporary *Murzilkas* as there is in the school readers. This will be examined in rather more detail below.

*Patriotism*

In the school readers, patriotism emerged as the central virtue presented to Soviet children. This is confirmed by a similar preponderance of stories, articles and verse with a patriotic motif in the contemporary *Murzilkas*. It would be repetitious and unnecessary to give further examples of these, which are very reminiscent of their counterparts in the readers. It is, however, worth looking in more detail at the treatment of the patriotic in *Murzilkas* of earlier years in order to find out how and when it came to occupy first place among the virtues.

In 1928, there was no hint that patriotism was going to become such a predominating theme. Nature stories and verses comprise the main element of the *Murzilkas* of 1928. The spirit of these is simple delight in the wonders of nature and nowhere is there any particular stress on the fact that the marvels of nature described occur in *Russia*. There is not the slightest attempt to use the child's interest in nature as a spring-board for patriotic character-education.

By 1938, however, patriotism was already flourishing as the key feature in character-education. There were none the less distinct and important differences between the treatment then and the treatment in the early seventies. Then, there was nothing so oblique as love for birch trees or the Volga, only unmediated political obsession. The three strands of patriotic education in 1938 were the foreign menace, the army, and Stalin. It has already been seen how the foreign menace was presented to the children in order to foster patriotism through fear of an external enemy and the creation of an analogue of war hysteria. Treatment of the army is dealt with below. It remains here to discuss the third major facet of patriotism in 1938, which was its dependence on Stalin.[2]

Whenever there is any element of the patriotic theme in 1938 issues, Stalin's name occurs for he is presented as an integral part of the children's Motherland and hence of Good. Whenever any positive political figure is named, Stalin's name is always to be found there as well. In various articles, he is the support of the

---

[2] For an extended, if dated, discussion of the depiction of Stalin for children, see Counts, *I Want To Be Like Stalin*, London, 1948.

Komsomol (October 1938:2), the inspiration of the air force
(November 1938:9), and the provider of a happy life for children
who display on their kindergarten walls 'Thank you, comrade
Stalin, for a happy childhood.' (August 1938:9.)

Features about Stalin make no pretence of being rational and
scientific. Their language is emotional and laden with (frequently
mixed) metaphors about light, spring, fire and struggle. For
example:

> Shine, our Stalin, with your bright glory,
> Your words flower in our hearts,
> We have for ever the right
> To happiness, rest and labour.
> Days are wonderful and songs are full
> Permeated by the fire of your rays.
> We elected to the Supreme Soviet
> Of the people beloved by the Motherland
> As first of them all – Stalin!
> (August 1938:2.)

Thus the foundation-stone for belief in Stalin is more of the heart
than the head although occasionally attempts are made to legitimate his omnipotence in terms of ideology. He is, for example,
linked with Lenin both as a prime pupil of Marx and as leader of
the Revolution (May 1938:2). On the whole, however, he was
simply an emotional cult figure.

Assuming that the postbag pages are genuine, children accepted
this view of Stalin; these pages include many verses and pictures
produced by children themselves which depict Stalin in these
same sentimental terms. Thus eleven-year-old Voya Malin writes:

> I write these lines and my heart is thumping
> And I can scarcely breathe for emotion.
> I write about the friend of the people
> Who has given us children happiness. (May 1938:11.)

Such was the cult of personality presented to children in 1938.
Stalin had not once been mentioned in the issues for 1928. (Nor
did Brezhnev or Kosygin feature in the seventies.) In 1938, however, he was the lynch-pin of patriotism, the arch-representative
of Soviet society. Any 'disloyalty' to him personally thus implied
treason and was punished as such. The cult was, indeed, designed

to make untenable, even fatal, the position that one was for Soviet power and Party hegemony but opposed to the politician, Stalin.

Of course, the concept of patriotism presented to children in 1958 had a dramatically different face: it was a birch-tree patriotism. In 1958, patriotism was cultivated by articles such as descriptive features about life on the Volga in which simple but proud accounts of all the freight carried by her and of the factories and hydro-electric stations alongside her are transformed into vehicles for character-education by the addition of such concluding comments as: 'And all this has been created by our Soviet people.' One aspect of 1958 Soviet patriotism, though (and this continued to find reflection in the seventies), was the frequent inclusion of stories from and about the non-Russian republics. Examples are a Georgian poem about a traffic policeman (May 1958:15), a Kazakh one about a postman (June 1958:14) and a series of stories about a little girl who lives in the tundra (February 1958:11–13).

Already, too, in 1958 there was the beginning of the utilisation of the space-travel theme for patriotic purposes: for example, there is a two-page article on the first sputnik, emphasising as much the fact that it was done by the Soviet people as the wonder that it was done at all (November 1958:14–15). Thus, by 1958 we have many of the elements of the pattern that has now become familiar. We have previously noted Durkheim's point that conflict between patriotism and internationalism disappears if patriotism is rightly conceived. All depends on whether patriotism is centrifugal or internally oriented. If it is internally oriented, 'one no longer must ask whether the national ideal should be sacrificed for the ideals of mankind, since the two merge' (Durkheim 1973: 77–8). In 1958 the two ideals come closer to merging than at any other period examined.

In the seventies, patriotism is presented as such an all-embracing ideal that it has elements of both the centrifugal and the internally oriented. Patriotic endeavours are certainly devoted to the country's scientific and economic achievements – but they are not wholly so. There are such striking elements of the political and the military in the Soviet concept of patriotism that it tends towards the centrifugal in its relations with other countries. The Soviet national ideal by no means merges indissolubly in every instance with the ideals of mankind. When no merger is possible, it is not the Soviet national ideal that is modified.

Patriotism, then, had no place in 1928, and was exaggeratedly emphasised in 1938 to serve the purposes of the Stalin cult and the witch hunts of the purges. The excesses had been repudiated by 1958 which did not, however, mean the disappearance of the theme altogether but its cultivation by more subtle means on a muted scale. By the early seventies, the theme had come to loom larger, though relying more on the foundations laid in the late fifties rather than those of twenty years earlier. None the less it had not lived up to the promise in 1958 that it might become the pure, internally oriented quality of Durkheim's conception.

## The military

In 1928 the military theme was not in evidence but, once again, the situation had been dramatically reversed by 1938. The military themes were then very significant – as one of the three patriotic motifs, the military is inextricably intertwined with the other two, Stalin and hostility to foreign elements.

The content of material on the military theme in the seventies is either backward-looking or else designed to stress the defensive role of the forces. However, the war stories of 1938 have a greater immediacy. They are not about exploits of a more or less distant past but describe events of the contemporary world. The Spanish Civil War forms the background for several stories – e.g. the serial 'Pedro' (beginning November 1938:3–5). Even the little bear, Murzilka, gets involved in the Civil War; in a cartoon he saves some presents from Spanish to Soviet children which were on board a ship sunk by the fascists (May 1938:19–20).

The fascists, whether in or out of the Spanish Civil War, are the prime enemy and are a constant presence in the magazine. Even a comparatively frivolous riddle about Rome comments: 'now fascism is rampant there' (March 1938:19). In a pathos-laden story, we hear of an orphan girl whose mother died years ago and whose father was killed by the fascists (February 1938:3–6). That all this met with some success is shown by a piece headed 'How we Hate the Fascists' contributed by a twelve-year-old boy in which he describes with what glee he and his friends attacked a snowman, making believe it was a fascist (April 1938:15).

In 1938 *Murzilkas*, enemies are near and concrete – actual named people, at home and abroad – whereas, in 1970 issues, they are remote and abstract – either long-dead foes or an impersonal external force potentially hostile to the Motherland. Hostile forces are in evidence in some stories in 1970, but they are all-pervading in 1938; little boys delight in exposing them to the grateful security forces. One such boy realises his dream by noticing suspect footprints in the snow (March 1938:14); elsewhere children detect 'enemies of the people' who are smuggling secrets hidden in a girl's doll to foreign 'tourists' leaving the Soviet Union (October 1938:7). The image of security men projected in these stories is essentially that of sympathetic father-figures – whose eyes harden remorselessly, however, at the scent of an 'enemy of the people' (October 1938:7–9).

A final significant point of comparison between the presentation of the military in 1938 and in 1970 is that in 1938 there was far more depiction of pleasure in actual fighting. In the seventies, the romance of the army was found in its flags and songs and traditions. In 1938, fighting itself was romanticised. A poem on 'Our Cavalry' ends:

> Our cavalry is not sad,
> For Comrade Stalin has sent them
> Not on parade but to war,
> To protect their country. (November 1938:6.)

Another poem illustrates the idea that one's loyalty to one's country is not sworn by oaths of allegiance but by action against the enemies who are always ready to attack an unguarded Soviet border. The young soldier who illustrates this theme seems to experience a kind of ecstasy in thus proving his allegiance by deeds (October 1938:8).

All in all, the military-patriotic motif was treated in a much more direct and physical way in 1938 with morally monstrous real enemies whom it is a joy to expose and fight; patriotism depended far less on the image of a beautiful Motherland, and its abstract defence. Some such treatment was to be expected at a time when fascist forces were, indeed, threatening the security of the USSR and the world. All the greater must have been the confusion in the mind of the Soviet child when a few months later, he learnt of the Molotov–Ribbentrop pact. Fascism had been presented as a moral enemy with which no political compromise was conceivable. A political deal with evil incarnate, as presented over the years in publications like *Murzilka*, can hardly have failed to be traumatic for the uncynical young. For some, at least, we know it was this turning point which set in motion doubts about the moral basis of the world – the world as depicted on the pages of *Murzilka* – and private speculations about political expedience and manipulation whose long-term consequences, after confirmation in 1956, can be traced in the private cynicism of some educated youth today. At the time, though, few youngsters could have been able to comprehend that the stress on vicious enemies was at least as much to aid Stalin's stringent social control at home as to prepare Russia for a war with fascism.

Military articles are absent in 1958: only in February, the month when Soviet Army Day (marking the end of the Civil War) is celebrated, are there articles glorifying the Red Army, and these are dedicated mainly to their heroic exploits of the past. Only at the end is it pointed out that they still protect peace throughout the world. Indicative of the lack of military emphases in these issues is the fact that an article on the development of flying does not even refer to the wartime uses of aeroplanes (May 1958:15–16). In 1958 no foreign spies lurk on the pages of *Murzilka*.

The military theme which occurred in the readers under such headings as 'The Soviet Army Protects the Motherland' is dealt with even more extensively in *Murzilka*s of the seventies. Indeed, it is one of the most noticeable aspects of the magazine's content. For fifteen months in 1970 and 1971, there was a series called 'Heroic Alphabet' which, month by month, dealt with all the Soviet peoples, telling of some noble deed by nationality during the Second World War. The style is dramatic and journalistic and each nationality mentioned, from Abkhazian to Yakut, is shown to have been selfless and dedicated in the Soviet struggle against fascism. Although the Second World War had finished twenty-five years previously, it is treated not so much as past history but rather as a very recent and still significant event. This clearly constitutes a deliberate attempt to keep alive the patriotic

spirit of the war years and in a way clearly designed to foster
Soviet rather than just Russian feelings.

The official aims of the series are summed up in the issue in
which the final part appears. The last letters of the alphabet are
preceded by 'a letter from a Marshal to Little Octobrists'. This
points out that, although there are many differences of language
and culture among the Soviet peoples, they 'all loved their socialist
Motherland the same'. The letter attributes credit to the Communist Party for teaching the different peoples to be friends
among themselves. Their friendship was strengthened by the war.
The Marshal then poses the question: what can the children learn
from this series? He answers it thus: 'Firstly, you should learn
from it a selfless love for your Soviet Motherland. Secondly, you
should learn from it fearlessly to defend your Soviet Motherland
from enemies.' (July 1971:26.)

It would seem that the explicitly stated aim of publishing the
series coincided, more or less closely, with the actual aim – that of
inculcating both an All-Union patriotism and an awareness of
the military menace represented by hostile forces whose enmity
must be seen as essential and unremitting. Children must be made
to understand that, while one might struggle against them 'for
peace', one could not appropriately apply to them the behavioural
norms of attempted reform, forgiveness and understanding
required in relation to those who misbehaved at home; the only
appropriate responses to structured hostility is patriotism and
readiness to fight and die.

Military articles in the *Murzilka*s of the seventies are not limited
to this series. In the May 1970 issue, thirteen-and-a-half pages out
of thirty-two are devoted to some aspect of war or of service life.
This is a special issue commemorating the end of the Second
World War, but there is no 1970–71 issue of *Murzilka* which
does not have at least several pages dealing with the military
theme. The Soviet Union certainly pays loud homage to peace
but not to the extent that its children are encouraged to be
pacifists. On the contrary, a readiness for military action is a
fundamental part of Soviet patriotism even if, as is always insisted,
this is only to be for defensive purposes. As well as a section of the
'Heroic Alphabet', the May 1970 issue includes articles on the
various Soviet war medals and on types of battleship. This com-

memorative issue does not, therefore, confine itself to the history of the Second World War; it also treats aspects of the contemporary Soviet armed forces. Other issues mention various groups in the armed services of the 1970s – infantry and missile forces, for example. The contemporary army, then, is given considerable prominence; its preventive role is shown as vital and is not permitted to be overshadowed even by the army of the last war and its members' heroic adventures.

Rarely are the military stories treated frivolously in any way. In one story there is a rather humorous personification of a tank which is described as enjoying war tactics and as being a 'hero' in its own right (February 1971:10–12). But by and large, the subject is treated with the maximum of seriousness. The Soviet brand of patriotism would never allow military uniform to be treated with anything but complete respect. (Nor would the light-hearted design of souvenirs using the national flag to joky effect – such as one sees frequently in Britain – be conceivable.) Although the general approach to character-education in *Murzilka* tends to be somewhat less serious than in the school readers, there are limits to this; and the military theme is one of those which, it is clear, cannot really be handled frivolously.

The armed forces are thus clearly a serious and prominent theme in Soviet character-education in the seventies but their treatment is linked to strengthening patriotic rather than internationalist feelings; one must be a good soldier for the defence of the Motherland. Nowhere is it suggested that the young Soviet child must grow up prepared to fight for the world proletariat. Indeed, this has not been a theme in *Murzilka* in any of the years examined.

### The Lenin myth

A theme closely intertwined with patriotism and figuring largely in the school readers is Lenin. Looking at *Murzilka* over the years enables the development of Lenin's portrayal to children as a semi-divine figure to be observed.

Only four years after his death, the Lenin myth had not appeared at all on the horizon of the NEP child. There was but one reference to him in the *Murzilka*s for 1928 in a poem, 'In the North', which briefly describes his exile (January 1928:9).

Nowhere is there any suggestion of the cult figure he was later to become – had, indeed, already become in 1938. Then, like Stalin, Lenin was presented not so much as a great man – political thinker, revolutionary strategist and statesman – but as a more than human giant on a pedestal, revered more for some inherent greatness rather than his contribution to particular historical achievements. The elusiveness of fact in the wrapping of magical abstractions partly served to give these figures the added emotional power of mystery but even more to ensure that no blemish marred the past's perfect legitimation of the present. Thus, as a great teacher, Lenin legitimated the greatness of his pupil, Stalin, in a way that a factual representation of their relationship would certainly have complicated. A typical example is:

### Lenin Lived

Lenin! Who does not know him?
From the Kremlin, where he soundly sleeps,
To the mountain tops of the blue Altai
The glory of Lenin brightly shines.

Higher than the mountains, wider than every sea,
Heavier than the very earth
Was our people's grief
When he died, our dear one.

Lenin died. But stronger than steel,
Firmer than the flinty mountain races
Came his pupil – splendid Stalin.
He is leading us to victories and happiness.

(October 1938:10.)

Similarly, the reader learns how a young Spanish refugee and his father on leave from the Civil War celebrate their happy reunion by going to Lenin's mausoleum (December 1938:3–5). Once Lenin's name began being used for the purposes of character-education, it very quickly became invested with certain supernatural powers. The speed with which this happened supports the view that it was in no way a spontaneous development among unsophisticated folk but rather the product of highly subtle, convoluted, daring of cynical thinking.

Khrushchev's secret speech in 1956 denouncing the cult of personality rid *Murzilka* of any contemporary cult figures but did not in any way rationalise the treatment accorded to Lenin. There were, though, rather more stories telling the readers about a few of his policies (e.g. on electrification and the mechanising of agriculture) to supplement the abstract, emotional presentation. A post-Twentieth-Congress example of the latter was a poem in which the reader is told that when, in a famous portrait, Lenin is seen with his arms round three children, it is as if he were enfold-ing all the children of the earth, embracing

> All those who carefully write near the Volga
> Or study their lessons by the Kura river.
> Il'yich embraced them and you also
> He embraced with all other children. (April 1958:3.)

Lenin was thus still firmly established as a figure with powers rising above those of ordinary people; this is one of the most constant elements on the pages of *Murzilka* from 1938 through to the 1970s. No examples of the mythologising of Lenin from *Murzilka* of the early 1970s are given here, since they would merely parallel those already quoted at length from the school readers. It is enough to add that there are frequent indeed such examples. The development of the Lenin myth differs basically from the development of other themes in *Murzilka*; it is a much more steadily developing theme, lacking the dramatic swings in emphasis characterising the other themes examined. In 1938, much of his role as a cult figure was, of course, shared by Stalin so that he had not yet achieved the solitary dominance he later won.

The myth of Lenin can be shown as appearing steadily; this does not mean that certain differences in his depiction throughout the Soviet period do not occur. In 1938, he was necessarily por-trayed primarily in high and formal abstraction in order to make the slogan 'Stalin is Lenin Today' seem convincing. In 1958, it was aspects of his character (which underline his differences from Stalin) that were stressed: the reader is told particularly of his common touch and his accessibility especially to children. In the seventies, both in the readers and *Murzilka*, there was perhaps an added highlighting of his reasonableness, common sense and practicality (his purported ability to make games for children and to listen to all rational appeals). These qualities are those which were widely acclaimed as the hallmarks of Brezhnev and his colleagues; it would give them an added weight if they could be implied to be part of a Leninist tradition.

It has been observed that myths are created when those exercising social control feel the need to legitimate their power. In 1938, there was, of course, a great deal to legitimate. The purges and the enforced collectivisation and resulting famines, for example, were to be hidden behind the myths created around Lenin and Stalin. In 1958, Soviet life was much more open – but the extent of Stalin's crimes and of the then leaders' part in them was not fully exposed. The myth of the seventies is concerned to demonstrate the historical continuity between the populist revolutionary power (i.e. the Soviet power of 1917) and the contemporary leadership. This involves making Lenin, as founder of the ruling Party, into a populist super-hero who acted on behalf of the masses but more wisely and firmly than they could themselves. The Party is thus legitimated as the heir to Lenin. It is shown to be the embodiment of Lenin's concept of a group of people committed to the masses but active more effectively and with a longer perspective because they are guided by Marxism. The Party and only the Party can (and will) lead the people to Communism. Lenin's image and Lenin's behests are constant symbols of revolutionary intent in a not over-revolutionary world.

*Atheism*

In the school readers, atheism was not found to be directly encouraged to any significant extent despite its supposedly fundamental place in Marxist ethics. It is only in 1938 that we find any material of a pointedly anti-religious nature.

One story is set just before the Revolution and is about a poor little girl at a convent school. She is treated cruelly by the nuns. In their play, the pupils display fierce malice towards the nuns; this is clearly felt by the author to be praiseworthy and legitimate. There is no question of turning the other cheek or suggesting that suffering might nurture a nobility of soul. The girl gets involved in revolutionary activity and is overjoyed when the Revolution frees her to become an ordinary child. 'I shall be happy' she says confidently (February 1938:7–9).

Another story is set in the more distant past and is about an Italian scholar who has fled a monastery from the Inquisition. It is made plain that he has not become a monk out of love of God but out of a desire for the knowledge only available in the monastery's library. He has read Copernicus who had been declared a heretic and has even gone one stage further than him by realising that the universe is endless. As a result, he has been excommunicated and the Pope has begun to prepare tortures for him. (It is noteworthy that the group of monks waiting to practise these tortures on him is called a *staya* ('pack'), a word normally used for a group of animals.) Eventually, he is betrayed but he refuses to save himself by denying his convictions. He is cruelly burnt (February 1938:13–15).

These stories, then, are clearly intended to arouse indignation at the horrors perpetrated by religion. It is ironic that attention was being drawn to such events at a time when the most vicious crimes of the Stalinist period were taking place. Although it is ironic in retrospect, it is also a perfect example of Stalin's lie technique in action. How could anyone doubt the credentials of a regime that was so explicitly concerned with fighting cruelty and unreason?! To the extent that the Inquisition – like fascism – was bad, so then must Stalin be good.

The presentation of this anti-religious material can be seen, too, as yet another facet of Stalin's use of fear and hatred to manipulate social attitudes. This in turn highlighted the external enemy with the purpose again of rallying a united Soviet collective against it. It also, of course, sought to dissuade any who might be tempted towards religion – the only remaining tolerated alternative focus of loyalty – from aligning themselves with anything so hostile to justice and humanity (qualities claimed by the Church which some of Stalin's citizens must have found particularly appealing at the time).

## Aspects of Soviet life

Here various features specific to Soviet life and reflected in *Murzilka* are gathered together. Some of these are of interest not just for the role in character-education which they may possess but also for the simple historical value of what they reveal of the flavour of Soviet society of their time.

There is, in fact, hardly any specifically Soviet content in the

*Murzilka*s of NEP Russia. The stories naturally reflect the conditions of their time and place, but only as unhighlighted elements
of background and not to convey a particular political message.
Many of the characters come from children's homes; those who
don't occasionally spend their leisure time collecting money for
the waifs *(besprizornye)*.[3] One story throws interesting light on
the child-care of the time: it tells of a lonely little boy who envies
children on the other side of a wall who are playing all sorts of
jolly, inventive games in a bright playground. At last, he can
stand it no longer and jumps over the wall to join them. But he
isn't a member and the caretaker throws him out, saying that the
boy's father has paid no subscription for him and so he can't play
there. The child replies that his father now has some money and
he will persuade him to let him join (July 1928:6–9). It is unexpected to the modern reader to find money looming so large in
a story about such a situation. One somehow expected the story
to end with the child being allowed to stay out of sympathy for
his unfortunate circumstances.

The postbag pages are a revealing source of information on the
extent of the penetration of the cultural revolution into daily life.
Thus one child writes that his parents have a radio (March
1928:26). Another urges all readers to clean their teeth regularly
(August 1928:31). Yet another writes of hooliganism at her school
and of how the teachers just do not know how to cope (October
1928:30).

The October Revolution is scarcely mentioned. One story tells
of a dog who acted in a heroic way in the Civil War, carrying
bandages and medicines at the front (January 1928:21–2). In
contrast with the October issues of the 1970s, which are crowded
with commemorative articles, the October issue of 1928 has just
one page alluding to the anniversary. This is in the form of a song
called 'October Day'; the words go as follows:

> Today is the united festival of workers and peasants,
> We are all workers' children and shall join their ranks,
> We are little children but from us shall grow replacements
> For the defence of freedom; our turn will come.

[3] The *besprizornye* (literally the 'uncared-for ones') were homeless children.
who became a major Russian problem after the Civil War.

So may everyone see that dear to all children
Are Soviet Russia and the struggle for her.
Banners, flags, songs, the Pioneer is summoned
And the children all cry, 'Always, always ready'.
(October 1928:27).

These, then, are the only mentions of the new Soviet system in 1928 editions of *Murzilka*. They have only the secondary, historical, interest referred to for there is certainly no sustained attempt – indeed hardly any attempt at all – to impress on children particular political attitudes. Nor is there any campaign in *Murzilka* against the opinions hostile to the regime which must then have been more explicit than in the 1970s after forty-five years of political propaganda and repression of anti-Soviet views. This may in some degree be explained by the different nature of anti-system views then and now. Then, anti-Soviet views were held by conservatives in reduced circumstances who still refused to accept the new order. Now, dissenting opinions are more probably held by disillusioned intellectuals in opinion-shaping professions who are much more likely to prove an active menace to those in charge of social control. It is those who desire radical change who chain themselves to railings, not people who pine for a return to the good old days. Thus, from the authorities' point of view, it is logical to provide a greater strength of armour against anti-Party views in today's *Murzilka* than in 1928. In the light of the overall lack of preoccupation with character-education in 1928, however, it is unlikely that the lack of propaganda countering anti-Soviet views was due to any conscious decision but rather to the general NEP attitude of *laissez-faire* which had not yet died.

By 1938, there has been a remarkable change; there is much that can be discussed here that is of interest primarily for its part in the process of character-education. A particular role is played by the presentation – often in cult terms – of certain contemporary figures as heroes. Stalin is, of course, the most significant of these but there are others, nearly all of them political leaders. The only important cult figure who was not primarily a political leader is Ivan Papanin. He was at the head of a group of scientists who, in 1938, set up camp on a drifting ice-floe, observing and experimenting in Arctic conditions. His feats, intrinsically stirring to the child's imagination and spirit of adventure, were used for character-education ends: what brave and skilful deeds our Soviet citizens accomplish to extend the resources and knowledge of the Motherland! Papanin certainly seems to have captured the enthusiasm of Soviet children in 1938, for his name occurs in five of the year's issues, in the postbag from the readers themselves, who seemed particularly to enjoy drawing him on his floe, as well as in features by the editorial staff. In many ways, Papanin is a counter-balance to the less attractive heroes with whom the children were presented that year. Courage in the face of physical hardship for the sake of knowledge is a quality which most would find appealing and worthy of being used to inspire young children. Papanin is not allowed to be an altogether apolitical figure though: it is stressed that his bravery was motivated by the desire 'to fulfil Comrade Stalin's task' (March 1938:2). His example to some extent thus serves to add lustre to Stalin's own name.

The other contemporary heroes with whom the child of 1938 was presented were overtly political. Current commissars were named in a way that does not happen in the other years examined. The most startling of these figures was Yezhov. To hear the head of Stalin's secret police, the man responsible for the most vicious stage of the purges, described as 'Uncle Yezhov' takes even the informed reader momentarily by surprise. In the spring of 1938, a whole page was devoted to him. The article (which appeared under a large determined-looking portrait) is quoted in full not only for the morbid curiosity value it has in retrospect but also for the light it casts upon the spirit of the times, even in the world of the schoolchild, and upon the facility with which the Party machine could turn a cold-blooded and opportunist nonentity into a hero overnight.

### Nikolay Ivanovich Yezhov

'Uncle Yezhov! I promise to you that I shall defend the Soviet frontier. I love you because you protect the frontier and our Stalin' – thus writes six-year-old Shura Potienko from Kiev to the Peoples Commissar for Internal Affairs, Nikolay Ivanovich Yezhov.

All Soviet children subscribe to Shura Potienko's letter. Our children passionately love the fighting spirit of our Scouts and their fearless leader, Nikolay Ivanovich Yezhov.

Comrade Yezhov is the friend of the workers, a firm Bolshevik–Leninist and one of the closest helpers of our beloved leader and teacher, Iosif Vissarionovich Stalin.

Comrade Yezhov was born in 1896. As a fourteen-year-old boy, he was already working at one of the Petersburg factories. In 1917, Yezhov joined the Bolshevik party.

Since then, he has for more than 20 years been in the leading ranks of the fighters for communism. He was commissar of a number of Red Army front-line divisions in the Civil War. The Civil War ended and Yezhov was entrusted with important party work.

In 1936, the Soviet government appointed comrade Yezhov leader of the People's Commissariat of Internal Affairs of the USSR. The enemies of the people felt that their end was near. They tried to kill comrade Yezhov but their conspiracy failed. The Soviet Intelligence, led by Nikolay Ivanovich Yezhov, has mercilessly destroyed enemy nests of Trotskyists, Bukharinites and Rykovites.

In 1937, the Soviet government awarded comrade Yezhov the Order of Lenin.

Comrade Yezhov works in the tradition of the very first Leninist intelligence officer, the famous Feliks Dzerzhinsky. (June 1938:2.)

The Soviet child could hardly foretell from this that Uncle Yezhov was himself to be dismissed (and later destroyed 'like a viper' by his colleagues) only nine months after this. Not just Yezhov but Kalinin and Molotov also had their portraits in *Murzilka* in 1938 (February 1938:2). Voroshilov shows a heroism in a story a month later (March 1938:3–6). But, of course, the prime political hero of the time is Stalin.

This utilisation of real contemporary figures as heroes had completely died out by 1958. Inversely the Lenin myth had increased in importance; the September 1958 issue discussed in detail at the beginning of the chapter is typical in lacking, apart from this, all specifically Soviet content.

The *Murzilka*s of the early seventies, like the school readers, present a wealth of material alluding to exclusively Soviet traditions and events. There are frequent poems about the jollity of May parades, regular articles on the Pioneer symbols, many hymns to the Party or to Lenin, and stories about Vladimir Il'yich as a child. There is also treatment of the Ninth Five-year Plan, which is discussed in an entertaining fashion designed to make it interesting and relevant to a young reader. 'Stories about the Ninth Five-year Plan', a monthly series of short articles on some aspect of the Plan, started in July 1971. The August 1971 article deals with products from the sea, for example, and the October 1971 one with oil. The first article in the series introduces the Plan and explains it as a kind of magical omniscient prophet:

Moreover, the State Plan knows that tomorrow you'll want to have not one pair of shoes but two, and it plans for the building of some more footwear factories. It knows that tomorrow people will want to have faster aeroplanes and so it plans for the construction of new jets. The State Plan plans the tasks for all plants, factories, building-sites and electric-power stations – for our whole economy. (July 1971: 13.)

In this historical outline, however, it should be noted that, between 1958 and 1970, material on specifically Soviet topics has moved from just articles about Lenin to a large number of stories and poems on a wide range of Soviet subjects. Although, of course, the individual figures eulogised in 1938 have not crept back in, the Party has – and notably so, for, as already remarked, the Party itself is deliberately mythologised in the current Soviet character-education process. The incorporation of specifically Soviet content remains an integral part of the character-education process as it has to a greater or lesser extent been since the thirties.

## Recent themes

### Stimulating reading

Before concluding our study of *Murzilka*, four topics which have a place only in issues of the magazine for 1970–71 and which are of particular interest are worthy of mention: let us take the least controversial of these themes first. As children's reading is the focus of attention of this work, it is of particular interest for us to examine the ways in which *Murzilka* tries to stimulate the habit of reading in children.

An issue in the spring of 1971 dealt at some length with the joys of reading: four pages, headed assertively 'A Book is Your Best Friend', were devoted to the subject (March 1971:2–6).

This article was the first of a series published in preparation for the fiftieth anniversary of the Pioneer organisation in May 1972. From that issue on, the magazine each month presented the Little Octobrist with some task to complete in order to prove his worthiness to belong to a Soviet children's movement. The first task assigned to him was to read a certain number of books, depending on his age, from a list prepared by the magazine. Making reading the primary task was justified in the feature by pointing out that books would help the children in all future assignments. Reading was thus shown as indispensable in life and having an important utilitarian function.

It is also significant that reading is not presented as being purely a private and individual pleasure. Some social responsibility is attached to reading a good book. This is demonstrated neatly by a story in which the teacher asks if any of her first-year pupils have read a particular fairy-tale. Vasya, to his great delight, is the only child who is familiar with it and he puts up his hand confident of praise from the teacher. He receives, however, a reprimand. If he enjoyed the story, why has he failed to recommend it to his classmates? (August 1971:2.) Thus, in this aspect of living, too, the collective is given priority. The feature also informs the Little Octobrist how physically to handle books in a responsible manner. Again, it does so in no overtly moralistic fashion but through an entertaining little verse which depicts books weeping bitterly because they have been made dirty and dog-eared by the little boy who owns them (August 1971:4).

One section of the article is an introduction to a library catalogue system. The remainder of the whole feature deals with the very first books for children about Lenin, claiming that they are still the favourite books of children whose grandparents once read them with delight (August 1971:3). Thus the only works singled out for individual treatment are books about, once again, the heroic myth figure central to the seventies' planned socialisation process.

This feature, though dealing with the child's personal out-of-school reading, is still predominantly concerned with social aspects of the reading habit, with how to use a library and how to handle books so that they remain readable for others as well as with the need to share a book which has given pleasure with the whole collective. It does not try to stress the private delights which reading can bring the individual.

In other issues of *Murzilka*, when the subject of reading was introduced it is usually its functional value as an educator which is highlighted. In an issue published at the end of 1970, for example, the instructional role of books is given an added contemporary appeal by taking the instances of space research:

A rocket flew to the Moon, gathered rock there and brought it back to Earth. This rocket was made by people who, from their very childhood, treasured books as the dearest thing of all and school as the dearest place. (December 1970:2.)

Just as the school readers contain material designed to strengthen the prestige of the children's organisations, so *Murzilka*, a magazine for Little Octobrists, contains material reinforcing the work of the school. The article referred to above continues with the patriotic reasons for diligent study.

About a country where all children study, they say, 'That's a very powerful and glorious country.' This is a just comment – for to an educated man, all is possible. And so it happens – top marks on the report-card of our girls and boys make the whole Soviet Union still stronger and more glorious. (December 1970:3.)

Thus the schoolwork of children is invested with a lofty role in the pursuit of a common Soviet cause. This is given even more concrete form by the proposition that children should aim to fulfil certain norms in the same way that their parents do on the shop floor. All children should aim at getting only top marks in honour of the next Party Congress. The Young Pioneers are said to have already made this resolution. The article suggests that the Little Octobrists should do likewise, for Communists would indeed rejoice at such a 'present'.

The purposiveness which is so evident in all spheres of Soviet life is, therefore, given a practical meaning for the child at an early age. He is told he is reading not so much for his own pleasure or betterment or for the abstract advancement of knowledge as for the benefit of society.

## Femininity

The other three topics arising from the *Murzilka*s of 1970–71 –

femininity, envy, and freedom – have a complexity not found in
the school readers and are unexpected subjects in a publication
for young children. In them, although the subject matter may be
difficult, the presentation is made simple and easily intelligible to
the more thoughtful child. These three topics could be classed
together under the heading, 'how to live powerless in a world of
power'. In the first passage, it is women who are the powerless.

In a 1971 issue, in the middle of an extract from a short story
by Yuri Karinets entitled 'I'm not Afraid of Grandfather Frost'
(already referred to above), there is a long digression on the
question of femininity. The passage is quoted below in its entirety
in view of its interest:

Have you ever noticed how girls move? In particular, slender girls,
slim ones? They move quite differently from boys. You and I – I
mean boys and men – walk simply, without thinking about how
we're walking. But girls think. And women also. Just have a look at
them on the street. They walk all the time as if they were looking in
a mirror although there is no mirror in front of them. Of course,
not all of them walk like that. But girls like that are uninteresting.
It's not worth looking at them. But it is always worth looking at the
others – how they walk, how they move, how they hold anything in
their fingers...Then they look as if they were imagining terribly
hard. Although, in fact, they aren't imagining at all. That is simply
how they move and that is all there is to it. They move very
musically, as if in time to music or to some song. Everything sings
in their movements – the turn of their head, their hands, their legs.
Haven't you noticed? I've noticed! I noticed it especially in Gizi.

Why is it so, do you think? It's because women are completely
different beings! Quite, quite different from you and me. In girls
there is a mystery! I can tell you this for certain. And this mystery
is one which we like. Many writers have thought about this mystery
– many, many people; not just I, but all mankind, has been thinking
about it for millions of years, and will always think about it and will
never solve it. Perhaps, of course, it will be solved. And then another
thing; if man does solve this mystery, he will at once be worse off.
The whole interest of the puzzle will be lost. We always want to
know everything, to solve all mysteries, but we never consider the
fact that a mystery is also a good thing. There are mysteries which
we always want to solve and yet never want to be solved! May such
mysteries remain for ever! (July 1971:8–9.)

The romantic mystique surrounding women in this text is not

at all what the uninitiated might expect in a Soviet work. Although, in socialist realist novels, women are often honoured in a rather sentimental way as the selfless mothers of the future Soviet men, one rarely meets a passage like this one which treats women neither as valuable members of society nor as practical home-builders, but rather as part of an 'eternal enigma' in a somewhat nineteenth-century romantic fashion. Surprising, too, is the author's strictly non-functional attitude to the way women walk. He finds it uninteresting if they walk in an asexual manner; it is as strange to find the matter approached with this attitude as it is to find any mention of the topic at all in a magazine for Little Octobrists (more than half of whom are girls). The generalisation at the end of the extract that some mysteries are best left unsolved seems to be a remark hardly in full accordance with the scientific materialist world-view which considers it possible, desirable and necessary to investigate and resolve all problems.

In several ways, the attitudes expressed in the above passage are far from typical of the approach to women in most Soviet writing, historically considered; but it does seem to be of significance that such opinions are freely expressed in a widely circulating magazine for young children. The story from which this excerpt was taken has not only appeared (in abridged form) in *Murzilka*, but also in covers as a complete novella and in serialised form in the journal *Koster* described in chapter three. The 'eternal feminine' is, therefore, certainly not dismissed in the USSR of the 1970s as an absurd bourgeois prejudice. The incredulity of the historical Lenin and his colleagues (including Kollontai) in response to a suggestion that such a passage would appear in a Soviet journal sixty years on can be imagined!

As opposed to an autonomous person image of women, Western advertisers, for example, present two simplified images: glamour girl and mother; all other human attributes are subsumed in these stereotypes. The everyday Soviet presentation of women is usually a Soviet version of the latter. Here we seem to be seeing the Russian version of the former being legitimised. Why? The most plausible interpretation is that belief seems to be growing in 'leading circles' that sex is being taken too casually in the USSR and is too easily available on a non-family (i.e. non-fertile) basis. If girls can be made mysterious and inaccessible enough, the marriage and birth rates might go up – and the children be brought up in a good old-fashioned disciplined environment. Men must be men, and therefore by extension, girls girls. Men with long hair and girls with short (and 'unisex' norms), they seem to think, will undermine marriage, disrupt the family and produce milksops, not warriors! (But, of course, few go so far as to consider dispensing with women in the labour force in the mass trades and professions.)

*Envy*

The second somewhat complex topic to be discussed is that of envy, an emotion well-known to those who feel themselves to be powerless in a world of power. It is, in other words, a sentiment common in societies marked by substantial inequalities and it is, therefore, of interest that *Murzilka* has included material for its readers on the complex problem of how to cope with this troublesome emotion.

One example of this material takes the form of a story; it is given added force by being written in the first person. It begins with the words, 'In my childhood, I envied everyone.' The directness of the first-person narrative makes it easier for the reader to be aware of and to admit to this feeling in himself as he identifies with the author. The latter recounts how he envied one child for his long arms, another for the speed of his running and a third for his keen ears (all unchangeable somatic attributes). The negativeness of envy is suggested by the reasons he gives why he envies these boys. Long arms make it easier to steal apples. Fast legs can run away more quickly once the apples have been stolen. And sharp ears are quick to hear the approach of the watchman. Above all, one boy, Pet'ka, is envied for his brain, which the author would have used to invent a berry-picking machine which, in one process, would gather the berries and hide them in the culprit's pocket. Whole days and even weeks are wasted in envying friends for their different characteristics and imagining what could be done with such talents. Then, one day, Pet'ka, appropriately the boy who is envied for his brain, confesses how he himself wishes he had the author's spare time. If only he had so much leisure, he would use it in so many worthwhile ways (December 1970: 21).

The implicit moral of this story is that envy achieves nothing except the discontent of the person involved. In society, there are two possible interpretations of envy. It can either be seen as useful and incorporated as a motive-force – into an incentive system – or it can be seen as destructive, in which case it must be undermined. The Soviet interpretation is largely the latter. Having decided that envy should be undermined, society can set about doing so in two ways; firstly, subjectively, through psychological counselling and the socialisation process or, secondly, objectively, by measures to minimise inequalities. The Soviet approach here is the former. Such a story as the above teaches that we all have our natural allotted functions and roles in society and should not be jealous of others' greater command over resources (in the adult world based on the division of labour into manual and mental – by implication the same kind of natural difference as arm-length). That one should not envy leading figures their privileges may well follow on from assimilating the moral not to envy Pet'ka for his brain.

Envy and inequality must not be exaggerated as themes in contemporary *Murzilka*s. That they are treated at all, however, and that they are treated in this particular way, is certainly of interest.

### Freedom

The final theme is that of freedom. It is dealt with in a story which attempts to explain in a child's terms the Soviet interpretation of Engels's dictum 'freedom is the recognition of necessity'.

Misha's mother is trying to clarify this for her son. He cannot understand the definition in relation to his morning exercises. He can accept that they are a necessity, but not that there is any freedom attached to doing them – for, in his view, there is only freedom when something is 'interesting'. His mother devises a way of making the exercises into a game so that he agrees that they are now interesting. The next day, Misha is eager to do the exercises and has himself thought of a game which can be incorporated into them (December 1970:24). By such a simple story, a difficult concept is made clear even to a young child. It demonstrates, in a situation from the child's own experience, how man can adjust his thought to make productive use of necessity.

It is one of the rare cases when an aspect of Soviet philosophy rather than Soviet ritual is discussed in *Murzilka*, and, as with the two previous areas, the fact that the topic is raised at all is of interest. It is not an easy idea and its treatment here suggests the importance which is attached to the child's grasping of the concept. Lack of freedom is, of course, one of the criticisms most frequently levelled at the Soviet system and it is, therefore, perhaps not altogether surprising that attention should be drawn to material presenting the Soviet approach to the question of freedom so that the child is armed for possible future attack (with the retort that freedom is possible but only within certain historically determined limits). The implicit message of the story is, of course, that one can, and must, learn to enjoy doing what one is told by those better fitted to judge what are the objective requirements of the historical process.

It hardly needs pointing out that the treatment of the last three topics is in direct contradiction to the implications of what Marx and Engels understood by historical materialism. The first example (which dealt with femininity) is so openly so that it cannot, yet, at any rate, be said to reflect more than a tolerated view. The second (on envy) is interesting because it touches on the difficult area of word-spinning where the incentive system ('good' in Soviet terms) and workers' altruism (likewise 'good' – and more in line with Marx's concept of a socialist society) have to be reconciled. The final story (on freedom) is perhaps the most critical and difficult area: Marx and Engels set out to criticise and expose what they saw as bourgeois myths about 'absolute freedom', and the 'free society' of capitalism which they saw as disarming the working class in its struggle with capital. They believed that only by exposing the 'false consciousness' to which the workers had been brainwashed and the mechanisms of this could the proletariat win freedom by understanding that they had no choices but that between succumbing or taking power. In other words, they were demanding an unrelentingly penetrating assault on the then prevailing ideology, on what they saw as a justificatory cloud of words thrown up as a screen itself; it is, indeed, turned upside down in the above story for it is used to suggest that one's head and not reality is the ultimate object of adjustment – hardly Engels's intention.

This study of *Murzilka* develops understanding of contemporary Soviet writing for children in two ways. Firstly, it sets themes discovered in the previous chapter in an illuminating, historical perspective showing that many of the moral values stressed today have not been constantly emphasised throughout the Soviet period but demonstrate a rather uneven pattern of development. Secondly, it has brought to light several themes of particular interest which have not emerged elsewhere.

# 6

## Conclusions

In this chapter the aim is briefly to draw together those aspects of Soviet children's literature which are particularly indicative of the nature of Soviet society in the seventies.

### Legitimation

The socialisation process in a monistic society like the USSR is, as has already been seen, highly purposive. One of the main facets of its purpose is legitimating the authority of the group which exercises state power. Meyer, an American political scientist, in fact suggests that the whole of the Soviet character-education machinery is but a self-legitimating device for the elite (Meyer 1965:355). This is, of course, an exaggeration but it does serve to draw attention to the very important legitimating role of Soviet children's literature. In Western social science, Max Weber distinguished three bases on which legitimate authority could be founded, and three corresponding types of such authority (Weber 1947:328–9). Firstly, *rational grounds*: a belief in the 'legality' of patterns of normative rules and the right to those elevated to authority under such rules to issue commands: this can be termed *legal authority* and, under it, obedience is owed ultimately to the office-bearer. Secondly, *traditional grounds*: an established belief in the sanctity of immemorial traditions and the legitimacy of the status of those exercising power under them: this can be termed *traditional authority* and, under it, obedience is owed ultimately to somebody because of his position. Thirdly, *charismatic grounds*: devotion to the specific and exceptional sanctity, heroism or exemplary character of an individual person and of the normative patterns of order revealed or ordained by him: this can be termed *charismatic authority* and, under it, obedience is owed ultimately to somebody because of his personality.

There are, of course, ideal types and real societies depend usually to varying degrees on more than one of these kinds of authority rather than on one of them to the exclusion of both of the others:[1] thus in Britain, the authority of the Queen can be seen as traditional and that of the Prime Minister as legal. In the Second World War, Churchill's authority was legal but also largely charismatic. In the USA the authority of the President is largely legal, backed up in such cases as that of John F. Kennedy by a strong element of the charismatic. One might expect Soviet authority to be almost entirely legal: the denunciation of the cult of the personality has cast a large shadow on charismatic authority and traditional authority is not easily assumed by what claims to be a revolutionary regime. Soviet writing for children, however, shows interesting attempts to realise the potential of all three types of legitimacy. Attention is certainly paid to legal authority in, for instance, stories and verses which sing the praises of both the Soviets and the Party. Charismatic authority may no longer be blatantly invoked for living individuals, but it is certainly exploited through the treatment of Lenin. Treated as if he were still alive, Lenin is first invested with a powerful charisma and then shown to be making demands on the young Soviet citizen that are identical to those made by the contemporary authorities. Neither is traditional authority neglected. This is used largely through the theme of 'Holy Russia'. Soviet rule in Russia is made into part of a great Russian tradition – there are stories which liken Red soldiers in the Civil War to medieval knights. The patriotic motif, in particular, is also strengthened by the traditional authority which is given to it through works demonstrating the love which Russians have always had for their country and have recurringly demonstrated on battlefields with their lives. There are also many efforts to create new 'traditions' with a

---

[1] Marxism, of course, sees the recognition of the authority of the ruler by the ruled in class society as the archetype of 'false consciousness' – the misprision of the real world caused by the distortions of perception produced by conflicting class interests: capitalists actually employ ideologies to brainwash workers. Only in a socialist society could the concept of temporary legitimate authority be considered; under Communism, by definition, there will either be no authority or all will possess it in equal measure.

specifically Soviet emphasis, as will be shown in more detail later.

Thus, in a number of ways, Soviet writing for children is used to further the legitimation of Soviet power and all three types of authority are called into action to help the cause.

In a pluralistic society like the USA, Canada or Britain, of course, the whole process is much more haphazard. The legitimacy of the US President, the Canadian Prime Minister, the British Monarch or any current political personality is not learnt to any great extent through direct features in children's books (although the mass media do play a part in maintaining the myths of consensus). A sense of legitimacy is picked up much more casually, as is in keeping with the nature of a pluralist society.

As far as children's literature is concerned, it would certainly be an exaggeration to suggest like Meyer that self-legitimation is the only purpose of the Soviet ruling elite's character-education programme. Its aim, however, is clearly very largely didactic in the broader sense that general character-education is kept in line with official demands on the future Builder of Communism.

Any secular morality must provide itself with the inspiration and authority that are a fundamental part of religious morality. Above we have dealt with the question of authority, let us now turn to that of inspiration.

## Inspiration

Any reading of Soviet children's literature shows that the Soviet authorities have realised the importance of their inspirational task and have found certain ways of providing secular sources of inspiration. The inspirational function of moral education is openly acknowledged: 'Great goals give birth to a great energy. Ideological and political education stimulates and directs people's creativity. All history bears witness to the fact that the maximum development of a person's creative abilities is inseparably linked with a high ideological commitment.' (Arkhangel'sky 1967:218.) This seems, perhaps, less close to Marx's view of ideas as part of a superstructure based on society's economic foundation of property relationships than to Max Weber's conception of the role of ideology in society: 'The magical and religious forces and the ethical ideas of duty based upon them have, in the past, always

been among the most important formative influences on conduct.'
(Weber 1971:27.)

In children's literature it is the image of the future which plays
the main inspirational role in Soviet morality, giving rise to such
verses as this one by Mikhalkov – a very prominent figure in the
hierarchy of Soviet children's authors.

> 'Communism'!
> What a word!
> How much it includes!
> Sometimes with hope,
> Sometimes severely
> It is pronounced,
> Bread for all,
> Gardens in the desert,
> A triumph of great ideas.
> All are equal!
> And there is no trace
> Of deprived people.
> Let enemies over the ocean
> Twist their mouths mockingly –
> It's too late or too early –
> But all the same it will come to pass,
> There are millions of us in the world.
> We are not alone on the march.
> We have the banners of fighting friends
> On high with our flag.
> 'Communism'!
> For us this word
> Shines brighter than a lighthouse.
> 'Be prepared!
> – Always prepared!'
> Glory to the Leninist Central Committee. (Kibareva 1969:6.)

One can easily query the effectiveness of such unsubtlety but
this is a typical example of many possible instances, showing the
deliberate replacement of heaven after death by a future heaven
on earth. It is the Soviet equivalent of the transcendent; it also
contains an important safety-valve element in its nature as inspirer
in that it inspires not only great effort for the benefit of the
future but also endurance of present hardship for the sake of the
future. The glorious Communist future certainly is a major part
of the inspiration element reinforcing Soviet morality.

The Motherland, as well as the Communist future, is also promoted as a spur to noble action. There is an abundance of stories showing how Russians devoted themselves to Mother Russia in the past. By these, children are encouraged to dedicate themselves to their native land – all the more so now that the Motherland, as the leader among socialist states, is so intimately bound up with the Communist future. Work is a joyful service of the Motherland. The army's blessed role is to defend her borders. It is possible that, as a more tangible and more traditional cause, the Motherland is, in the last analysis, more effective an inspiration than Communism after sixty years of not wholly smooth progress towards it. In discussing Soviet legitimation, it was also noted how prominent a role was played by patriotism (especially in the provision of traditional authority); it is clear that the dominant place of patriotism in Soviet character-education is due largely to the way in which it helps to fulfil the two important tasks of providing secular Soviet alternatives for both inspiration and authority in morality.

The other major element providing inspiration in the Soviet Union is, of course, Lenin. Here use is made of the age-old device of inspiring through hero figures. The prevalence of tales about Lenin is one of the most distinctive characteristics of Soviet children's literature; there has been no parallel hero of such stature in the West since Jesus. There are large numbers of children's books depicting him. Many other books, for adults, discuss the best way to portray him to children. An early and ever-popular book in this genre for children is *Nash samy lushchiy drug* (*Our Very Best Friend*; Krupskaya 1963), a biography of Lenin. It contains many portraits of him, especial prominence being given to those which show him with children. The chief aspects of his character which are stressed are: devotion to the Marxist cause, care for comrades, zeal for life, approach to everyone as an equal, true understanding of workers and peasants, love of reading (especially poetry and novels with a good social content), self-discipline, love of a simple life, diligence in study, love of children, love of all people (except the enemies of the Revolution) and gaiety. Krupskaya wrote this book in order to improve the standard of works for children about Lenin, which she deplored for their triviality. (In such stories, too much of

Lenin's time was spent looking at sunsets and embracing little children rather than engrossing himself in Party work.) Krupskaya's own book does not avoid all possibility of such criticism because it, too, is concerned more with highlighting Lenin's humanity than his teaching, but it certainly treats him in less of a myth-creating way. Most stories depict him as a solace, an inspiration, a model for our own behaviour and as a still-living force, the last element strikingly demonstrated by the common slogan, 'Lenin Lived, Lenin Lives and Lenin Shall Live'. All these aspects of his portrayal are paralleled by earlier depictions of Jesus. It is as if the Soviet authorities have consciously tried to provide a Communist Christ-figure to appeal to the masses. As a result, Lenin is certainly not presented to Soviet children in any rational way which objectively describes his political behaviour or his writings.

The aim is to inspire not to create a historically realistic picture. Soviet society could be said explicitly to tolerate some half-truths. Zhdanov, for example, in a speech to the First All-Union Congress of Soviet Writers (1934), said that life must be presented 'not simply as objective reality...but rather as reality in its revolutionary development. The truthfulness and exactitude of the artistic image must be linked with the task of ideological transformation, of the education of the working people in the spirit of socialism.' (Zhdanov 1950:15.) Such a doctrine permits falsification if it furthers the political cause. Soviet mythologising reached an extreme in the Stalin era, as was seen in chapter five. Of Stalin's image, as presented to children in the East European countries, Neuburg writes:

He was the embodiment of Dialectics, the Central Hero, the Greatest Whatever mankind possessed. He was deity on earth, in whose worship some Bulgarian kindergartens developed a whole ritual. Children were told to shut their eyes and pray to God; they did, and nothing happened. They were then told to shut their eyes and pray to Uncle Stalin; when they had, they could open their eyes and were given their sweets for the day. (Neuburg 1972:75.)

As we have seen, political figures of the seventies do not as individuals serve as inspirational figures although the Party can be viewed as a latter-day version of the 'men of gold' (remembering that any good Soviet person can realistically aspire to acquire 'gold' in his veins). To sum up, the Communist future, the Motherland, Lenin and, to a much lesser extent, the Party are the theories which are promoted to serve the Soviet Union's inspirational needs.

## Violence and death

Let us now move to those topics which are universally contentious among theorists of children's literature. In chapter one it was noted that violence and death are topics about whose suitability for children's literature there is considerable disagreement. What is the Soviet approach here? The military theme is potentially violent. Let us look at the popular story by Baruzdin, *Shel po ulitse soldat* (*A Soldier Went Along the Street*), a book for pre-school children. This is a history of the Soviet army. Each section deals with some incident in the Red Army's development from the storming of the Winter Palace onwards; each section opens with 'A soldier went along the street', the child-loved device of repetition. The closing is quoted here in full to illustrate both the way violence is not stressed in the portrayal of soldiers and also the way that soldiering is presented as an enjoyable duty, part of a great tradition – and yet certainly not something just of the past.

A soldier went along the street. A familiar soldier. Where have we seen him? It seems that he resembles that soldier who took the Winter Palace in '17. And that one who came back victorious after the civil war in '22. And that soldier who defended our borders in 1930. And that soldier who defended our Motherland at Lake Hassan in 1937 and on the Karelian Isthmus in 1939 and '40. And, of course, he is like the heroic soldier of the Great Patriotic War. And he's also like the young soldier jet-pilots and defenders who came to the aid of their friends.
Yes, he's like your grandfathers, fathers and older brothers.
But all the same. . .
A soldier went along the street. It is you.
A few years will pass. For some of you, ten years, for some – twelve, for some – a few more and you will become a soldier.
Not in order to attack other countries but in order to defend your own country.
You will become a soldier.

You will become a soldier of the heroic Soviet Army.
You will become a soldier of the Soviet land.
You will become a soldier of the great Soviet people.

(Baruzdin 1969:45-7.)

This excerpt sums up the presentation of soldiers to Soviet children. In war conditions, the soldier is shown as merciless towards enemies – but is always kind towards children, even those of hostile nations. He is depicted as an important figure because of his present-day relevance and his life is shown as having a romance that is due to tradition and honour rather than blood and iron. The point can be made that violence in Soviet children's literature is not presented as wrong *per se* but as depending on its moral significance in its context.

Thus, in an anthology, *Zhivye stranitsy* (*Living Pages*; Kibareva 1969), there is no fear of portraying violence in the story of a coloured boy-waiter in South Africa. His story has the telling title 'They have Taken Away even his Name'. He was amazed when the author addressed him with the polite form of the second person pronoun (*vy*); this contrasted with the way he had been summoned from a neighbouring table: 'Come here, monkey.' He had been sold to the bar owner when his whole tribe was being persecuted. He was very talented; he would draw anyone's portrait in twenty minutes if they paid – unjustly – the barman. Injustice and cruelty are the themes of this passage which ends poignantly: 'I remember his eyes, large and dark. If only you could see how suffering, sorrow and inexpressible human pain is in them!' (Kibareva 1969:273.) In the same anthology there is a letter, purportedly sent in by a little Venetian girl recounting how she and her brother go daily to sell souvenirs to tourists on St Mark's Square. Pathos is laid on very thickly. Their father is ill because of his heavy work in the factory – but the family is too poor to be able to send him to rest in the Dolomites. When they left their house, their mother was not yet up because she had been up very late the previous night over her work as a laundress. It takes the children two hours to get to work. They do not earn much but are happy because they can take home at least a little (Kibareva 1969:328).

Death is a subject largely avoided by modern Western children's literature (except by the horror-comics). It is also a rare topic in Soviet children's literature – but seems not to be skirted with quite the same squeamishness there. L. Panteleev in 'Our Masha' has his young heroine come to terms with the inevitability of death (Panteleev 1967). A fish, which has been caught but which she intended to put back in the stream, dies. Masha is convinced that this is rectifiable. 'We'll cure it. Doctor Oh-it-hurts [a popular character created by Chukovsky] will cure it.' But it has to be explained to her that there are some situations where even Doctor Oh-it-hurts is of no avail. Panteleev himself comments on this episode: 'Are we not making a mistake in encouraging Masha's passionate, committed love for everything alive? No, we are not. Let her be at times unhappy but in this way and only in this way can one educate a person's character.' (*Detskaya Literatura* 1973: No. 6, p. 5.) Death, however, must be natural; cruelty is inexcusable. Panteleev adds: 'A young torturer or murderer of butterflies cannot grow into a good, kind, big-hearted adult. I am convinced of this.' He goes on to describe an incident which suggests that violence must not be part of the child's world – despite the more 'realistic' approach of certain adults.

A girl a little older than Masha caught a butterfly and in front of the eyes of the other children tore off its wings.

'Stop it, what are you doing?' I asked the girl. She was surprised. 'What of it?'

'What do you mean, what of it? As if it were right to torment butterflies!' Masha attacked her with a voice trembling from indignation.

And then the mother of the girl interrupted our conversation. Up till now she had been quietly talking with her friends but she suddenly looked round and said sharply:

'Butterflies? Don't kill them? What strange talk! And even, forgive me, out-of-date talk. Don't you know, comrade, that butterflies are destructive?'

'Yes, I know, I've heard, Butterflies are harmful. Although I must admit that I don't really believe that in nature even one link can be superfluous, unnecessary, harmful...But if there truly are saboteurs in nature, if they really must be destroyed, then let adults do it. Just as adults, and not children, wage wars, catch criminals, judge them and punish them...'

This incident is notable for its statement of the need to shield children from unpleasantness – they must not become callous and corrupt. It is also worthy of note that, for Panteleev, this unpleasantness includes not just the killing of butterflies, but also war and the punishment of offenders.

The examples quoted in this section illustrate well the Soviet axiom that the end justifies the means. Violence is not described to titillate but to show the superiority of the kindly Soviet state. Except when used to this end, violence is absent from Soviet literature for children which preaches consideration and gentleness – except towards the enemies of the Soviet state.

### Adult problems

Closely allied to the problem of violence in children's literature is the presentation to children of adult problems – in particular, sex. From our own reading experience as erstwhile Western children, we know that such adult problems as sexual relationships and quarrelling between parents not long ago hardly featured in children's stories. In the stories of our childhood, if not of our children's, parents nearly always lived in perfect harmony and sexual questions were taboo.

Notably at variance with the usual Soviet treatment was one popular Soviet story first published before the Second World War – 'Golubaya chashka' ('The Blue Cup') by Arkady Gaidar (*Pioner* 1936: No. 1). This describes a man and his daughter going for a walk together in order to get away from the mother, who nags them. The little girl persuades her father to tell her what life with her mother was like before she was born; she convinces him that the mother still loves him, despite the visits she receives from an airman. The story's ending is happy in that the family atmosphere is friendly again when all are reunited after the walk. This is, then, no ordinary depiction of an unproblematic marriage; its allusions to adult problems and to jealousy are extraordinarily frank.

As might be expected, it was not accepted by all Soviet parents and teachers as being suitable for children. Many parents felt that it was 'a bomb' tearing apart their parental authority and undermining at their roots the basics of family life and morality (*Literaturnaya gazeta*, 26 June 1937). An angry mother wrote: 'It is shocking to offer such things to children. . .I should not like my son to understand the author's mood and to begin inspecting all the people who come to visit me and to become suspicious: children's faith must be preserved.' (*Detskaya literatura* 1937: No. 13, p. 40.) Some librarians also felt that the book was not suitable for children – particularly because of its bringing jealousy into the open. One made the following judgment of the book: 'The moods of jealousy which creep in throughout the book are impermissible in a children's book.' (*Idem.*) At first the defenders of the story were in a minority but they gradually gathered force. A. Zhavoronkova wrote: 'It is not at all obligatory to depict in children's books only ideal parents...Faith in parents...disappears as a result of discord in the family life of a specific family and not as the result of reading a book.' (*Detskaya literatura* 1937: No. 18, pp. 41–2.) It is now held that her views were 'more convincing and reasonable' than those of the story's opponents (Makarova 1973:170). Nevertheless, many feel that children will require a teacher's guidance to help them understand the work properly and, although the story is a striking and popular example of adult problems being presented in children's literature, it certainly is atypical. The more usual opinion is that children should be protected from knowledge of such disharmony. Perhaps only a writer as masterful as Gaidar, who could handle such a theme skilfully enough, could escape disapproval.

The question of protecting children from adult problems arises most frequently when children reach their teens and are tempted to read works intended for adults.[2] Should the child be encouraged to read as widely as he desires or should curbs be put on him? The official Soviet pedagogic policy here is argued by A. O. Pint (Pint 1971: 218–19). He quotes a letter to the national teachers' newspaper which asks the editorial board to settle an argument between the writer and her husband: they have a young relative to stay with them – a girl of about sixteen who has clearly read little but is devouring Zola's *Nana* and *The Womb of Paris*. The woman correspondent considers that a more mature age should be reached before reading such works – but her husband laughs at her for this, saying that it is better to let the child develop freely. Who is right? The editors refer the problem to a children's

[2] It should again be recalled that no really explicit literary material about sex is published in the Soviet Union – even for adults.

librarian, who replies by telling of an eminent pianist who was once asked to perform a difficult programme at a music school. When he learnt that his audience would have had no previous experience of composers like Skryabin and Liszt, he refused to play such a programme. He knew that it would mean nothing to the unprepared listeners and might prejudice them against such music for life. So it is with literature, argues Pint in the person of the librarian. The reader must be prepared for tackling such deep and distinctive writers as Zola, Flaubert and Maupassant. An intelligent guiding hand is indispensable. The librarian declares: 'I am categorically against "free development". Not all freedom is good. Occasionally it may lead to sad consequences, to vulgarization and cynicism.' She believes that adolescents should be protected from 'unsuitable food' and that teachers, librarians and, above all, parents should be skilled at doing this. Once a sixteen-year-old girl had asked to borrow John Braine's *Room at the Top*. The librarian asked her why she wanted to read it (although there was no Braine in the children's library and she could simply have refused). She wanted to read it because a friend had recommended it. On discussing the girl's reading experience, the librarian found she had not read very much and advised her to read some more straightforward works first: perhaps one day she would be mature enough to read John Braine.

Similarly, before one reads Zola or Flaubert or Maupassant, one should be familiar with the works of Turgenev and Tolstoy. Young people of fifteen and sixteen quite rightly do not consider themselves children and they are at this age interested in everything – particularly the mystery of human relationships. But Zola and Maupassant should not be the first to tell them about these. If one finds one's child reading these authors, one should not exclaim in horror and snatch the book away, one should simply say 'Let us look at something else that will make all this much clearer.' So, if adolescents are treated reasonably, it is argued, their interest can easily be diverted. It is quite explicitly felt to be necessary to divert their attention from works which deal too closely with sex.

Why should sex be mystified in this way? Why should it seem preferable to treat it with lies and silence rather than straightforwardness? The reasons are complex and are, of course, bound up with a society's overall attitude to sex. However, when a society is intensely goal-directed, it tends to encourage strong sexual self-discipline – as if feeling that men and women have only a limited supply of energy, as little as possible of which should be 'wasted' on something as self-indulgent as sex. In particular, young people are discouraged from practising (or even reading about) sex so that they can concentrate on study and on becoming more economically productive citizens. The goal-directedness of the USSR would thus seem to be a prime cause of Soviet official mystification of sex. In a similar way the American settlers imposed strict sexual standards. Correspondingly, in England, the Victorian morality, with its orientation on abstinence for capital accumulation, pursuit of the goals of Empire and the national destiny, mystified sex more than is the case today when the consensual morality lacks a unifying goal. It is perhaps un-surprising that books are now beginning to be produced for English-speaking children in which the heroes can come from broken homes and in which adolescents can have sexual feelings. According to Reich, sexual repression is the basis for political passivity and strict parental authority in the patriarchal family is the training ground for accepting state authority (Reich 1933: 28–31). Although many find Reich unconvincing in his con-demnation of any encouragement to discipline in sexual be-haviour, there certainly does seem to be some correlation between the political and the sexual attitudes of a society. It seems to me, however, that this is not so much to do with the nature of political authority in that society as with the degree of purposiveness in its ideology – be this officially enforced or consensual.

### Treatment of individual values

From our study of the content of contemporary Soviet children's literature, comment can now be made on some implications for the Soviet child socialisation process as a whole. Firstly, some definite tendencies have emerged as to the relative importance of the various qualities of the Builder of Communism listed in chap-ter two. Patriotism is clearly the prime virtue in practice. It is subordinate to no other quality, whereas all the others hinge on it. It is, for example, the supreme embodiment of collectivism. Love of work is essential mainly because, through work, one's love for the Motherland is proven. If for their importance to patriotism alone, these two virtues also receive prominent treatment in the readers and *Murzilka*. Discipline is not given a section of its own in the former but it is implicit in a wide range of stories on various themes – from military to classroom life, from cosmonautic adventure to behaviour at home. Internationalism is only a minor theme in the school readers; stories under headings that suggest internationalism – e.g. 'International Workers' Friendship' – turn out in practice to be material reinforcing patriotism. Atheism is the least-mentioned characteristic of the Builder of Communism. There is an almost total lack of anti-religious propaganda. This may be because the authorities felt that religion was withering away of its own accord. If so, it was a feeling which, as is shown below, has not been supported by research. Alternatively, they may have felt that too virulent a campaign would antagonise rather than convert believers – a view which certainly seems to have been borne out by history. Whatever the reasons, atheism is a rarely mentioned virtue.

A second implication is that the way in which the characteristics are presented involves a necessary submission to a higher authority. Even in relation to collectivism, the children are told that collective decisions are the correct ones, but that they need guidance from above (Lenin had to reason with the peasants, to show them why they should change their minds about building a church). In the teaching of work-morale and discipline, the stress is inevitably on subordination of self to duty. However, in the Soviet presentation of patriotism, the implication is also one of submission to something more important to oneself. This emerges from the articles on loyalty to Soviet institutions in which the people are subtly shown as needing wiser leadership from above. It is clearly advantageous for the authorities to develop in their future citizens the unquestioning acceptance of leadership; we have seen how they attempt to do so from the examples given throughout.

Submission to a leadership and reliance on patriotism are not what Marx would have expected of the morality of a socialist system. What about the virtues which would seem more fundamentally socialist, such as equality and non-acquisitiveness?

'Equality' is not a key word in the way that 'Motherland', 'collective' and 'labour' are. It is mentioned in relation to work in the form of the statement that all jobs are equally valuable to society. Elsewhere it is stated, in passing, that of course there are no longer any distinctions between black and white, between rich and poor in the USSR (*NR*: 77). But this is not a theme on which Soviet children's writing dwells, for the obvious reason that there are still glaring discrepancies in Soviet life – between, say, urban and rural conditions – and it would be unwise to overstress an equality which, as even young schoolchildren will realise, does not exist. Moreover, an emphasis on equality will shake the rationale of the need for wise leadership, for incentives and an elite, and for this reason too it is not a theme which the readers press home.[3]

Non-acquisitiveness is likewise not overstressed; but this is probably on different grounds. Occasionally, however, the child is told that in the Soviet Union one says 'our' not 'my' (*NR*: 77), and there is also a rather interesting story in which one pupil exchanges his old pen for his neighbour's new one. The latter boy is very upset at this. The children reading the story are asked who is in the right – and it is significant that *neither* of the characters is presented sympathetically (*Fl.* 86–7). The little boy who lost his new pen is certainly not supported – for one should not care so much about material possessions. Non-acquisitiveness *is* thus a Soviet as well as a socialist virtue. However, shortages are not nowadays so great that much attention has to be paid to it for political reasons, nor are goods so abundant that attention is needed for moral reasons.

A further point following from the data in these chapters is that there are areas of inconsistency or double-think within the framework of values as presented to the child. Striking examples of this occur in relation to the treatment of the themes of war and peace. Pupils are encouraged to identify with military heroes at the same time as they are told that they must revere peace. The number of items which seek to justify the existence of an army in peacetime would suggest that there is, perhaps, awareness of a certain conflict of values here. The theme of work gives rise to

[3] See Lane, *The End of Inequality?*, Penguin, 1971, for a full discussion of the various types of inequality still obtaining in Soviet society.

more double-think. Pupils are told that all jobs are equal. They are also continually urged to study as hard as possible for the higher the marks they receive, the more they will be able to give to their Motherland. The discerning child must experience some confusion.

A deliberate cultivation of the unrealistic in contemporary Soviet character-education seems to appear in the school readers and in *Murzilka*. Thus, for example, all children's dreams of the future are shown as coming true. All in all, children are given an image of Soviet life that is totally rosy – no suggestion is made of any possible future personal disappointments, let alone of any remaining imperfections in the social and political system. As the child grows older, he will inevitably find that life is not as consistently benevolent as it has been painted. His disillusionment may be on a purely personal level – he may not be accepted by university even though he has obediently studied hard, for example – or it may be due to a growing political awareness – he may, perhaps, soon realise that the USSR is not simply a country 'where there is no longer any distinction between rich and poor'. When he emerges from the rose-tinted world of the children's book and Pioneer detachment into the less serene real world, is not the Soviet child liable to experience a deep shock, shaking the foundations of the messages instilled into him from his first years at school?

Linked with this question of the unrealistic in Soviet children's literature, there is a good deal more evidence to suggest deliberate myth-creation with Lenin as the central element. He is presented to the children as a Demiurge or Saviour – more in religious terms of inspiration and comfort than as a great political figure and thinker who served the people well, let alone as a politician not infrequently over-ruled by his cabinet colleagues and making human mistakes. Other elements of the myth concern the Soviets, and, more especially, the Party, which, as we saw, has divine characteristics of infallibility, omniscience and omnipotence – but by far the most important part of the mythology is Lenin.

Finally, it must be noted that there is no remarkable radicalism in the values and norms presented. Attitudes to politeness and keeping one's promise are, for example, given a Soviet context but differ little from traditional bourgeois attitudes. They are not very prominent themes in the readers, but the fact that they appear at all is significant. Similarly, presentations of attitudes to women and to home life differ only in certain points of emphasis from Western bourgeois norms. Indeed, they are less radical than the works of some Western children's writers who are deliberately writing stories for children that are not permeated with traditional middle-class emphases on good manners, uncritical disciplined behaviour and respect for women and home life.

# Part III

## THE IMPACT OF SOVIET CHILDREN'S LITERATURE

# 7

# Sociological surveys

The aim of this chapter is to assess how successful Soviet methods are in educating schoolchildren through children's literature. It first tries to assess the specific success of Soviet children's literature as a vehicle of moral values before looking at some Soviet sociological surveys which evaluate the success of the character-education process as a whole. The content of this chapter is thus extremely problematic and conclusions drawn can be only provisional. One longs for much more extensive and systematic survey data. It is nevertheless felt that the points that can be made are significant and do reveal much that is of interest about Soviet socialisation.

## The direct impact of children's literature

Just occasionally, one encounters instances in which people declare that some significant action on their part was inspired directly by a book which they had read. Thus some sixth-grade schoolboys in the USSR organised an *artel*[1] after reading Chernyshevsky's *Chto delat'* (*What Is To Be Done*). In a similar vein, a youth from Tomsk wrote to the national youth daily: 'Not so long ago, I too was "living it up". I had long hair and was rude to those around me. I'd rather not talk about what my friends and I did for "amusement". But then I happened to read Yu. German's book *The Cause that You Serve*. I became literally a fanatic about medicine. I renounced my old ways and began to study.' (*Komsomol'skaya pravda*, 11 December 1970.) But the most striking and large-scale example of Soviet child behaviour

[1] Co-operative association, usually of workers or peasants.

being motivated by a children's story is the Timurite movement of the Second World War.

The book which inspired this was Arkady Gaidar's short novel *Timur i ego komanda* (*Timur and his Team*). This is the tale of a young boy and his friends who perform all sorts of good deeds to help the families of men who had gone to the front. The first instalment of the novel appeared in *Pionerskaya pravda* on 5 September 1940. It was immediately popular and a film was quickly made from the book and shown first in the winter of 1940/41.

As early as January 1941, the Soviet press was noting that Gaidar had done something far greater than merely creating a children's story or film scenario:

He has thought up a new game for children, an entertaining and moving game based on our very best feelings – on love for our motherland and for Soviet man, on the firmest comradeship. It is a game which inculcates in its participants justice, bravery, inventiveness, physical skill and endurance, spiritual sensitivity and resoluteness – all qualities which we want so much to see in our children.

(*Literaturnaya gazeta*, 19 January 1941.)

Almost immediately, then, the book was looked on not just as a story but as a pattern for action by live Soviet children. Indeed, as soon as the story had appeared, teams of children modelled on Timur's team did spring up in Kharkov, in villages in Moscow, Omsk and other regions.[2] In August 1941, there was a large meeting of Timurites in Kiev. Gaidar was present and addressed them thus:

Children, Pioneers, glorious Timurites! Protect with still greater attention and care the families of the fighters who have gone to the front. You all have skilful hands, sharp eyes, quick feet and clever heads. Work tirelessly, helping your elders. Fulfil their tasks unconditionally, reliably and exactly. Mock and despise those softies, loafers and hooligans who stand on the sidelines at this hour, chattering without working, who hinder our common sacred cause.

(Ukh'yankin 1961:5.)

Most schoolchildren were anxious to do their bit for the war effort and they were given much official encouragement. *Pionerskaya*

---

[2] The information on the Timurite movement is based on a pamphlet by S. P. Ukh'yankin, *Pionery Timurovtsy*, Moscow, 1961.

*pravda* printed exhortations similar to Gaidar's. Timur teams were created in each school and their number grew daily. School No. 2 in the Siberian town of Stalinsk was asked how many Timur teams it had. It answered: 'The day before yesterday there were 18, yesterday there were 26 and today there are 38. Who knows how many there will be tomorrow?!' The mass nature of the movement grew and grew. On 8 November 1942, an All-Union 'working Sunday' of Timurites was held. Over two-and-a-half million children took part and, on this one day, accomplished some huge tasks: for example, they cut 74 943.2 cubic metres of firewood for schools and for families of men at the front. That year also other remarkable feats were reported – they collected 4268.1 tons of scrap metal, 355.4 tons of wild medicinal plants and 2719 poods[3] of grain. They unloaded 297 metric tons of coal and 63 of peat, they stacked 50 tons of wheat and they cleared snow from 29 000 square metres of railway track.

By 1942, there were more than two million Timurites in the RSFSR alone. Many examples of work done throughout the Union appeared in the press. For example, a soldier came to Kiev bearing nine hundred letters for families living in that area. In the course of one day, a hundred Timurites delivered them all. In newly liberated Taganrog, they spent one whole night clearing the city. Activities were not limited to helping the families of those at the front; they also included visiting hospitals, collecting scrap metal and other tasks useful to the war effort. V. P. Potemkin, the People's Commissar of Education for the RSFSR, told the Moscow teachers' *aktiv* in February 1943 of the deeds of seven hundred teams of Sverdlovsk Timurites, involving more than fifty thousand children. Pupils from school No. 24, for example, had collected clothing for needy children who were not coming to school, looked after evacuated youngsters, sewed tobacco pouches and sent them, along with paper, pencils and toothpaste, to frontline hospitals – and kept up a constant correspondence with men at the front.

Their work received official approval. The old Bolshevik, Yaroslavsky – moralist, author of the hagiographic *Landmarks in the Life of Stalin* and one of the very few who managed to survive the purges – in 1943 wrote a New Year address to the Pioneers,

[3] 1 pood=36 lb=16.4 kg.

saying: 'It would be good for you to organise more Timurite teams – but not show ones; they must be real ones. You can thus be very useful to your Motherland.' Care was taken to ensure that the children didn't feel they were just playing a game but that they were really helping their country. Thus Party organisations would give special tasks to the groups. Socialist competitions were organised. Teams throughout the Soviet Union were linked by badges and by specially composed popular songs such as this favourite:

> Many gay Timurites
> Are everywhere in the big towns;
> There are many of us in *auls*[4] and villages,
> In the Siberian *taiga*[5] and the steppes.

Although the book's chief relevance was to wartime conditions, the movement did not die immediately the Second World War ended. The children continued to look after the families of soldiers. But, in 1946, the movement became somewhat weaker. One of the reasons for this was felt, it was said, to be the failings in the Pioneer organisation as a whole – which, according to an announcement of the Central Committee of the Komsomol, had become full of cliches and formalism (hardly surprising when we remember how *Murzilka* in 1938, like all the press, had had to pander to suspicion and hatred and had used officially approved cliches – for their comparative safety, if nothing else). The training of Pioneer leaders was also considered to be weak. An attempt was, therefore, deliberately made to turn the once spontaneous Timurite movement into a permanent sector of Pioneer work.

In 1954, after Stalin's death, the Timurite movement did again begin to acquire a mass character. By 1957, the Eighth Plenum of the Central Committee of the Komsomol was somewhat concerned about the development of the movement. One of the major discussions centred on how to attract children to such activities. The inspiration usually came from reading the novel. It was suggested that this initial interest should be encouraged by asking children questions such as: 'How would Timur have acted if he'd learnt that in kindergarten No. 6 there were children who

---

[4] Mountain villages in the Caucasus.
[5] The coniferous forests of Siberia separating the tundra from the steppe.

tear down the flags and destroy the trees?' Examples relevant to the present-day child's experience rather than to his wartime predecessor's should be taken, it was argued.

Today groups still exist based on school, Pioneer unit or home district. At the Twenty-second Congress of the Komsomol the content of Timurite work in the post-war period was defined as 'care for adults' – specifically, for pensioners, for war- and labour-invalids and for those with particularly large families. The Timurites of the fifth class of school No. 5 in Ordzhonikidze correspondingly decided, it was reported, to seek out pensioners and offer help; some pensioners rejected it but most accepted happily. The Timurites of the village of Kozyl'yary in the Chuvash Autonomous Soviet Socialist Republic were reported to be active in the distribution of books among the local population.

There is considerable prestige attached to being a member of such a Timurite group. I. M. Slepenko, an educationalist, in an article on Timurite work tells the story of Lida, who was refused membership because she didn't help enough at home: stirred to action by this, she soon became a reformed character (Slepenko 1958:68–9). Much thought is put into the organisation of the movement by the educators. It is felt that too long an involvement in one particular project will lead to loss of interest. And so the Cheboksary Timurites visit pensioners one week and the Blind Club the next. Each Timurite works for no more than two hours a week. It is stressed that the pensioners are not mere passive acceptors of the children's good deeds; they also exert a positive educative influence on them.

Various romantic ideas and games are encouraged to stimulate further interests in the movement. For example, the leader of one class sent the pupils a letter as if from Timur himself. Special gatherings are arranged on Timurite Day (22 February, Arkady Gaidar's birthday).

All this shows how one novel has profoundly affected Soviet child behaviour over quite a long period. Certainly the movement was not purely spontaneous. It was quickly recognised as having much potential for mobilising resources, for educating children in collective action, humanitarianism and various skills, and it was therefore given considerable official encouragement and support. None the less, Gaidar's slim little novel, which is still very popular, deserves the credit for providing the stimulus to a very significant mass movement.

## Children's heroes

Timur may no longer be such a dramatic spur to action but he is still often cited by children as a favourite hero. As has been seen, providing children with heroes is one of the preferred methods of character-education through Soviet children's literature. Who are the other heroes who have succeeded in capturing the imagination of Soviet children?[6]

There is, firstly, a series of books in the Timur tradition, all of which have proved popular, if not to quite such a remarkable extent. One of these is Sergey Golitsyn's book *Sorok izyskateley* (*Forty Explorers*). Forty children form a squad of Pioneers which believes that the world consists of two types of people: 'explorers' and 'sluggards'. Explorers are people who love to do new things and to embark on all sorts of exciting projects. Sluggards, on the other hand, are apathetic, lead a dull life and deserve only contempt. These Pioneers determine to be explorers and they set out on an expedition to discover a lost masterpiece by an anonymous painter. After many unusual adventures, they find the painting and even ascertain the painter's name; the painting gets hung in the local museum. When the book appeared, it provoked a big response from Soviet children who wrote to the editors of the Pioneer journal *Pioner* asking how they could be explorers and determining not to be sluggards.

There is a similar atmosphere of desire to help the community in *Govorit sed'moy etazh* (*Seventh Floor Speaking*) by Anatoly Aleksin. This tells of a group of children who secretly take over an attic in their block of flats and set up a radio station. Through their broadcasts to the flats in the block, they create a jolly community spirit throughout the new big building.

Yet another book in the Gaidar tradition is *Stozhary* (*Old Timers*) by Aleksey Musatov. The hero of this is Konshakov who lives on a collective farm and is a devoted young follower of

[6] Much information on this topic is to be found in Bogdanov, 'Literary Characters Influence the Life of Soviet Children', *Journal of Educational Sociology*, November 1961, Vol. 35, pp. 162–4.

Michurin, the famous plant-breeder and follower of Lysenko! Konshakov has himself certainly inspired many Soviet children to take an interest in and help with the work on the farm.

Three other books still provide popular heroes for Soviet children. Yuri Gagarin used to say that his hero was the pilot in Boris Polevoy's *Povest' o nastoyashchem cheloveke* (*Story of a Real Man*), still one of the favourite heroes of Soviet young people. The pilot was modelled on Aleksey Maresyev, a legendary legless Soviet pilot of the Second World War. The hero of Maresyev himself was Pavel Korchagin, the character created by the young blind writer Nikolay Ostrovsky in *Kak zakalyalas' stal'* (*How the Steel was Tempered*). This is a romantic novel about a young man serving the Revolution and bearing his own suffering bravely. Ostrovsky's own hero, he said, was the Italian revolutionary martyr in *The Gadfly* written by the American Ethel Lillian Voynich in 1897, and many times republished in Russian. The Gadfly, Korchagin and Maresyev have become traditional heroes and are likely to remain among those who inspire Soviet teenagers and make them long to demonstrate their courage in similar ways – even though these three do not have the same immediate relevance to the average contemporary child's situation as do the more recent works. The power of the earlier books of the Gaidar type is their ability to make everyday life interesting, worthwhile and romantic.

It would be of considerable interest to assess the effectiveness of reading matter as an element in the character-education process. It is not possible, however, to isolate this one factor and properly to evaluate its influence without discussing the success of the system of character-education as a whole. Here five surveys of the general moral development of Soviet children are analysed. In the next chapter is assessed all the available evidence for the success (or the failure) of Soviet character-education in inculcating specific virtues of the Builder of Communism (see chapter two). In the discussion which follows here, it must be remembered that the written word is only one agency in the whole process and cannot be held responsible for all the observed behaviour. It is nevertheless felt by the Soviet authorities, at any rate, to be a very major element in the whole system.

### Soviet criteria for evaluating children's moral development

One report is available concerning criteria for measuring the moral development of schoolchildren (Khanchin 1970:48–53). It was written by V. S. Khanchin of the General Pedagogy Research Institute attached to the Academy of Pedagogical Sciences. His research was prompted by his awareness of the inadequacy of the methods of assessing a pupil's moral level. Existing methods consisted mainly of assessing the pupil's essays and opinions as expressed in the classroom or Pioneer meeting; they were clearly biased in that they were all affected by the pupil's desire to please the teacher. How could such methods be improved? Khanchin's primary assumption was that the only reliable indicator of morality is action. How does the pupil in fact behave? It was decided that, for educational purposes, analysis of moral behaviour needed two foci: the external manifestations of moral level (actions, gestures, mimicry, indifference); and the nature of these manifestations (their intensity and duration, and the circumstances giving rise to them).

On the basis of laboratory experiments, together with systematic observation, Khanchin evolved a method of standardising the measurement of moral qualities. The teacher administering the survey has to mark each pupil in relation to four elements in his behaviour by ticking that description of it in a given situation which most closely fits observation; a procedure then converts these indications into a numerical value, placing the subject at a given point on a scale for each element of behaviour. The elements considered are set out below.

(1) *Pupil's action in a concrete situation (e.g. willingness to share)*: shares his sweets and belongings equally with his comrades; sooner helps himself than others; will share but helps himself to the most and the best; doesn't share but doesn't hide his sweets and belongings; hides them so that no one knows or sees; demonstratively doesn't share.

(2) *External manifestation of moral character (e.g. comradeliness/alienation)*: considers the wishes of his comrades, shows initiative in friendship but is flexible; the same but is not flexible; complies with the projects of his comrades but

doesn't show initiative himself; holds himself aloof and is indifferent to others' projects; is envious of others' successes and makes a point of acting in his own way; inconsiderate of others.

(3) *Extent of the manifestation of his moral level (e.g. feeling of affection)*: concerned about the position and experience both of those distant and near to him; concerned only about his relatives and very closest friends; indifferent to all those around him; shows schadenfreude at the failures of others.

(4) *Nature and strength of the stimuli necessary to evoke moral behaviour (e.g. motives for helping a colleague in work or study)*: shows spontaneous desire to help another; acts under the influence of the teacher; acts in expectation of a reward or other advantage; acts in fear of reprimand or punishment.

A trial run of this test was carried out in 1968 on 1014 pupils from the fourth, fifth and sixth classes in two schools. Each pupil was placed in relation to each element of behaviour on a twelve-point scale according to methods worked out 'by competent experts'. Preliminary examination of the results showed certain clear tendencies, of which the most striking were:

(a) in all three classes, the level of moral development of the girls was higher than that of the boys;

(b) where the average of points in a class was higher, the gap between boys and girls was less;

(c) scores on the first three elements of behaviour increased from the fourth to the sixth classes but, on the last element, they dropped in the older classes; and

(d) the most significant indicators of the level of moral development were those revealed in relation to the third and fourth elements of behaviour (that was confirmed by the researcher's factor-analyses of the data obtained).

This experiment was only a preliminary one; Khanchin intended to use it to work out simple and reliable criteria for assessing moral behaviour. The results of the test are here of less importance than the test's construction in that, in the latter, the criterion of moral behaviour resides in the subject's relationship to the group. A moral person is one who is a willing member of the collective; one who holds himself aloof is considered as having a low level of moral development. Especially noteworthy is the order of the characteristics relating to the first moral element, willingness to share. It is considered worse demonstratively not to share than secretly to keep one's sweets all to oneself. The Soviet point is that an aggressive non-sharing would disrupt the group whereas a secretive selfishness does not do so. This is a further interesting, though minor, example of the greater importance which Soviet morality attaches to the wellbeing of the group rather than the soul of the individual.

Even the modest preliminary results so far published are extremely suggestive. They indicate an overall improvement in the moral level as the child progresses through school suggesting a gradual acceptance of official norms. They also show marked sex differences in the effectiveness of conscious socialisation: girls are more ready to accept the official values than boys – as is the case in the West, where comparatively few girls have (until recently) become delinquent. One of the main causal factors believed to lie behind different rates of delinquency for each sex in the West is the different sex-role stereotypes with which boys and girls are presented; boys are to be daring and brave, girls primarily home-lovers. It has been shown how, in the USSR, children are provided with not dissimilar sexual stereotypes from those in the West: little boys must grow into soldiers on the Soviet borders who are not afraid to die for their country if necessary; little girls may grow up to be tractor drivers – but they must also, and first and foremost, be always caring and dependable mother figures.

### Assessing children's moral development

Another researcher has also been concerned with how to assess the moral development of the pupil: she is V. I. Petrova, who works in the Research Institute of General Problems of Character-Education attached to the Academy of Pedagogical Sciences. She has mostly been involved in trying to work out a means of measuring the moral development of an individual pupil over a given period and uses two criteria of moral development: comradeliness and a sense of justice.

One of the most revealing features of her results (Petrova 1971: 23–8) was the way they highlighted a problem in the use of questionnaires. To measure his level of justice and comradeliness, each child was observed playing. The children were organised in a team game of darts. Each had the right to throw a predetermined number of darts and to aim to get at least a predetermined number of points. If the child got the points with fewer throws, then he had the right to additional throws, but had the choice of either going on throwing himself or conceding his excess throws to someone who hadn't been so lucky as to be chosen for the team. Though the children all knew that it was 'right' to concede, forty to fifty per cent did not, in fact, do so. When presented with a similar, but imaginary situation – what would they do if given the choice between helping a friend or going to the cinema or playing football – ninety-eight percent of the same group of children said they would choose to help their friend.

Thus Soviet children – like, doubtless, the subjects of all inquisitions – either consciously or unconsciously biased their verbal answers towards the responses they felt to be desired by their questioners.

## Changes in moral development over the Soviet period

Some very interesting work has been done by R. G. Gurova (of the same Institute) on trying to compare the moral level of Soviet youth with that of their pre-revolutionary and early Soviet counterparts (Gurova 1971:41–51). She repeated some small-scale experiments carried out by P. N. Kolotinsky – a psychologist who, between 1904 and 1929, studied the interests and ideals of school-leavers. In his book on the results of this work (Kolotinsky 1929), he analysed results for the years 1913, 1916, 1921 and 1926. Gurova repeated the experiment for the year 1969.

The experiment consisted of presenting the pupils with the following form, which allowed them plenty of space for writing fully on each of the topics.

(1) My favourite writer.
(2) My favourite piece of literature.
(3) My favourite poet.
(4) My favourite poem.

(5) My favourite scientist.
(6) My favourite hero.
(7) My favourite heroine. } from literature, history or the present day.
(8) My favourite motto.
(9) My favourite scientific book.
(10) The quality which I value in people above all others.
(11) My favourite school subject.
(12) My favourite occupation.
(13) My favourite entertainment.
(14) My favourite topic of conversation.
(15) What I want to be.
(16) What I shall be, at least in the near future.
(17) What is the purpose and the point of life.
(18) What would I like to have in life above all else.
(19) My attitude to religion.
(20) My attitude to love.
(21) My attitude to marriage.
(22) My attitude on the relationship of parents to children.
(23) My attitude on the relationship of children to parents.
(24) My attitude to school.

In addition, the pupils in 1969 suggested two more questions:

(25) My attitude to politics.
(26) Does man need immortality?

Requests for certain information of sociological significance also appeared on the questionnaire – social origin, sex, parents' education, success level at school – but the questionnaires were completed anonymously.

TABLE 3   *Respondents to Kolotinsky–Gurova investigations of moral level of Krasnodar youth*

| Year | Total | Boys | Girls |
|------|-------|------|-------|
| 1913 | 46 | 0 | 46 |
| 1916 | 41 | 0 | 41 |
| 1921 | 38 | 17 | 21 |
| 1926 | 46 | 11 | 35 |
| 1969 | 44 | 12 | 32 |

*Source*: Gurova 1971, p. 43.

The size of the 1969 sample was chosen as the average of the samples used by Kolotinsky. All the pupils in each year came

from Krasnodar, but, as table 3 shows, the proportion of the
sexes varied from year to year. The survey was small, but Gurova
claimed that a much larger survey throughout the Soviet Union
showed that the Krasnodar answers were typical and did not
notably deviate from the larger sample.

Questions 1 to 7, 9 and 10 were intended to give information
on the ideals of the school-leavers. How had these varied over
time? The most striking change in the answers to the 'favourite
writer, poet and scientist' questions was that, in 1969, far more
names were mentioned. In 1913, schoolgirls named 84 writers,
58 poets and 12 scholars; in 1969, the respective numbers were
149, 89 and 32. Far more pupils in 1969 declared that they had
no single favourite author but liked many for different reasons.
The same tendency applied to favourite poets; throughout the
years, however, the poet named most often has remained the
melancholic and romantic Lermontov, apparently possessing a
particular appeal for adolescents, the more generally acclaimed
Pushkin being placed second. But each period brought forth its
own favourites as well. In 1913 Nadson was frequently mentioned: he was a poet of the 1880s who 'became the spokesman
for a generation that was rotting in the atmosphere of defeat and
stifling reaction, and yet vividly recalled the heroic deeds and the
sacrifices of its elder brothers...Though he was wordy, inflated,
exclamatory, his lines were moving'. (Slonim 1962:30.) He has
now been replaced by poets of a more contemporary relevance,
Mayakovsky, Esenin and Simonov. In 1969, as opposed to
previous years, every pupil named at least one favourite poet.

As far as scientists and scientific literature were concerned, the
range of men and works mentioned by contemporary young
people was significantly wider than in the past: they named
Darwin, Mendeleyev, Copernicus, Einstein, Lomonosov, Leo-
nardo, Lobachevsky, Erasmus, Popov, Pierre Curie, Tsiolkovsky,
Belinsky and Pisarev, among others.

Very few literary heroes have stood the test of time but those
who have are Hamlet, the heroes of Jack London, Andrei, Pierre
and Natasha from *War and Peace*, Anna Karenina, Tat'yana
from *Eugene Onegin*, Elena Stakhova and The Gadfly. Onegin
himself and Pechorin (*The Hero of Our Time*), frequently named
in the past, now appear no longer – despite the popularity of

Lermontov and Pushkin.[7] Modern children choose largely from Soviet literature – such heroes as Pavel Korchagin and others mentioned earlier in this chapter. Heroes from history have also significantly altered: Alexander the Great, Julius Caesar and Henry IV have been replaced by Marx, Lenin, Bauman, Dzerzhinsky (the founder of the Cheka[8]), heroes of the Civil War and Second World War, and cosmonauts.

What qualities have been valued over the years? The most regularly named qualities in 1969 were honesty and love for people. Intelligence and determination were named in all years – but, in 1969, they were qualified by the proviso that the possessor use them to the benefit of society. Two other qualities mentioned in every survey were kindness and dignity. Many further characteristics figured in 1969: these were patriotism, goal-directedness, dedication, bravery, comradeliness, respect for other people, sincerity, tact, uprightness and optimism – but independence, good manners and harmony no longer appeared. In 1913, only eight qualities were named; in 1916, ten; and in 1969, twenty-six.

These findings reveal some significant changes. The 1969 youngsters had enjoyed a much broader education; they were enthusiastic about a far wider range of writers and scientists. The fact that they did not name just one favourite author or highly-valued quality suggests a greater maturity of outlook. The heroes and qualities praised also seem to indicate a large measure of success for the Soviet character-education system: the favourite heroes are those displaying patriotism and dedication to the national cause: gone are the heroic figures of any other culture. The qualities valued also are the social ones which are continually promoted in the schools and in literature for children. Most interesting of all, perhaps, is the case of patriotism: this did not appear at all in 1913 but was prominent in 1969. Similar tests done in Britain or the East Coast of the US would doubtless have shown an opposite tendency. The actual ideals of modern Soviet youth are, to judge by this test, largely the collectivist ones encouraged by those who run the educational system.

[7] This indicates success in teaching admiration for the positive type of hero as advocated by socialist realism. This would tend to lead to an impatience with the 'superfluous men' of the nineteenth century, of whom Onegin and Pechorin are the prime examples.

[8] The secret police of the early years of Bolshevik power.

Certain questions were specifically devised to show directly the social values of the young people studied. These were the ones on the purpose of life, attitude to politics, greatest wish and favourite motto. It was felt that the choice of motto in particular would indicate a young person's social attitude. Kolotinsky put all the mottoes into one of four categories (see table 4), based on orientation to other people and to society. As can be seen, an extra category was added after the 1969 survey, since thirty per cent of the mottoes then were felt to be primarily concerned with self-education.

TABLE 4 *Pupils' favourite mottoes grouped by social orientation. Figures are percentages*

| Social orientation | 1913 | 1916 | 1921 | 1926 | 1969 |
|---|---|---|---|---|---|
| 1 Altruistic | 39.4 | 65.4 | 35.7 | 18.9 | 27 |
| 2 Egoistic | 27.3 | 23.1 | 17.8 | 32.5 | – |
| 2a Self-educational | – | – | – | – | 30 |
| 3 Progressive | 21.2 | 11.5 | 43.5 | 37.8 | 34 |
| 4 Indeterminate | 12.1 | – | 3.5 | 10.8 | 9 |
| All | 100 | 100 | 100 | 100 | 100 |

*Source*: Gurova 1971, p. 46.

Unfortunately, only a few of the actual mottoes were quoted in Gurova's article and no information was provided as to which category each was assigned to. Examples of those which she did quote are:

| Year | Mottoes |
|---|---|
| 1913 | All or nothing. Live as you like to. Happiness is not in money. |
| 1916 | The end justifies the means. Be honest. |
| 1921 | Take from life all that is given. Independence and struggle. |
| 1926 | Be strong. Look everything in the face. Forward to Communism! |
| 1969 | Never despair. If I am for myself, then what am I? One for all, all for one. Be the master of your will and the slave of your conscience. Fewer flowery phrases, more simple, everyday action. Smooth your sharp corners which might hurt people. Study, study and study. |

It would be interesting to know how 'all or nothing' or 'the end justifies the means', say, were classified. Without such information, it is difficult to comment meaningfully on the results. It is doubtless significant that there are no 'egoistic' mottoes for 1969 but one wonders whether the 'self-education' ones might have been classed 'egoistic' by Kolotinsky.

The answers to 'what is the purpose and point of life', as grouped, perhaps reveal more (see table 5).

TABLE 5 *Views on the purpose of life grouped by social orientation. Figures are percentages*

| Orientation revealed | 1913 | 1916 | 1921 | 1926 | 1969 |
|---|---|---|---|---|---|
| 1 Personal, egoistic | 36 | 29.7 | 61.1 | 50 | 6.8 |
| 1a Self-perfection | – | – | – | – | 6.8 |
| 2 Altruistic, social | 18 | 3.7 | 11.1 | – | 86.4 |
| 3 No purpose | 28 | 55.5 | 16.7 | 35.7 | – |
| 4 Other[a] | 18 | 11.1 | 11.1 | 14.3 | – |
| All | 100 | 100 | 100 | 100 | 100 |

[a] Not classifiable into any of the above categories.
*Source*: Gurova 1971, p. 46.

The question itself did not seem to have much meaning for many of the children in Kolotinsky's surveys – about one in five replied that life did not have any point except death. Such 'pessimism' did not appear at all in 1969 – but again, a new category was introduced to deal with some of the answers in 1969. Again, one wonders whether this new category of 'self-perfection' would not previously have been covered by 'personal, egoistic'. 'Personal' or 'egoistic' is derogatory in the Soviet context, whereas 'self-education' or 'self-perfection' can meet with official approval – obviously not too large a figure was wanted in the disapproved category in 1969. Nevertheless, the table does suggest to what a large extent Soviet youth has assimilated the socially committed concept of the purpose of life.

Gurova felt that the 1969 responses could have been better categorised as follows:

(*a*) *to serve the Motherland* ('to serve the fatherland', 'to justify the hopes of the government', etc.);
(*b*) *to be of use to the people* ('to struggle for peace', etc.);

(c) *to find one's vocation* ('to know as much as possible and to use one's knowledge practically', etc.);

(d) *to improve oneself* ('to become a real person', 'to make man into Man', etc.);

(e) *to seek personal achievement* (only three answers here: 'to succeed in everything', 'the goal of life is happiness', and 'to get into university').

The results of Gurova's survey are, she feels, supported by the findings of the Institute of Social Opinion attached to *Komsomol'-skaya pravda*, which in 1960 investigated what young people felt to be their purpose in life (Chikin and Grushin 1962). They had responses to questionnaires from 16 574 people, of whom only four-and-a-half per cent said they had no purpose in life. Their overall results were as follows. First place went to 'keeping a pure conscience'; second to 'doing one's duty to one's native land'; and third to 'securing happiness in one's private life'. These results, however, do not reveal very much to the Western reader without a more detailed explanation of the Soviet school-leaver's concepts of 'conscience' or 'duty' or 'happiness'.

The question about 'my attitude to politics' was introduced only in 1969 and so comparisons are not possible. It is, however, of interest to see why Soviet children consider it essential to be knowledgeable about politics. Two did not answer this question, but twenty felt that an interest in politics was necessary for perhaps basically personal reasons ('to help to establish peace throughout the world', 'when too many are apathetic, the way is clear for fascism', etc.).

The enquiry about 'what I should like to have in life above all else' was introduced by the pupils of 1926; their answers were significantly different from those of their counterparts in 1969. In 1926, sixty-three per cent answered in material terms, asking for riches, money, etc., whereas in 1969, only one gave such a reply: 'I'd like a good flat.' Gurova points out that this does not mean that contemporary youth has no interest in material possessions, but simply that these do not dominate them. They asked, on the other hand, for knowledge, education, interesting and useful work, free time for study, art or sport, faithful friends and peace on earth. None of these were mentioned in 1926. Similarly, in 1969, no one mentioned beauty, physical strength or good manners, all of which featured in 1926. In 1963–64, V. G. Lisovsky and S. N. Ikonnikova asked 2035 young people what they felt to be essential for their happiness (Lisovsky and Ikonnikova 1969:90); their top responses were 'work they enjoyed', 'contentment in private life', and 'the respect of those around them'. Their results coincided with those of Gurova in stressing the lack of preoccupation with material possessions and a desire, above all, for rewarding work.

Questions 11 to 15 were included in the questionnaire in order to ascertain the interests of the subjects; these have shown notable changes over the period studied. In the early years, 'what I want to be' was responded to by many with an adjective such as 'rich' or 'happy'; no such answers appeared in 1969, when the pupils named only various professions. The work of teachers, doctors and engineers has been consistently popular but new to 1969 was the large number of pupils expressing an interest in scientific work of some kind. The professions connected with the arts – acting, painting, music – have now in comparison moved into the background. These findings are again supported by other work; the scientific bias is confirmed by V. V. Vodzinskaya who questioned 124 Leningrad pupils on work aspirations and discovered that the first ten places were given to scientific or engineering jobs (Vodzinskaya 1970:85–6). In her investigation nobody seemed to want to do manual labour, as is confirmed by numerous other surveys of job aspirations.

The same tendency towards a greater interest in science was evident from the answers to the question on favourite subject: these nowadays come down quite strikingly in favour of mathematics. Spare-time pursuits also reflected a similar trend. Many pupils in 1969 reported reading scientific books as one of their favourite hobbies, whereas few, compared with the twenties, mentioned an interest in the arts. As might be expected from improved facilities, sport and tourism were also frequently named as favourite pastimes, whereas they rarely were in the past.

Unfortunately, Gurova did not report on the answers to the questions on love, marriage and parent–child relationships. Was this because they did not reveal the development of attitudes she desired or was it that she did not consider these topics as important as the others? She did, however, provide a brief note on the 'my

attitude to religion' question. The 1969 pupils' addition to the
questionnaire of 'does man need immortality' suggested that they
were at least interested in religion; the answers – perhaps significantly – are not given. The 'attitude to religion' responses caused
Gurova to admit to a certain alarm: she found them, by and
large, far too passive, with too many of the type 'I don't believe,
but others may, if they want to'. She advanced anti-religious
education as a most urgent area for further research.

Gurova also repeated another interesting experiment of the
NEP period, originally carried out in Leningrad in 1927. Pupils
from the seventh to the tenth classes, 1445 in all, were asked to
write an essay: 'What would you do if you had a magic cap?'
(Montelli 1930). This title did not seem so appropriate for contemporary youngsters; in 1967, therefore, the 1247 pupils involved were invited to write as their essay 'What would you do if
you could do anything?'

The general conclusion drawn in 1927 was that most pupils,
when writing, concentrated on satisfying their curiosity and their
personal needs. Fifty-six per cent showed a desire to widen their
experience (to travel to the Moon or Mars or simply to exotic
parts of the world); thirty-two per cent were concerned about
their personal well-being (a wide range of desires here – from
'having a good meal' and 'having a comfortable bed' to 'getting
to heaven'!); twelve per cent showed some kind of social commitment in their answers (e.g. to go abroad and get everything
that our country needs').

Once again, the more recent answers demonstrated a far
stronger sense of social duty; forty-five per cent of the pupils
claimed that they would primarily act for the benefit of society
and twenty-four per cent wanted to widen their experience; only
eighteen per cent showed concern for their personal well-being.
The following were said to be typical of the high social orientation
of the 1967 answers: 'establish peace and freedom in the world',
'cure all illness', 'give their lives back to all those who died for
their Motherland', 'go to Greece and save the Greek patriots from
the fascists', 'go to Peking, remove Mao Tse-tung and give him
over for re-education', 'arrange things so that people never died
before their time and so that children of all countries could
study'. Their US, Canadian or British cousins, if given the same

test, might well have echoed the first two ideas – but would hardly be likely to express concern about their war dead, Greek patriots or Mao Tse-tung! The 1967 answers are also said to have shown a new trend: this was concern to use experience gained for some socially useful purpose – e.g. 'to acquire great knowledge of science and make a lot of scientific discoveries', 'to penetrate the secrets of the Universe and determine where the boundary between living and non-living runs'. Even those whose answers in 1967 were categorised under the heading of 'personal well-being' showed a wider sphere of interest than those surveyed forty years before. They were concerned not so much with themselves as with their friends and relations: 'to give all my acquaintances, relatives and close friends health, and I myself to get into college'.

A very significant element of the 1967 answers was the rejection by many of the idea of omnipotence. Why should Soviet people need such magic powers? 'In our country, every person and society as a whole can achieve its goals without any magic tricks. The best thing would be to eliminate the possibility of omnipotence, using it to make only one condition – that no one else would ever possess it again.' (An indirect reference to Stalin?) Many more mature pupils saw the complexity of the problems raised. They realised that even depriving mankind of all illnesses would have certain negative results – for medical research also leads to all sorts of invaluable knowledge about nature, physiology and so on. One sixteen-year-old wrote rather impressively:

Let us suppose that the gift of omnipotence were given to an honest person, a man on the side of progress. In a trice, he would rid mankind of imperialism, Chinese dogmatists, nuclear weapons, illness, narcotics, drunkenness, gambling, crime. . .And then, throughout the world eternal peace would reign, there would be an abundance of everything necessary – and the extinction of mankind would be inevitable, because man's role would now be nought. He would no longer be a builder of a bright future but would be a dweller in it.

This essay, along with many others, shows a sophistication of approach, absent in 1927, which testifies to significant educational progress in the Soviet period.

Of course, there are problems in relying on data found by such surveys and questionnaires. Even when they write anonymously, subjects may be tempted to write so as to present themselves in the best light – they know that teachers will recognise their hand-writing (Gurova admits this possibility) – and to give the answers which they suspect the enquirer requires. Even allowing for this, these tests do seem to show a high level of social awareness among Soviet school-leavers. This emerges clearly from the last experiment and also from the answers to the questions on heroes, valued qualities, favourite mottoes and pastimes, and on aspirations for the future in the Kolotinsky–Gurova experiments. There can be no doubt but that the Soviet system of character-education has, over the past forty years, succeeded in affecting the attitudes of youth to a significant degree.

### The value-judgments of schoolchildren

E. V. Bondarevskaya and Z. B. Krupenya of the Rostov Peda-gogical Institute have investigated the value-judgments of school-children in the belief that these are a good indicator of the pupils' level of moral development. In the course of their research, they observed more than a thousand children in the eighth to the tenth classes of eighty schools in Rostov-on-Don and the surrounding area. The pupils' value-judgments were assessed in a number of ways – through questionnaires, essays, and individual or group discussions (Bondarevskaya and Krupenya 1970:56–65).

One of the most revealing questions to which they were asked to give a written answer was 'Which behaviour defects are most characteristic of the pupils of your school (class)? How do you explain those faults and how would it be possible to eradicate them?'

The first significant aspect of the responses to this was that, as table 6 shows, a large number of pupils did not answer the question, saying, perhaps (as did one boy from the ninth class): 'This is the first time that I have been asked such a question, and don't know what to say because I have never thought about it before. In my opinion, such questions need a lot of thought.'

Bondarevskaya and Krupenya explained the high refusal-rate by reference to an inadequacy of pupils' training in criticism, both of others' behaviour and of their own. The increasing pro-portions of those failing to answer the question as one moves up

through the classes they attribute convincingly to changing attitudes to the collective amongst these groups. 'Pupils in the eighth
class are, to a certain degree, on the brink of transition from the
adolescent to the older-pupil age group.' In the adolescent collective, there is not yet the sharp distinction between the *aktiv*

TABLE 6    *Senior pupils' responses to question on defects in group-behaviour,
Rostov-on-Don. Figures are percentages*

| Response | All pupils (1294)[a] | Eighth classes (523)[a] | Ninth classes (332)[a] | Tenth classes (439)[a] |
|---|---|---|---|---|
| Faults acknowledged | 73.7 | 80.0 | 71.5 | 67.7 |
|    unspecifically | 2.2 | 1.5 | 2.3 | 3.0 |
|    specifically | 71.5 | 78.5 | 69.2 | 64.7 |
| Faults denied | 4.4 | 4.0 | 4.0 | 5.3 |
| No answer | 21.9 | 16.0 | 24.5 | 27.0 |
| All | 100 | 100 | 100 | 100 |

[a] Number of pupils.
Source: Bondarevskaya and Krupenya 1970, p. 56.

and the *passiv* which is evident in the older classes. The interests
of most adolescents are centred, in the main, on the school; a
voluntary alienation from the collective is rarely encountered.
Moreover, the new position, brought about by the move into the
eighth class, signifies the beginning of life as a senior pupil and
stimulates an active interest in school affairs. This is why the
number of eighth-class pupils who didn't answer the question is
comparatively small. By the later classes, the position has changed
somewhat.

In the ninth to tenth classes, there occurs a splitting up of pupils
according to their various interests, opinions, position in the collective and attitude to school. Their interests and allegiances are
sometimes outside the collective in which they study. Occasionally,
these out-of-school allegiances so take hold of the boy or girl that he
or she becomes indifferent to the collective and stops living by its
interest. (Bondarevskaya and Krupenya 1970:59.)

The researchers add that, as the adolescent grows up, he becomes
less 'black and white' in his judgments and more reluctant to
make firm criticisms; this may also be a factor contributing to the

relatively large number of older pupils who would not answer the question.

Pupils, in pinpointing what they saw as the most serious short-comings in their group, did not limit themselves to the faults of their contemporaries but also mentioned those of their teachers and the youth organisations (see table 7).

TABLE 7 *Areas of main group-behaviour defects identified by senior pupils, Rostov-on-Don. Figures are percentages*

| Area of defect | All pupils | Eighth classes | Ninth classes | Tenth classes |
|---|---|---|---|---|
| 1 Study | 31.7 | 35.0 | 29.0 | 31.0 |
| 2 Social work and out-of-school activity | 27.0 | 34.0 | 23.0 | 24.0 |
| 3 Relationships between pupils | 8.8 | 4.0 | 16.0 | 6.4 |
| 4 Qualities of the personality | 29.0 | 25.0 | 29.0 | 33.0 |
| 5 Work of public organisations | 2.6 | 0.2 | 2.5 | 5.0 |
| 6 Work of teachers | 0.9 | 1.8 | 0.5 | 0.6 |
| All | 100 | 100 | 100 | 100 |

*Source*: Bondarevskaya and Krupenya 1970, p. 59.

Area 1 includes such failings as lack of interest in study, not working to the utmost of one's capabilities, copying and talking in lessons. Some pupils were reproached for not being sufficiently aware of the social importance of study. Area 2 comprises any failing in attitude or behaviour in connection with work in the Komsomol or with any social responsibility.

The pupils found indifference and lack of consideration parti-cularly reprehensible in their relationships with one another; these are the characteristics most frequently cited in areas 3 and 4. One ninth-year pupil said: 'If a classmate is ill, he must be visited and told what homework has been given. We must ask him how he feels and if he needs any help. We do all this – but do it like a chore or an obligation. It should be done quite simply, from the heart. We should show more sensitivity to those around us.'

Unfortunately, details are not given about the faults found

with public organisations (area 5). Although the figures for these are low, they are interesting in that they demonstrate a growing dissatisfaction with such organisations as the pupils get older.

The researchers felt that the failings of teachers to which the children drew attention (area 6) were in some cases just and in others not. They considered it significant that these complaints (mainly of lack of objectivity) came particularly from pupils of the eighth year – a time, they maintained, when adolescents tend to be especially sensitive.

By and large, the criticisms showed that pupils had assimilated the belief that social responsibility is a primary virtue – though they were evidently conscious of the fact that they and their colleagues did not put it adequately into practice. It was a lack of social commitment that they condemned first and foremost; poor schoolwork, for example, was criticised not so much in itself as for being an indication of an insufficient sense of social duty.

Most revealing of all, perhaps, were the causes to which the pupils attributed the faults they made. These are broken down in table 8.

TABLE 8   *Pupils' attributions of causes of group-behaviour defects, Rostov-on-Don. Figures are percentages.*

| Cause | All pupils | Eighth classes | Ninth classes | Tenth classes |
|---|---|---|---|---|
| Pupils themselves | 46.0 | 52.4 | 40.1 | 45.4 |
| Incorrect organisation of co-operative activity and relationships between pupils | 18.2 | 15.6 | 15.7 | 23.3 |
| Teachers | 6.6 | 6.0 | 7.1 | 6.8 |
| Negative home influence | 21.0 | 18.6 | 25.2 | 19.3 |
| The Komsomol | 7.4 | 7.2 | 11.0 | 4.0 |
| Other causes | 0.6 | – | 0.7 | 1.1 |

*Source*: Bondarevskaya and Krupenya 1970, p. 61.

As table 8 shows, nearly half the pupils attributed faults to inadequacies in their own personalities – saying, for instance: 'I explain all the failings mainly by the fact that the pupils are lacking in strength of will.' Bondarevskaya and Krupenya interpret this as showing a high level of moral development, although this seems out of line with the Marxist emphasis on the importance of social conditioning. Such self-judgment is not, however, an attitude which the Soviet authorities would discourage; it distracts attention from other sources of dissatisfaction. Clearly this was the response which the researchers wanted and the pupils may have sensed this. The pupils rarely blamed the official agencies of socialisation, represented by the Komsomol and the teachers, possibly suspecting that such a response would displease the authorities carrying out the investigation. In particular, it seems justifiable to doubt the reliability of the figures because, although forty-six per cent of the pupils claimed that they considered that the cause of their failings lay in themselves, only sixteen per cent went on to suggest stronger self-training as a means of eradicating these failings – over forty-seven per cent said that an alteration in the teachers' approach would bring about improvement. One ninth-year pupil said: 'School life is dull. If there's a school social evening, you go unwillingly and are embarrassed to dance under the fixed gaze of the teachers. School life should somehow be re-organised to make it more interesting.' A classmate added: 'To get rid of faults, we need something interesting to oblige us to work and to think.'

Bondarevskaya and Krupenya divided the essays they received into three types. Firstly, there were those containing a statement of behaviour defects but with discussion of them only at a superficial level. The following is a typical example of this category:

In our school, there are certain behaviour defects. Pupils are late or talk during lessons. Some play truant, get poor marks and don't turn up to do their tidying duty. Not all take part in the campaign to keep the town green. I explain all these failings by the fact that they do not heed the advice of their elders. It is possible to correct all these faults.

Secondly, there were responses demonstrating that the pupil himself had the necessary emotional reaction to the failings: in such essays, it was evident to the researcher that the pupil personally deplored the faults he described instead of simply presenting them as bald statements. An example of this category is one eighth-year pupil's reply:

In our school there are, of course, faults. There is unpunctuality and bad behaviour. School life has stopped interesting some of the pupils

– who already consider themselves adults. And yet where else but at school can one find such an interesting, intriguing and, if I may say so, undiscovered world?! All these faults I explain by the fact that pupils are out not for the school but for themselves. If each one put even a little effort into doing something for the school, for the collective, life would become more interesting for himself too...

Thirdly and finally, there were responses showing an ideologically 'correct' approach to the question: such answers included an evaluation of the personality as a whole – not just mentioning isolated actions, but also such general ideological failings as an uncritical approach to bourgeois culture or an absence of the Communist spirit of purpose. Of such a type is this answer from a tenth-year pupil:

One of the behaviour defects is the bad level of social activity among certain pupils. It is unpleasant even to speak with a person who has opted out of social work. For social work is, as it were, a foundation for the future Communist society, where one must work not from compulsion but from desire. To eliminate faults, the pupils must be interested so that study and social work become for them a necessity of life. Otherwise it is impossible even to think about building a Communist society.

(It is interesting to note in passing that this essay, like most of those quoted in Bondarevskaya's article, spoke of how to cure 'their' faults – not 'our' faults.) Most pupils, however, were seen to progress beyond the stage of simply stating the faults which they see in a detached way; they show a personal sense of regret at these failings and have at least some suggestions to make about how to eradicate them. But only just over a quarter were found to progress to what the researchers termed the third stage in which this is all slotted into the official ideological framework.

Bondarevskaya and Krupenya consider their work relevant in that it reveals the necessity for more thorough work in character-education – which should increase the proportion of third-stage responses. To us its results are interesting not only as a Soviet assessment of the Soviet system but also for what the answers show about Soviet schools in practice, counterbalancing the idealised picture of school life obtained from looking at plans and programmes. It does also demonstrate, though, that Soviet children seem, by and large, to have accepted the practical Soviet values as such – although most do not interconnect them in terms of the articulated world-view of Soviet Marxist–Leninist theory.

## Attitudes to socially useful work

O. A. Abdullina of the Moscow Lenin Pedagogical Institute chose pupils' approach to socially useful work as a fundamental indicator of their overall level of moral development. Her work is interesting both for its results and for the light which it throws indirectly on the organisation of 'social work' in Soviet schools. From teachers, class leaders and, especially, the children themselves, she collected written and oral comments on each pupil in the survey (Abdullina 1971:40–8).

Firstly, she demonstrated how easily class leaders can make mistakes in their judgments of pupils. For example, Galya V. was considered to be 'an efficient, principled girl, always contributing to the discussions of the *aktiv* and demanding in her attitudes to her comrades'. But when her classmates were asked to comment on whom they liked to have leading their 'social work', several replied in this vein: 'Galya loves to command and to shout, to show her "I". But I don't want one of us to be the commander and another the subordinate. It is better to do everything all together and on an equal basis.' The class leader began watching Galya more closely and realised that, although she was good at organising and ordering the others around, she seldom did any of the difficult work herself.

Secondly, Abdullina brought out the necessity of not only observing the child's actions but also seeking out his motives. Andrei K., for instance, was capable and energetic and liked to be at the centre of any social activity, but it was gradually realised that he was motivated more by egoism than love of the collective. Once, he and his classmates from the sixth year were organising a three-day trip into the country. Andrei was in charge of the arrangements and showing much initiative and drive. The teachers decided to link the trip with the seventh year's excursion; Andrei suddenly refused to continue to take part. When asked why, he answered, 'Why should I go? There'll be strong boys from the seventh year. I wouldn't be needed.' In other words, his social vigour was inspired by his desire to be the centre of attention.

In the attempt to discover a little more about pupils' motivation, Abdullina requested the children in the sixth and seventh classes whom she was studying to write an essay entitled 'My Social Work'. They were told that their essays would be discussed at a class meeting and were urged to be frank and to give reasons for their answers. Most of the pupils wrote fully and openly. Two examples follow. Firstly, Olya from the sixth class wrote:

This year, I have carried out the duties of class monitor. I like supervising the duty roster and my classmates. It doesn't always work smoothly. Sometimes they won't listen to me or are late for their duty but, all the same, I feel a great responsibility for the class. In general social work teaches me a lot...If I work badly, then my friends will stop trusting me, and it's bad when you're not trusted.

Olya is praised for the selflessness of her sense of duty. Kolya, in the seventh class, on the other hand, writes:

I am the editor of the class newspaper. I enjoy this work because, when you do the newspaper, everyone reads it and praises it. I particularly liked doing the New Year issue because the producers of the best newspaper got tickets for the party at the Palace of Congresses in the Kremlin. My newspaper was best of all those in the competition and I got to the party in the Kremlin.

He showed himself, it is pointed out, to be motivated mainly by love of praise or the promise of reward.

Next Abdullina drew attention to the pupils' own opinions about the organisation of 'social work' in the schools. In the sixth and seventh classes of two Moscow schools, twenty-four per cent of the pupils expressed satisfaction with the organisation of social work. The remaining seventy-six per cent came up with complaints that tasks were carried out not by the whole collective but by individual pupils or groups; that the social tasks were assigned not by the collective itself but by the class leader; that the carrying-out of tasks was not controlled or assessed by anyone; and that the tasks were distributed without sufficient regard to the particular interests and capabilities of individual pupils. The second complaint suggests that less control from above is wanted by the pupils whereas the third may suggest the opposite. Thus no firm conclusions can be drawn from these complaints – except the fact that there is considerable dissatisfaction on the part of pupils with 'social work' as organised by the schools.

From 'lengthy and detailed' study, Abdullina discovered two main areas of contradiction in this field. Firstly, there were pupils who acted well but whose understanding of moral concepts was lower than their behaviour suggested. Secondly, there were those who had thoroughly mastered principles and theory, but whose behaviour did not always live up to this. When attempting to assess a pupil's moral level, the researcher must thus omit neither the theoretical nor the practical side of morality in order to get a full picture of his character.

These five pieces of Soviet research have all been concerned with finding ways of assessing children's morality. Each has chosen a different indicator and each, while showing certain positive results of the Soviet process of character-education, has also uncovered inadequacies in the system.

# 8

# Development of specific character traits

The information derived from the Soviet research described above can be linked with other evidence to try to assess the level of success in respect of each of the six main qualities of the Builder of Communism. In looking at these qualities now, one is reminded of what was learnt about them in preceding chapters; for example, that the Soviet concept of patriotism implies an un-qualified commitment to the Party leadership, or that inter-nationalism and atheism have become unimportant goals in practice when compared with the other four.

## Collectivism

Chapter two identified collectivism as a fundamental Soviet virtue and study of the content of writing for the Soviet child has shown that the world is presented to him as a set of collectives – from the home, the classroom, the Pioneer group, the collective farm or the home town right up to the supreme collective of the Mother-land. In his relationship with each of these he is urged to find it a duty and a joy to serve and to subordinate himself to the greater good of the majority. Is it possible to measure the extent to which Soviet youth has assimilated such attitudes?

One of the most notable overall conclusions of the surveys described above is the way in which the senior schoolchild does seem to have assimilated the collectivist values desired by the authorities. On the whole, he does seem to judge people in terms of their relations with social groups and to look for his own fulfil-ment through contributing to society. The impression is that few Soviet young people feel that they ought to 'drop out' of society or 'do their own thing' in order to 'find themselves'. The ideology is outward rather than inward looking; the evidence of the above surveys suggests, despite all necessary qualifications, that that aspect of the official Soviet value-system has been accepted by Soviet youth.

At the level of language, Chukovsky has evidence to show that even the youngest child has made the Soviet collectivist idiom his own. He records, for instance, how one little girl asked, when she heard that her father was too ill to go to work one day, 'What about the Five-Year Plan?' (Chukovsky 1963:54). He uses the following incident to describe 'the extent the new feeling of social ownership has penetrated into the consciousness of the Soviet youngster' (*ibid.* 56). A boy has just seen an elephant at the zoo for the first time. He looks at the beast closely and eventually asks:

'And whose elephant is he?'
'He belongs to the State.'
'That means he is a little bit mine, too.' (*Ibid.* 57.)

From one of the writer's own conversations with Soviet children, the following example can be added. I once invited a ten-year-old Soviet girl to visit me in England. She objected that she would miss her friends. 'Bring them with you', I suggested. 'That would mean bringing the whole working class' was her immediate response.

But, as Soviet moralists would stress, one must judge by actions not words. The American specialist in child-upbringing, Urie Bronfenbrenner, gained an impression of a high level of collectivist behaviour on the basis of both unstructured observation and more precise experimentation (Bronfenbrenner 1971:77 *et seq.*).

An important aspect of collectivism in the Soviet context is participation in some kind of socially useful work. This may be anything from collecting medicinal herbs to playing an active part on a Pioneer committee. The child is encouraged to such activity in his school and youth group and it is expected to remain a habit through adult life. Abdullina's survey, described above, provided some indication of certain inadequacies in the organisation of socially useful work within the school.

While the child is at school, it is difficult for him to avoid some degree of participation in socially useful work. When he leaves school, however, he may decide to opt out if his character-education has not been successful. In 1965/66, a survey of nine hundred scientific workers, all aged under thirty and working in various institutes in Moscow, was carried out (Vasil'ev *et al.* 1967: 94). When asked by anonymous questionnaire whether they took part in socially useful work, their replies were as shown in table 9.

TABLE 9    *Responses of Moscow scientific workers to questionnaire on participation in socially useful work*

| Response | Percentage |
|---|---|
| I don't take part | 14.0 |
| I occasionally take part | 24.0 |
| I regularly take part | 29.7 |
| I hold elective office relative to some aspect of socially useful work | 32.3 |
| All | 100 |

Source: Vasil'ev *et al.*, 1967, p. 94.

Thus it would seem that a substantial majority conform to the idea that it is desirable to take part in some socially useful work in one's leisure time – although, of course, one cannot tell from these answers whether this is done with an eye on career prospects or out of a deeply ingrained sense of duty.

Despite the fact that the above evidence, especially that relating to the highly educated, clearly suggests that some success has been achieved with respect to character-education in collectivism, regular reports of anti-social behaviour still appear in the Soviet press. These are certainly not on the scale occasionally suggested in the New York *Daily News* or the London *Daily Express* but they have equally certainly not been eradicated. Thus one reads about youths who have been arrested for robbing coinbox telephones and then destroying the equipment (*Izvestiya*, 26 July 1970), or about an airline pilot who refused to transport vital medicine to a sick child because it wasn't specifically allowed for by the rule book (*Pravda*, 8 May 1968). Occasionally, there is evidence for a more widespread unwillingness to subordinate personal gratification to collective welfare. In April 1972, for example, a large number of college graduates refused to take up their state labour assignments because these required three years in remote, often harsh conditions (*Izvestiya*, 23 April 1972). The fact that no statistics are available regarding such anti-social behaviour might suggest that more takes place than the authorities care to admit.

Personal experience has probably in small ways shown every visitor to the USSR that certain collectivist attitudes do, in fact, prevail that at first strike those coming from the more individualistic West as strange: many visiting students, for example, have been scolded by strangers in the street for having hair too long or skirts too mini or too maxi. Most have witnessed some scene on public transport where an improperly socialised citizen is reprimanded by a fellow passenger with a collectivist outlook because he is smoking or has not paid his fare. The inexperienced winter visitor who ventures out inadequately clad is soon advised of his foolishness. The sum of all the evidence would thus suggest that even though there are notable exceptions most Soviet citizens do grow up with an identifiable collectivist tinge to their outlook on life.

Constant underlining of the supreme importance of the collective may have encouraged collectivist attitudes but it has also resulted in neglect in the process of character-education of ways of dealing with the personal conflicts of the individual. This seems to be producing official Soviet concern in two main spheres – love and sexual relationships, and manners.

It is only in the early seventies that the press began to call for at least some sex education. In the fifties, articles on the subject argued that children should not be told very much about sex; parents should answer questions without embarrassment but also without too much detail. Children, it was firmly stated, should not be allowed to sleep on their stomachs, and girls should be debarred from riding bicycles (Atarov 1964:53). In 1964, one writer asserted his agreement with Aleksey Tolstoy – that 'here are matters about which it is not good or necessary to speak'; he deplored a spate of articles and letters on the topic of sexual behaviour in the Perm' newspaper *Molodaya Gvardiya*, maintaining that more emphasis on sport and intellectual creativity would 'save' young people from sexual pre-occupations, and quoting Lenin's conversation with Clara Zetkin: 'Healthy sports – gymnastics, swimming, outings, physical exercise of all kinds – a diversity of intellectual interests, study, analysis, research – and all this, as far as possible, in combination. All this gives young people more than interminable speeches and discussions on sex.' (Quoted in Hollander 1969: 196–9.) But more publicity is now given to those who realise that sport and hard work do not provide a full simple and neat solution to the whole problem of sexuality and sexual morality. In 1967, the new biology syllabus did reintroduce the section on 'The Development of the Human Organism', omitted since 1960, but a male teacher in the journal devoted to school biology deplored the fact that the only literature on the biology of sex for young people was a translation of foreign material (*Biologiya v shkole* 1967: No. 3).

In the Soviet context, though this teacher was not completely a lone figure, he was fairly exceptional and progressive simply in the fact that he welcomed the idea of sex education in schools. In a Western context he would, of course, have seemed rather conventional, for he also said: 'The abstinence of young people from sexual life is not only desirable but useful and has no negative consequences.' Of masturbation, he asserted: 'This weakens the organism physically and spiritually, distracts from study and work and causes feelings of depression, dissatisfaction and weakness. This harmful habit may appear because a youth lacks an interesting occupation, is isolated from the collective or has certain other tendencies.' He too quotes Lenin's remark to Clara Zetkin that lack of control in sexual life is 'bourgeois' and 'a sign of decay' (*idem.*). Biology lessons on their own are not enough. The biology teacher must be helped by the literature teacher because, in literature lessons, 'high ideals of love, friendship and fidelity are revealed to the students during analysis of a series of literary works' (*idem.*).

It would seem that many teachers are still reluctant to deal generally and directly with the intimate questions of sex with their pupils. *Izvestiya* was unusually outspoken in a report about two young girls 'debauched' by much older married men, blaming this on the fact that schools have devoted no attention to the important personal side of morality. (*Izvestiya*, 19 November 1968). *Pravda* criticised the irresponsible attitude of one young man; his parents opposed his marriage because they felt the girl was 'beneath' him. The couple still married and quickly had a child, believing that a baby would reconcile them with the grandparents. The latter stood firm however, declaring that their son would receive no further financial help from them. This persuaded him to abandon his wife and child. Both parents and school had failed to give a worthy moral lead to personal relationships (*Pravda*, 6 December 1971). These are just some examples of a topic that has received prominent coverage in the Soviet press in the last few years.

Some Soviet sociologists are dissatisfied not only with the fact that irresponsibility and delinquency have not disappeared from sexual life but also that a double standard still remains in relationships between men and women (see, for example, Golod 1968). The double standard is, in some ways, actually being perpetuated by attitudes of sex roles inculcated in much contemporary Soviet writing – apparently as part of the campaign to 'strengthen the Soviet family'. In socialist realist fiction, love is usually presented in a way that often seems simplistic and naive to Western readers, who are accustomed to a more complex treatment of emotional conflict in literature. This is apparently mainly because the Soviet writer who is too concerned with the intricacies of personal life is likely to be criticised for individualistic self-indulgence.

When discussed at all, love is idealised in a romantic and, at the same time, straitlaced way. The standard attitude seems to be one of agreement with Makarenko that he who is cynical about a woman will be cynical about life as a whole. Indicative of the typical approach to personal relationships is this advice to teenage boys:

Moral boorishness and lack of control in the sphere of love brings enormous harm to our society. He who believes that love is only a pleasure is giving birth to sorrow, unhappiness and tears.

Respect your girl, protect her honour and dignity, her human pride.

The girl who will attract you is your future wife and the mother of your children. (*Vospityvat' vospitannost'* 1971:43.)

Motherhood is very much officially idealised. It is emphasised that, although there must be equality between the sexes in the Soviet Union, men must still treat women with respect, opening doors for them and offering them seats on buses, because a woman deserves deference as a mother, actual or potential, of future citizens of the USSR. The above-mentioned pamphlet adjures:

'Cherish [your wife's] honour and beauty. The mother of your children is a woman, two, three, four times over: as many children as you have, so many times is she a woman.' (*Ibid.* 44.)

Thus in the main, Soviet character-education either ignores questions of love and sex or else mishandles them. But some writers now feel that an ostrich stance can be as harmful as a tactless approach: 'Silence about what plays an important part in everyone's life cannot fail to have its consequences.' He continues with vehement rhetorical questions:

But where do we have any books aimed at adolescents and called upon to satisfy their intelligent interest in questions of sex, their justified curiosity, so horrifying to some hypocritical educators? Isn't it clear that the lack of such literature is an anti-human pheno-menon and testifies to an indifference to the great force and tre-mendous human significance of natural human feelings in everyone's life? (*Lit. Rossiya,* 7 December 1966.)

Various reasons, of course, play a part here. There is almost certainly fear on the part of the authorities of relaxing what is a basic mechanism of social control – sexual repression – as well as the previously mentioned apprehension over debates about funda-mentals. The official desire since the mid-thirties, recently even more stressed, to 'strengthen the family' has also greatly affected policy here. But, within the Soviet value-system itself, the emphasis on collectivist behaviour and the initial belief that personal con-flicts were somehow of relatively little social importance have meant that school and press have both so far failed to deal satis-factorily with problems of sexual relationships.

For similar reasons, other perhaps less important aspects of the niceties of personal behaviour have been understressed in the Soviet education system. Immediately after the October Revo-lution, indeed, many Russians felt that attention to details of manners was evidence of bourgeois pretensions. This attitude has to some extent endured. A review in a national newspaper of a new book on etiquette argued that such a book was very necessary because 'there are even those who consider that to be polite and to mind manners is a remnant of bourgeois prejudice.' (*Izvestiya,* 23 January 1972.) This certainly does not represent the approved approach nowadays. The review continues by declaring that it does not agree with those who find whether one wears a hat or not irrelevant. It believes that the basic rules of etiquette have been formed throughout man's history for good reason. This certainly seems a far cry from the style of 'proletarian simplicity' of original Bolshevism.

There are also those who press even for lessons in conduct at school; the national youth press published some correspondence discussing whether there should be such lessons or not. Students of a television club in Kirov wrote requesting such lessons and asking for them to be as regular a part of the syllabus as classes in physics, chemistry, or Russian literature (*Vospityvat' vospitannost'* 1971: 22). Even those who rejected the idea of lessons in etiquette agreed that 'cultured' behaviour was essential. One correspondent, a pedagogue from Moscow, E. Gudakov, wrote that he did not like the idea of separate lessons, but 'Of course, one can and must teach adolescents to help girls on with their coats, to stand aside for elders, to hold their knives and forks correctly and to give thanks for attention.' (*Ibid*. 23.)

Thus there is a clear increase in concern about the details of daily behaviour as, judging by the press reports, acts of petty rudeness and 'uncultured' conduct are a not uncommon cause of trouble for Soviet educators. The rituals of daily etiquette may become meaningless (like propaganda cliches) but do serve the useful purpose of smoothing relationships and making everyday contacts more easy and relaxed. Whether a balance will be achieved between over-emphasis on ritual details and total disregard for the niceties remains to be seen.

There are, to sum up, two sides to the coin of the impact of collectivism on Soviet culture. Firstly, collectivism is to a large extent accepted as a value (it is, after all, part of a long Russian tradition). Secondly, however, it has led to a certain neglect of the problems of the individual which is giving rise to some difficulties in modern Soviet society.

## Discipline

In chapter two, discipline was seen to be closely linked to the virtue of collectivism, since it is through self-discipline that one is able to subordinate one's own selfish desires to the greater good of the collective as a whole. In literature for children, discipline is an implicit virtue rather than an explicitly promoted one. It does not have sections specially devoted to it in the school readers (as patriotism does) nor is the young reader regularly reminded that discipline is an essential Soviet virtue (as is the case with love of work). However, it is implicit in numerous stories, particularly in those describing war or space heroism.

The whole concept of discipline is a difficult one. It includes both self-discipline and a willing submission to officially imposed discipline. In both these areas, there is evidence to suggest that character-education in discipline is not adequate. In so far as it is related to collectivism, it has had some success. (It would seem that sixty-two per cent of young scientists are disciplined enough to devote regular amounts of their spare time to socially useful work, for example.)

The chief indicator that discipline is in some cases lacking is press concern about hooliganism. In 1966, the press reported a decree of the Praesidium of the USSR Supreme Soviet 'On Increased Penalties for Hooliganism' (*Pravda* 28 July 1966). This declared that 'The working people of our country justly demand that hooligans and rowdies bear strict responsibility for their actions. It is necessary to build up an atmosphere in which every case of hooliganism is decisively cut short by state bodies and Soviet public.' (It is worthy of note, in passing, that a collectivist and work-related solution is offered to the hooligan problem; people arrested for such offences can be used without pay for jobs like street-cleaning on the decision of the Executive Committee of the local Soviet.) As a result of these sterner measures, one journal claimed that delinquency figures in 1970 had been cut by half since 1967 (*Sem'ya i shkola* 1970: No. 12, p. 12).

Nevertheless, there are still regular press reports of hooliganism. Sometimes these are grave. The article referred to above also describes the murder of a little boy by two young delinquents, one of whom was only in the sixth class; the murder seems to have been purposeless mugging since there was no question of any theft. In 1970 there were reports of armed bank and payroll robberies in Moscow, Odessa and Rostov-on-Don. The problem seems to be that rifles are easily purchased in sporting-goods stores; it would appear that, although undisciplined usage of firearms is not the problem it is in many areas in the West, it is still a cause of concern to the Soviet authorities. From a number of reports it was found that, to the investigators' concern, some young people did not regard pilfering from school as a crime (*Uchitel'skaya gazeta*, 3 July 1975:3). Sometimes, however, the offence seems trivial. One report complains about girls who have never been taught how to behave and who sit with their legs crossed! (*Komsomol'skaya pravda*, 11 November 1970.)

Occasionally, the rights of collective power are abused by children who are too immature to discipline themselves. Thus, one report tells of a children's home where the pupils' council ordered that the heads of their comrades who have misbehaved should be shaved. They also beat up one boy who ran away (*Literaturnaya gazeta*, 12 June 1968).

But the major cause of concern regarding hooliganism is the traditional northern offence of drunkenness. This is a recurring theme of even the central press and, despite heavy penalties for those who brew, let alone sell, home-made alcohol, there does not seem to be much sign of the problem being solved (see e.g. *Izvestiya*, 6 January 1970; *Vechernyaya Moskva*, 14 July 1975 etc.). The extent of the problem is summed up by this passage:

In our country, people drink because of sadness and joy and because they are on a date. They drink because they have just been paid. They drink because there's a frost or because a child has just been born. If there are no children who have just been born, they drink anyhow. Some people drink because they are still mourning over the last war, some because they feel cold and some because they have just taken a bath. Some drink when relatives gather together, or when a pig has been killed. And some even start the celebration of Women's Day with drinks. (*Izvestiya*, 9 November 1966.)

Children often begin to drink at a young age. It is estimated that seventy to seventy-five per cent of young people of school age consume alcoholic drinks (*Molodoy kommunist* 1975: No. 9, pp. 102–3).

The whole question of discipline aroused the national youth paper's attention in 1970 when, in a new housing-development area in Volgograd, idle youngsters wandering round the streets had thrown acid on to a girl's clothing. This provoked a survey by the city's Komsomol which discovered that almost twenty per cent of those questioned said that they spent part of their time aimlessly on the streets. TV was the favoured leisure pursuit of fifty-four per cent. Only eighty-six of a thousand adolescents (nine per cent) engaged in sport regularly and only seven per cent expressed any enthusiasm for creative technical activities (*Komsomol'skaya pravda*, 24 October 1970). All in all it would seem that hooliganism has not proved simply a 'relic of the past' and its continued presence in Soviet society suggests that the discipline aspect of character-education is not wholly adequate, either in its inculcation of self-discipline habits or in persuading all to submit willingly to authority.

## Love of work

Dedication to work has been seen throughout, both in the discussion of the prime Soviet virtues and in the examination of the content of Soviet writing for children, to be basic to Soviet morality – for, in normal peacetime circumstances, it is through work that the individual is seen as demonstrating his loyalty to the collective, the system, the Motherland. Thus, at school, the child is constantly exhorted to study diligently and his textbooks and magazines frequently tell him about varied, interesting jobs that he will be able to do when he leaves school. To what extent is such character-education successful? Does one encounter in Soviet schoolchildren the attitude familiar to many teachers in North America or Britain – that school is boring and homework an infringement on one's liberty? When the youngster begins work, does he in practice find the satisfaction he has been trained to expect to feel in it?

As regards schoolwork, reports from Western observers as well as those in the Soviet literature suggest that discipline is considerably stronger than in many a Western classroom and that, whatever a pupil's private thoughts about homework may be, he will nevertheless do it (see e.g. Bronfenbrenner 1971:77). Again, it is once he leaves the structured school situation and has a greater freedom of action that his behaviour will be most revealing of how successfully his character has been formed.

Here, too, there is conflicting evidence. A half-page of letters discussing work appeared in *Izvestiya* in the spring of 1971. One twenty-year-old girl wrote that work was necessary only to subsist and that the main thing in life was to have a good time while one was young (it is to be noted that she was no loafer but a factory assembly worker). A letter from Zaporozh'e agreed with her: 'everybody works only to gain a living. The lofty words come only from the lips. There is something quite different in the heart... There may be some 15 per cent of people who look on work as a pleasure, but they (most of them) are the kind who have troubles in the family at home.' However, three letters singing the joys of work were printed to counterbalance these two disenchanted ones. Whatever their proportion, it is clear that some youngsters remain unconvinced by the school readers about the pleasure of labour (*Izvestiya*, 11 May 1971). An article on young people's attitude to work complains about those who work only in order to live and enjoy themselves, and not because they like work. They have the deplorable attitude that 'the smart man doesn't climb a mountain, he walks round it'; the writer feels that such an attitude has become too popular among some young people (*Izvestiya*, 14 March 1971).

It would seem that pupils leave school saying, at least, that they have expectations that work will bring them satisfaction. To the question 'Are you convinced that you will be able to obtain your favourite specialisation and then get work in it?', ninety-four per cent of the boys and girls questioned by Vasil'ev answered 'Yes' (Vasil'ev *et al.* 1967:107). But it seems that expectations are not by any means always realised. Of the young people studied (who included all kinds of working youngsters from collective farm labourers to scientists), seventy per cent were proud of their specialism and satisfied with the work they themselves had to do (*ibid.* 107–8). This is a sizeable majority – but it still leaves thirty per cent dissatisfied.

Work in children's literature is presented as a delight and honour in itself rather than mainly just as a means of gaining one's living. Is this an approach which is assimilated by Soviet youth? Vasil'ev questioned 2665 young working people on the purpose they saw in their own work. Of these, 399 (fifteen per cent) mentioned wages only; 830 (thirty-one per cent) said that the main thing was interesting work, although wages could not be forgotten; 617 (twenty-five per cent) referred only to the content of their work (*ibid.* 108). Unfortunately, we are not told how the other 819 (thirty-one per cent) answered. Nevertheless, on the basis of the available data, it is possible to draw some comparisons between this general survey and another in which only young scientists in their twenties were asked a similar question. Of these, only two-and-a-half per cent named earnings as the fundamental reason for working (*ibid.* 87), compared with the fifteen per cent in the more widely based group. This suggests that young scientists found a sense of purpose in their work that was far above the average – despite the official Soviet view that, in the words of the Mayakovsky poem, 'All jobs are equal'. This is borne out by Joel J. Schwartz's assertion, given weight by the Soviet national press, that some Soviet school-leavers who are rejected for higher education stay out of the work force because they have a snobbish attitude towards labour (Schwartz 1973:43).

A number of sociological investigations prove the success of the Soviet character-education system in creating a desire to study. Research has shown that about eighty per cent of school-children want to continue studying after they leave school but in practice only about half were able to do so (Turchenko 1973, p. 85; *Narodnoe obrazovanie* 1977). The success in teaching the benefits of study has thus perhaps been too great for the large numbers who will have their hopes disappointed.

Another body of sociological research into job evaluations suggests that there is rather less success in teaching the other tenet of Soviet character-education relating to work, namely that 'all jobs are equal'. Novosibirsk University from 1962 to 1970 led an investigation into the job evaluations made by schoolchildren throughout the Soviet Union. Occupations were rated on a ten-point scale and the findings are shown in table 10. It is quite clear from this table that Soviet children do not feel that all jobs are equal; on the contrary their ratings correlate fairly closely with the level of training required to do a particular job.[1] This is not, perhaps, surprising in view of the fact that exhortations to study to become 'better' qualified and, implicitly, 'more able' to serve the Motherland are given more prominence than those promoting the egalitarian theme. Love of work is presented by *Soviet* theoreticians (and is seen by Marcuse) as the key value

---

[1] See Lane and O'Dell, *The Soviet Industrial Worker: Social Class, Education and Control*, London, 1978, for a more detailed treatment of occupational prestige in the contemporary USSR.

around which all the others revolve. It certainly does have a very significant place in the Soviet value-system and therefore it cannot but detract from the success of the character-education process if there is equivocation in the approach to the subject which children acquire at school.

TABLE 10 *School-leavers' evaluations of occupations on a ten-point scale*

| Occupation | Average rating | Occupation | Average rating |
|---|---|---|---|
| Physicist | 7.64 | Driver | 5.25 |
| Pilot | 7.62 | Character-educator in | |
| Radio technician | 7.62 | children's establishment | 5.04 |
| Mathematician | 7.34 | Turner | 4.58 |
| Geologist | 7.22 | Electro-mechanic | 4.46 |
| Doctor | 7.20 | Worker in communi- | |
| Worker in literature or | | cations | 4.42 |
| art | 7.04 | Weaver | 4.36 |
| Teacher at institutes of | | Tailor | 4.02 |
| higher education | 6.75 | Tractor driver | 4.02 |
| Construction engineer | 6.59 | Bricklayer | 3.57 |
| Mechanical engineer | 6.41 | Catering worker | 3.24 |
| Teacher in secondary | | Smith | 3.14 |
| school | 6.03 | Carpenter | 2.96 |
| Metallurgist | 5.96 | Shop assistant | 2.75 |
| Miner | 5.54 | Book-keeper | 2.56 |
| Chemist | 5.52 | Municipal worker | 2.27 |
| Train driver | 5.46 | Clerk | 1.96 |
| Steel founder | 5.35 | | |

*Source*: Omel'yanenko 1973, p. 120

On the one hand, as we have seen, it is repeatedly stressed that work, whatever form it may take, is noble for even the most lowly and unskilled labour is essential to the building of Communist society. In the school readers, one of the most striking differences between pre-revolutionary and contemporary Russia is shown to be the respect which all workers now enjoy compared with the privation and unjust treatment they used to suffer. The press also occasionally makes an example of someone who has failed to show the required regard for manual labour. On the other hand, children are at the same time constantly urged to study diligently because, it is reiterated, the more they learn the more they will be able to serve their country and the greater will be their contribution to the construction of Communism (and the higher may be their pay, of course – 'according to labour performed'). The implication of this is clearly that a job's value and prestige is greater, the higher the level of knowledge and skill necessary to do it.

The child must thus experience conflict. He is taught both that he must revere manual labour and that he must strive to become as highly qualified as possible. It is hardly surprising that there are reports of snobbishness about jobs, of women who do not like to admit that they work as cleaners, of girls who refuse to marry insufficiently qualified men – even of the forging of academic diplomas. This seems to be, in essence, a conflict of theory and practicality. Any socialist ideology must preach equality of status for all types of labour. But it is also clearly essential for a rapidly advancing modern industrial society to encourage the training of technical and other highly skilled specialists because the country's economic advancement depends very much on this group. The elements of contradiction which thus emerge are caused by the demands of the legitimating ideology conflicting with those of practical need.

This dual standard must have its effect on young people. Those who end up on the shop floor may well face disillusionment, having been presented with such a rosy image of the glory of labour. On the other hand, some might also feel they had, to some degree, failed their country – or themselves – in not becoming highly skilled. Most outsiders would probably agree that, on the whole, the official Soviet respect for both labour and learning was healthy and admirable but that the hypocrisies involved in coping with the scientific and technical revolution could at the same time prove counter-productive.

## Patriotism

Patriotism, or love for the Motherland and its leaders, was identified in chapter two as a basic characteristic of the desired New Soviet Man; examination of the literature has shown this to be, in fact, the most highly promoted of the Soviet virtues. Has this promotion met with success – or has the word 'patriotic' in practice become in the East, too, the near-pejorative epithet it is among many young people in the West?

It would seem probable that it is not as hard to foster patriotism as some of the other desired Soviet characteristics; most people of most countries could at some time in their lives sympathise with their own version of Scott's verse:

> Breathes there the man with soul so dead
> Who never to himself hath said
> This is my own, my native land!

Affection for the familiar places where one grew up would seem to be a far more widespread feature of human psychology than, say, love of discipline or denying oneself for the good of a collective. It would seem likely that, at least as far as love of Motherland goes, it is not inherently difficult to imbue youth with patriotic feelings. And it seems that, in the USSR, such feelings are fostered with success.

It would seem probable that, for many, this natural geographical loyalty develops smoothly into a political loyalty. An American political scientist, for instance, sees a general lack of child cynicism towards political figures whatever adult views may be; he attributes this to a 'painfully benevolent portrayal of the wider environment in contemporary children's literature' (Greenstein 1969:43). Vasil'ev finds that youth demonstrates its patriotism through a preparedness to defend the Motherland – with arms, if need be. He adds: 'Military themes on the radio and television and in the cinema enjoy great popularity among youth. Young Leningrad televiewers named as their favourite programme *Stories of Heroism.*' (Vasil'ev *et al.* 1967:110–11.)

A 'shining demonstration of patriotism' was an All-Union tourist campaign in which young people visited 'places of revolutionary, military and labouring glory of the Soviet people'. More than three million young boys and girls traversed the paths of the Second World and Civil Wars. As a result of the campaign, more than twenty-seven thousand museums, rooms and corners dedicated to military glory were created, six thousand monuments, obelisks and memorial plaques on battle-sites were set up, thousands of warrior graves were put in order and the names of formerly unknown war heroes were established (*idem*). The large participation perhaps proves only that the Party was anxious for such demonstrations – but there is evidence that Soviet patriotic education does have some genuine results. Even such a writer as Frederick Barghoorn, an American political scientist who certainly does not view the Soviet system with much favour, agrees that Soviet socialisation, combined with wartime successes, industrialising and space-research achievements, has ensured that the majority of Soviet citizens at least passively accept that their system is on the right lines (Barghoorn 1966:34).

A Soviet journalist who had travelled abroad, but who has not always been in favour with the authorities, found that the spirit of patriotism – in its broad Soviet sense – was what most characterised Soviet youth. He wrote:

There is also such a concept as duty to the people, to the country and to oneself. It seems to me that this is the chief thing that distinguishes our young people from Western bourgeois young people, and not the fact that ours go to Young Communist League meetings while the Westerners dress in black sweaters and tight pants and dance rock'n' roll and the twist. (Nekrasov 1964:253.)

This is very much the writer's own impression from personal contact with Soviet young people. Whereas Western youth tends to be anti-establishment and anti-patriotic, their Soviet counterparts seem to accept the basic values of Motherland and State. One Soviet girl in her twenties summed up the prevalent attitude by saying: 'When my country is criticised, it hurts me as if it were a personal insult.' Even young children seem to have assimilated at least the Soviet patriotic idiom. Quite unprompted, one ten-year-old began to tell me how wonderful life was going to be under Soviet Communism. 'Everyone will work and there'll be no money. You'll be able to go into a sweetshop and just help yourself to whatever you want.'

Some indication of pupils' acceptance of the patriotic virtue is given by an analysis of schoolchildren's essays on the theme 'What I am going to be'. Pupils were asked to name their future profession and give reasons for their choice (D'yachenko 1971:17–29). The results are summarised in table 11 and show that patriotic motives rank very highly in the reasons given for choice of profession. The importance of the actual percentages here

TABLE 11 *Pupils' motives for career choice. Figures are percentages*

| Motive | Class 6 | | | Class 7 | | | Class 8 | | |
|---|---|---|---|---|---|---|---|---|---|
| | Boys | Girls | Total | Boys | Girls | Total | Boys | Girls | Total |
| Love of Motherland and people | 5.5 | 34 | 18.1 | 15 | 58.8 | 38.7 | 13.3 | 43.75 | 26.0 |
| Love of labour | – | – | – | 15 | 8.81 | 11.3 | 13.3 | – | 6.45 |
| Love of animals | 5.5 | – | 3 | – | 3 | 1.6 | – | – | – |
| Love of nature | – | – | – | 10.7 | 3 | 6.45 | – | – | – |
| Love of technical work | 16.5 | – | 9.7 | 10.7 | – | 4.8 | 13.2 | – | 6.4 |
| Interest in minerals | – | – | – | 10.7 | 3 | 6.45 | – | – | – |
| Interest in travel | 5.5 | 6.6 | 6.2 | 7.1 | 3 | 4.8 | – | – | – |
| Interest in art | 5.5 | – | 3 | – | 3 | 1.6 | – | – | – |
| Interest in a school subject | – | 6.6 | 3 | 3.57 | 3 | 3.2 | – | 6.25 | 3.2 |
| Passion for the profession | 5.5 | – | 3 | 3.57 | 6.1 | 4.8 | – | 12.5 | 6.4 |
| Striving to satisfy one's desires | – | – | – | – | 3 | 1.6 | – | – | – |
| Undefined motive | 11 | 26.4 | 18.1 | – | – | – | 6.6 | 6.25 | 6.4 |
| No motive | – | 13.2 | 6.2 | 18 | 2.4 | 9.6 | 47.0 | 31.45 | 42.0 |
| Aspiration towards victory, to show one's courage, endurance etc. | 45 | 13.2 | 30.3 | 10.7 | 3 | 6.45 | 6.6 | – | 3.2 |

*Source:* D'yachenko 1971, p. 22.

must not be over-rated. 'I want to serve my Motherland' could, after all, be given as a reason for choosing almost any job whereas 'interest in minerals' or 'love of animals' are much more circumscribed motives. None the less it is significant in itself that quite a large group of the pupils whose essays were examined chose to mention patriotic feelings as a motive for job choice. Perhaps the most revealing data in the table is that which testifies to successful sex-role socialisation. No girls professed any interest in technical work and it is mainly boys who were anxious to show the 'manly' characteristics of courage and endurance. The fact that girls substantially predominated in expressions of patriotic feeling supports the point already noted that girls seem generally to be more successfully educated in the desired Soviet virtues.

Unfortunately, of course, there are no Soviet opinion pollsters gauging public views on Soviet political leaders or tendencies. Nevertheless, it seems probable that active disillusionment with Party leaders and their policies affects only a minority. The majority of Soviet citizens seem to grow up to feel not only that the Soviet Union is an especially beautiful country, but also that, despite some shortcomings, she does have what is basically the most just political system in the world.

*Internationalism*

In chapter two it was seen that the Soviet value of internationalism was presented as being fully compatible with the value of patriotism, although given a less prominent position in the Moral Code of the Builder of Communism. The children's literature examined, moreover, has made it clear that internationalism is always subordinated to patriotism whenever there might be any question of a clash between the two values. Does the character-education system succeed in achieving the perhaps somewhat precarious desired balance between these two qualities in the minds of young people?

Vasil'ev found that about eighty-two per cent of his young scientific workers regularly followed the international scene, while only one per cent were not at all interested (Vasil'ev *et al.* 1967: 95). His survey is a little difficult to interpret, since he says that a further twenty-five per cent were 'only interested in the most pressing questions', but the conclusion that a very large proportion of educated young people are actively interested in foreign affairs is inescapable. This is not in itself at variance with the system's aims so long as this interest is contained within a framework for aspects of foreign life officially described as 'progressive'. Thus, Moscow Pioneers are praised for writing in the autumn of 1970: 'Dear Angela Davis, We are very anxious for you. We shall obtain your freedom. We invite you to visit our Pioneer Palace. Our hearts are with you.' (Verba and Pikovsky 1973:81.)

Love for all one's foreign cousins is not however to be encouraged. The 8th of February has been marked in many schools as the Day of the Young Anti-Fascist and the Warrior for Freedom and Peace (ibid. 69). 'Youth is Exposing Imperialism' has become a much promoted slogan of the Komsomol (ibid. 80). In response to this and to the fiftieth anniversary of the Pioneer organisation, Karaganda pupils set up an operation called 'Your Contribution to the Peace Fund'; an information sheet about this declared:

To all councils, brigades and committees of the Komsomol,
To clubs of International Friendship,
To all pupils of the town of Karaganda!
Friend! Comrade! Contemporary!
You live in a happy, free country. Above you is a clear sky and a bright sun. More than once have black forces threatened the freedom of our Motherland, but she has preserved her independence and peace thanks to the solidarity and friendship of all her peoples.
However, the world is troubled. Remember, contemporary: you and your friends also have to answer for peace on the Earth.
Together with adults, continue the sacred cause of struggling for the strengthening of peace.
Reinforce friendship between children of the workers of the whole world, of all nationalities.
Spread wider the work of the Clubs of International Friendship in your schools by participation in the campaign 'Youth Exposes Imperialism'.
At the proper time, reject all the important events which threaten peace, raise your voice in protest against the bloody and evil deeds of imperialism, against the unleashing of a new world war: hold meetings to show solidarity with those peoples who are fighting for their freedom and independence, collect the signatures of those who are on the side of peace.
Bring the strongest contribution you can to the cause of the

strengthening of peace, organise working troops and put the money you earn into the Soviet 'Fund for Peace'.
May the struggle for peace and happiness on our planet become the aim in life of each of us. (*Ibid.* 81–2.)

Local youth is said to have responded well to this appeal – though this, of course, may be said mainly to demonstrate the efficiency of the Soviet system for organising youth campaigns. Every school in the town participated and 'hundreds of roubles' were contributed to the fund; one is curious as to how it was spent. Behaviour which involves a carefully measured amount and type of internationalist feeling is clearly encouraged.

But young people's interest in international affairs is not limited solely to 'exposing imperialism' or even to reading Soviet newspaper reports of happenings abroad. Soviet youth has, from the authorities' point of view, too great an interest in foreign goods. Many a Western visitor has been amazed at the enormous black-market prices offered for blue jeans or a Rolling Stones record. The satirical magazine *Krokodil* regularly jibes at those for whom any goods that are imported (*importny*) are at once desirable. The following couplet is mocking both this and another major Soviet status symbol, gold fillings: 'They felt his name should be exalted/Because his gold tooth was imported.' (Smirnov 1968: 17.)

The attraction for the rebellious section of Soviet youth of the foreign is neatly summed up by this description of a slightly deviant youth in the novel, *A Starry Ticket*: 'I saw him dodging in between the cars, a nimble figure, in gaudy check shirt of Czechoslovak origin, tight trousers of unknown provenance, a pair of light Austrian shoes. Only his head was Russian, but it was shorn in a French crew-cut style.' (Aksenov 1962:7.)

In view of the modish fascination with the products of the Western clothing and pop-music industries, it would seem that the precarious balance which would constitute a 'correct' approach to things international has not fully been achieved in the Soviet Union. Patriotism is central in the practical teaching of Soviet morality; it is therefore probable that any contradictions in the presentation of this will have an especial effect on the development of Soviet youth. There would, in fact, seem to be at least one important political contradiction in this area – the predominance of patriotism as opposed to internationalism is clear but lip-service must still be paid to internationalism.

Publicists and theoreticians emphasise that a dedication to Russia does not preclude a firm sense of internationalism; they claim that not only are the two compatible, but that both are basic to a true Soviet world-view. In practice, however, it is clearly the nationalistic end of the scale which is highlighted. Thus, in stories about pre-revolutionary times, for example, it is self-evident that Russia was better off under an autocrat than she would have been under a more enlightened foreign ruler.

Depictions of life abroad are mainly aimed not at providing understanding of and sympathy for customs and outlooks that differ from Soviet ones, but rather at illustrating the superiority of the Soviet way of life.

Children, as has been seen, are often portrayed as having instinctive bonds with each other, whatever their nationality. These are not, of course, shown as being separate from and above adult political divisions, however, for these bonds are still ultimately determined by the Soviet system which is shown as the protector of justice and peace and childhood. Even when internationalism is given some prominence, it is very closely linked with and even shown to hinge upon Soviet patriotism: really, everyone should be a Soviet patriot – for the Soviet Union is the spiritual Motherland of all working people.

Although national feeling is the central element of Soviet morality, there is clearly a certain double-think here – of which some Russians are themselves aware. Ehrenburg, writing about Stendhal, for instance, says: 'The controversy over Stendhal's cosmopolitanism is the old quarrel about the true nature of love for one's homeland: does such love entail contempt for other peoples and eulogy of the faults and shortcomings of one's fellow-countrymen?' (Quoted in Stillman 1958:235.) This problem is, indeed, an old one in the Russian context; Brzezinski and Huntington suggest that the authorities exploit it to their own ends in their stress on patriotism in character-education: 'Here, the regime can tap deep-seated feelings of ambivalence, insecurity and inferiority–superiority which have characterised past Russian attitudes to the West.' (Brzezinski and Huntington 1964:90.) This is done by consistently making patriotism into a much more political virtue than it has traditionally been; modern love of the Motherland is shown to be love more of the Kremlin than of the Steppes.

The fact that Marxism has little room for patriotism must be understood by more Russians than Solzhenitsyn:

What is the combination of Marxism with patriotism but a meaningless absurdity? These two points of view can be 'merged' only in generalised incantations, for history has shown us that in practice they are diametrically opposed. This is so obvious that in 1915 Lenin actually proclaimed: 'We are anti-patriots!' And that was the honest truth. And throughout the 1920s in our country, the word 'patriot' meant exactly the same as 'White Guard'. (Solzhenitsyn, *The Sunday Times*, 3 March 1974.)

In several ways patriotism is thus a conflict-laden value in Soviet morality and this becomes particularly significant when one bears in mind the prominence given to patriotism throughout the children's literature discussed. Although not something discussed in the Soviet educational press, this contradiction must be a factor underlying some failures in the socialisation process – particularly among intellectual youth. It also may account for such phenomena as the exaggerated value attached to imported Western goods by sections of Soviet youth. More generally, it involves a clear ambiguity in thought to which no satisfactory official answer is provided – and, as such, must cause confusion to any thinking young Soviet citizen.

Durkheim, like Soviet theorists, believed that patriotism and internationalism need not clash as values – but only if patriotism were internally rather than centrifugally orientated. Unfortunately, this does not seem to be consistently the case with contemporary Soviet patriotism. Certainly there is cause for hope: Soviet theorists constantly stress the peace-loving nature of the Soviet people and stories for children reiterate that love of peace is one of the characteristics of the Builder of Communism. But this is not, of course, represented as a passive, turn-the-other-cheek virtue. It is a love which will demand determined struggle because there are still hostile forces in the world which seek to make money from war and gain power through aggression. Such forces must not be tolerated; they must be actively fought against (the phrase 'the struggle for peace' has long ceased to sound paradoxical to most Soviet ears). Such reasoning provides the link between love of peace and readiness for war in the Soviet argumentation and the rationale for much detailed discussion in the educational press of the best methods of carrying out 'military-patriotic education': for example, the First Secretary of the Kursk regional committee (*obkom*) of the Komsomol recommended the encouragement of military clubs at school. Here children would play war games and study weapons. They would also visit local war-invalids. The clubs should have their own banner and rituals. The First Secretary also favoured 'military sport' summer camps for children. He urged teachers not to become complacent in this field; there were still too many schools and Pioneer groups which did not concern themselves adequately with military education (*Pravda*, 19 February 1972).

An article in the leading journal of educational theory, entitled 'Preparing Youth for the Defence of the Motherland' reviews a large number of books on the military-patriotic education of youth – which, again, suggests the importance which is attached to this topic. Its author approves, in particular, of the large number of books and articles on this subject being published in the non-Russian republics (*Sov.ped.* 1970: No. 9, p. 146). Does this, perhaps suggest that the authorities feel that the need for such education is greater in non-Russian areas?

Military education is believed by Soviet educationalists to foster a sense of patriotism. An article on military education concludes thus: 'All work on military-patriotic education which is conducted in the schools helps us to develop pupils who are ardent patriots of the Motherland and to prepare them for self-denying labour in her name and for the glorious defence of her sacred frontiers.' (*Narodnoe obrazovanie* 1970: No. 9, p. 73.) Interestingly, once again, the use of religious terminology is found. Military enthusiasm and patriotism are seen as being closely bound up; they are very greatly emphasised in comparison with internationalism and love of peace, the parallel virtues which Soviet sources officially proclaim but, as yet, do relatively little to promote. Thus it would seem that, as practically presented, Soviet patriotism is centrifugally rather than internally orientated. As with patriotism and internationalism, the love-of-peace preoccupation-with-military-affairs antimony can hardly avoid provoking conflict in the minds of Soviet youth.

## Atheism

Chapter two documented the fact that an atheist outlook is officially an essential part of the Builder of Communism's worldview. Unexpectedly, very little anti-religious or specifically atheistic material was found in our examination of Soviet children's literature. Has this neglect resulted in a level of atheist consciousness unsatisfactory from the authority's viewpoint? Or does it simply imply that religious opinions are fast fading, disappearing of their own accord and not felt to require official discouragement via the children's press?

Both official sources and survey data make it clear that it is the former which is the case. The level of atheism among schoolleavers today is far from that desired by the authorities. In a pamphlet, *The Twenty-fourth Party Congress and the Tasks of Atheist Education*, S. I. Nikishov says that religious prejudices are the most persistent 'relics of the past'. He argues that, though successes in creating the Builders of Communism have been great, better atheist education is urgently required (Nikishov 1972:25).

Frequent newspaper reports also suggest the lingering of religious beliefs – or attraction to religious rituals – among the young. Just as foreign denims and hard rock records are coveted among a section of Soviet youth, so it is fashionable to wear a cross. *Krokodil*'s cartoon hippies not only have long hair and bare feet, as in the West, but also a cross round their necks. This fashion, the national youth papers opine, is potentially dangerous (*Komsomol'skaya pravda*, 16 October 1970). The Komsomol and state can certainly be hard on some believers: one girl was expelled from the Komsomol and her teacher-training college because she got married in church. It was argued that this was just, even though she was not a real believer; a teacher must not have a conciliatory attitude towards religion (*Komsomol'skaya pravda*, 6 January 1971). It seems that many people, even if they profess themselves to be non-believers, are attracted by religious ceremonial, especially by christenings and funerals. In a study of a village in Belorussia, twenty-two out of sixty-five supposed non-believers thought that religious rituals were worth preserving (*Izvestiya*, 12 November 1971). Many young people occasionally attend church from an academic interest in Old Russia; others are clearly moved by the services. Despite this, children's ignorance about religion and atheism was found to be great. Children in their third year at school were asked to define various words connected with religion 'mixed up with other words to do with vestiges of the past like "bribe taker" or "merchant"' (Ogryzko 1970). *Ateist* ('atheist') was defined, among other things, as 'a large bird that comes in the spring' (the Russian for 'stork' is *aist*). *Altar'* (the same as in English) was confused with *vratar'* ('a goal-keeper in soccer').

The whole question of religion among young people has been studied by Soviet sociologists, who have shown that only a little over forty per cent of tenth-graders are convinced atheists (Ogryzko 1970:67). Given that the Soviet schoolchild will be likely to ascribe to himself the required atheist views if he is in any doubt as to what he should put, this percentage seems surprisingly low. A study of schoolchildren in Leningrad shows that religion is still a part of the background of the majority (see table 12). These figures are particularly striking when we remember that they are for Leningrad – probably the most sophisticated city in the USSR.

TABLE 12    *Religious background of schoolchildren, Leningrad*

| Background | Class 5 (170 pupils) | | Class 8 (120 pupils) | |
|---|---|---|---|---|
| | (No.) | (%) | (No.) | (%) |
| Believers in family | 18 | 11 | 22 | 18 |
| Ikons at home | 20 | 12 | 15 | 13 |
| Families observe religious holidays | 91 | 54 | 30 | 25 |
| Attend church | 8 | 5 | 28 | 23 |
| Christened | ? | ? | 69 | 58 |

*Source*: Ogryzko 1970, pp. 70–6.

Because of such figures, the Party has expressed anxiety to develop atheist character-education. The Party Programme for 1969 states:

It is necessary to conduct systematically widespread scientific-atheistic propaganda, to explain, patiently, the untenable nature of religious beliefs that arose in the past because people were weighted down by the forces of nature and by social oppression and were ignorant of the true causes of natural and social phenomena. Owing to this, we ought to be guided by the achievements of contemporary science which far more fully reveal the picture of the world and increase man's power over nature, leaving no place for the fantastic imaginings of religion about supernatural powers. (*Programma KPSS* 1969:200–1.)

Writers on the subject feel that atheist education should be of two types – positive and critical:

The positive element is the creation of a soil in which it will be very difficult for religion to strike its roots and the development of immunity against religion. In other words, this is the character-education of the new man. And the critical element means the direct overcoming of religious ideas, sentiments and cultural ideas proper. (Ogryzko 1970).

There is widespread discussion on this theme. The educational press has frequent articles on it. The librarians' professional journal also has advice on overcoming religious survivals: the librarian is counselled on how to cope with the religious child (Filippenko 1972:28–31). First, she should give him books on the wonders of nature and such scientific wonders as the Kon-Tiki expedition. Care should be taken not to offend his sensibilities. Then he should be directed to works of fiction which will develop in him a clearer understanding of the psychology of the believing individual – e.g. Ostrovsky's *Kak zakalyalas' stal'* and Polevoy's *Povest' o nastoyashchem cheloveke*. While they are in a period of doubt, the librarian must give them something to fill the gap, as it were – to develop in them a sense of social responsibility and collectivism. Finally, they must be guided to works on scientific materialism so that they can see religion in its place in historical development.

The apparent partial failure of the atheist facet of Soviet character-education does seem to be causing concern, for it would seem that the system has here experienced its most striking lack of success. There has been much talk of extending anti-religious propaganda; it will be interesting to discover whether this will, in fact, be reflected in the school readers and in *Murzilka* in the next few years.

This chapter can, in most respects, draw only rather impressionistic conclusions about overall levels of success or failure. Given the campaigning nature of the Soviet press, it is usually easier to highlight the weak points in the carrying-out of any official drive; however, it has been possible to give some indication of the effectiveness of the operation of the Soviet character-education system. It is, for example, evident that differing levels of success have been achieved with regard to the different Soviet virtues. Despite obvious difficulties of measurement, it would seem that patriotism and collectivism are widely adhered to. Discipline appears to be strong – with a notable exception in the handling of alcohol. Regarding attitudes to work, more success has been won in encouraging a love of study than in instilling a conviction that all jobs are equal. Internationalism has not been channelled completely efficiently in the desired way as there is a fascination for foreign goods and culture that is certainly at variance with the authorities' intentions. The other area of notable failure has been in creating atheist convictions. From the above conclusions it seems clear that the Soviet authorities have had most success in giving Soviet expression to those values which have a long Russian tradition – namely patriotism and collectivism. Love of study is arguably the one value which has been introduced since 1917 on a very wide scale. Atheist attitudes and a sense of the equality of all work are not part of the Russian tradition and these have not been successfully imposed on the popular consciousness. This is undoubtedly due in part to their novelty to the Russian value system, but it must also be a result of what we have seen to be a relative neglect of these values in the socialisation process.

# 9

## Secular morality and myths

Having conducted a fairly extensive survey of the nature of
character-education as conveyed in literature for Soviet children
and having, as far as is possible, assessed its impact, it remains
now to return to two general problems which were pin-pointed
in the introduction. The first concerns the question of how to
build a morality in a secular society. The second closely related
problem deals with the creation of 'foundation myths'. It is
intended in this chapter both to draw attention to relevant
aspects of Soviet society and, on the basis of these, to highlight
some general implications for the creation of a morality system
in any modern secular society.

### Durkheim's secular moral education

It is over half a century old but there is one thorough Western
general study of the setting-up of a secular system of character-
education. This is Emile Durkheim's series of lectures first
delivered at the Sorbonne in 1902–03 and collected under the
title *Moral Education*. As it is a highly stimulating work, and also
seems to me to throw some light on problems met by Soviet
practice, the major points of his argument are now briefly set
forth. Firstly, he establishes the general requirements of a secular
morality; secondly, he isolates three fundamental elements of
morality; and, thirdly, he discusses how to develop these in the
child. In speaking of general requirements, Durkheim's prime
contention is that it is not simply enough to strip the supernatural
from morality – some alternative must be provided in order to
give the virtues and their teachers essential justification and
authority. The controllers of society could discover in this argu-

ment rationalisation for a 'foundation myth' to authorise their own power – but they would not find support in Durkheim for anything irrational or untrue in their myth. Reason is to be man's guide in setting up a secular moral education and Durkheim reasons that 'society must have an ideal towards which it reaches' (Durkheim 1973:13). Religion not only lends authority to morality, it also inspires; secular character-education must take over both these functions. We have seen how Soviet character-education strips itself of God and certainly provides alternative sources of authority and inspiration. We have also found, however, that certain curious ambiguities – not foreseen by Durkheim – have crept into the Soviet justification and authorisation of their morality.

Considering many methods as to how the necessary secular virtues can be inculcated, Durkheim stresses that lesson-content can and must be used as a means of moral education – although he writes: 'Doubtless it would seem surprising at first that classroom education could possibly promote moral education.' (Durkheim 1973:249.) As Roy Nash has pointed out, even our own supposedly objective textbooks – perhaps just through their selectivity, and their omissions – subtly put across one particular set of social attitudes (Nash 1972:230–2); any doubts in the reader's mind about the possibilities for moral education through lesson-content must surely have been removed now we have studied Soviet school readers.

Discipline, attachment to social groups and autonomy are the three elements of morality isolated by Durkheim. Discipline he considers fundamental, not only because of the benefit it brings to society but also because it is to the individual himself 'the condition of happiness and of moral health'. His argument is that a sense of limitlessness profoundly disturbs man and that totally undisciplined behaviour brings him not satisfaction but disillusionment. He supports this thesis with reference to his study of the causes of suicide (Durkheim 1973:38–41). He does not praise an unthinking discipline – indeed, he seems to give us an Aristotelian golden mean where the virtue is central on the scale, joining the twin excesses of blind discipline and blind liberality (*ibid.* 45). The golden mean of this scale is, it must be noted, not so much obedience to some external authority as self-control. This virtue can only be achieved, claims Durkheim, by those who have learnt to submit to an external discipline in their youth (*ibid*. 49–50). Contemporary liberal opinion might frown on his admiration for discipline but his argument reads in a convincing way. Disciplining children, in my opinion, must not be viewed solely as a means whereby those in power seek to maintain their own authority. It is desirable for the development of mature adults who can live happily and fruitfully in society. The danger lies mainly in the easy abuse of discipline. Those in a position of authority over others can all too simply come to enjoy the experience of power and to exert it for its own sake. To punish a child because he kicked his grandmother is one thing; to do so because he forgot to date his homework is another. A secondary danger is that discipline could become too rigid. Discipline, by definition, demands a certain standardisation of rules of behaviour but it must not be considered that these rules apply to all times and all places: 'Not only does man's range of behaviour change, but the forces that set limits are not absolutely the same at different historical periods.' (*Ibid*. 52.) It is simpler, however, to lose sight of reason and the change of circumstances and to assume that the rules of behaviour of our own childhood are ideal for our children. In this way, too, discipline can be easily abused. Discipline has been dwelt on here, partly because of the possibly controversial importance which Durkheim attaches to it and partly because we have seen it to be one of the prime virtues of the Soviet value-system; as such it must not be facilely dismissed as a convenient means of social control, used by those in positions of power, to exploit the rest of society. It undoubtedly can serve this function but, if unabused, it also brings positive benefits to the individual and to society.

The second of Durkheim's three fundamental elements of morality is 'attachment to social groups'. He states that 'to act morally is to act in terms of the collective interest' (*ibid*. 59). Again he finds that this virtue brings health both to society and to the individual. The benefits for society as a whole are clearly cohesion and the strength of unity but those for the individual perhaps need some expansion; Durkheim's argument develops from the idea that man gains in depth and understanding from social contact. It is social rather than ascetic life that is most profoundly enriching to the individual personality and, once again, he uses his analysis of suicide-rates to prove his point (*ibid.* 68). But the good of society has not just an inspirational role in Durkheim's morality. He declares: 'If society is the end of morality, it is also its producer.' (*Ibid.* 86.) Society is to be the source of both the inspiration and the authority previously provided by God, and Durkheim sums up its dual role in almost biblical language:

On the one hand, it [society] seems to us an authority that constrains us, fixes limits for us, blocks us when we would trespass, and to which we defer with a feeling of religious respect. On the other hand, society is the benevolent and protecting power, the nourishing mother from which we gain the whole of our moral and intellectual substance and towards whom our wills turn in a spirit of love and gratitude. In the one case, it is like a jealous and formidable God, the stern law-maker allowing no transgression of His orders. In the other case, it is the succoring deity to whom the faithful sacrifice themselves with gladness.' (*Ibid.* 92–3.)

Such exaltation of society is often mistrusted by Western liberals, who are so alarmed by what they feel to be its inherent danger of leading to an unthinking fascist or Communist attitude that they do not allow it as a virtue. However, Durkheim's statement of the role of society in morality is, indeed, very much akin to what has become one of the basic Soviet virtues, that which is usually termed 'collectivism'.

The final of Durkheim's three elements of morality is that which he calls 'autonomy'. This is dealt with in less detail and is the most tenuous of the three elements. It concerns the idea that an act cannot really be considered as moral if we are forced into it (*ibid.* 112). '"Autonomy" is a realisation of why we should behave in a certain way and through it, we do not perhaps act differently, but our acts cease to be a humiliation or a bondage.' (*Ibid.* 118.) Durkheim finds the source of autonomy – simply – in science and reason. Religion was irrational – largely because it assumed the existence of something unchangeable (*ibid.* 106) – and so could not be a source of autonomy. Science, he claims, takes all features of life, including change, into account, and is therefore a true source of autonomy. We have seen that Soviet morality likewise claims to be based on science but it neither stresses autonomy in theory nor encourages it in practice in the character-education process. This omission may well, as is shown below, be an important factor underlying some of the behaviour problems which Soviet society does display.

### Independent thought

Throughout this work it has become apparent that the fundamental characteristic of the Builder of Communism is to be his world-view – that the primary aim of character-education in all its forms is to train young people to an acceptance of a single, uniquely 'correct' Soviet outlook on life. All else, including the development of creative thinking about problems, is subordinated to this. The conviction that there can be only one correct opinion, only one correct answer to all basic problems may, in certain respects, make life simpler for the average citizen. There is after all a kind of comfort, perhaps familiar also to practising Catholics, in an absolute faith in the correctness of an opinion received from above. But education in such unquestioning attitudes to the official doctrines can stifle the child's ability to think independently and creatively. This is a problem which has been causing concern to Soviet educationalists for several years. Sometimes textbooks are to blame here; *Pravda* (28 February 1968) criticises a literature textbook for the ninth grade for leaving nothing to the child's imagination. This book tells the pupils even how they will feel on reading the selected passages. About Alexander Ostrovsky's play *Groza* (*The Storm*), for instance, it says: 'The scene of the last meeting between Boris and Katerina arouses in us the feeling of contempt.' In one critically minded Soviet novel of the sixties we are encouraged to feel a certain disapproval of one of the characters who has quite easily managed to shine in the Soviet situation without showing a spark of initiative:

Your life, Vik, was the old folk's invention. They planned it for you while you were still only a babe in the cradle. So you got your distinctions at school, you got your distinctions at college, you went through all the regular motions on the great road that leads to the Academy of Sciences – that is, to being a corpse which has earned the general respect of the community. . .But I tell you you've never once in your life decided anything for yourself, never once risked anything. (Aksenov 1962:31–2.)

P. L. Kapitsa, the world-famous physicist – also well known for his interest in educational questions – has also emphasised that it is essential to promote originality. Speaking to a 1970 conference in Hungary on the training of physics instructors and referring in particular to the teaching of physics in schools, he complained that problems in textbooks usually involved only the selection of the right formula. Setting less standard tasks would help to bring out a more inventive approach (*Voprosy filosofii* 1971: No. 7, pp. 16–24).

This encouragement of independent thought does not mean that pupils are to be allowed to come to *any* conclusion. If Soviet schools do adopt textbooks and methods which train children to think things through more, the training will be to reason from firm Soviet first principles to obtain the 'correct' conclusions for particular cases. However, any such training may eventually lead to the questioning of the basic principles – a risk that has caused this approach to education to be shunned from the 1930s.

Theorists of higher education blame the schools for the pedestrian nature of many students' work. From the early thirties, schools have considered a student's acquisition of an extensive range of facts as essential – to the detriment of the student's development in reasoning. The syllabuses are so heavily loaded that there is little time, it is argued, for the pupils to learn how to think for themselves. It is felt now, however, that it is impossible to teach a child all the facts he will need and so the aim should be to train the mind rather than the memory. Soviet educationalists stress that it is more important for the child to see the whole forest than the trees. Thus both at home and at school children should be encouraged to work out the answers to their questions themselves rather than being told the solution as soon as they ask.

When little attention is paid to developing independent thought, the problem of an over-rigid attachment to written rules or instructions from above is likely to arise. The Soviet press, both in fiction and in news-reporting, is full of examples of situations where officials have refused to bend rules – even in cases where it was indisputably reasonable to diverge from the regulations. A most dramatic instance of this occurs in Yevtushenko's *A Precocious Autobiography*. He is describing the horror of the scene amongst the immense crowds that are pushing forward to see Stalin's coffin:

At that moment, I felt I was treading on something soft. It was a human body. I picked my feet up and was borne along by the crowd. For a long time, I was afraid to put my feet down again. The crowd closed tighter and tighter. I was saved by my height. Short people were smothered alive. We were caught between the walls of houses on one side and a row of army trucks on the other.

'Get the trucks out of the way!' people howled. 'Get them away.'

'I can't. I've got no instructions', a very young, fair bewildered militia officer shouted back, almost crying with desperation. And people were being hurtled against the trucks by the crowd, and their heads smashed. The sides of the trucks were running with blood. All at once, I felt a savage hatred for everything that had given birth to that 'No instructions' shouted at a moment when people were dying of someone's stupidity. (Yevtushenko 1965:96–7.)

A similar tragedy caused by bureaucratic inflexibility forms the plot of Vladimir Tendryakov's story *Ukhaby* (*Pot-Holes*). In this, an injured man dies because officials and doctors refuse to step over the line and help him when it is not strictly their responsibility, as defined in their book of instructions.

Rather more light-heartedly, Zoshchenko points up bureaucratic rigidity. In the story *Galosh*, he describes the intricacies of red tape which he had to go through in order to retrieve a shabby lost galosh from a lost-property office. By the time he has produced the papers necessary to prove that he did really lose a galosh, he has mislaid the other one.

In the non-literary press, too, there can be found many examples of people who do not have the initiative to bend rules when the occasion demands – thus causing, at best, a humorous or frustrating situation or, at worst, a real emergency or tragedy. The often ludicrous lack of flexibility of the bureaucracy is, indeed, a frequent target of the satirical magazine *Krokodil*. This tradition is often sanctioned by reference to the fact that the only poem of the *avant-garde* revolutionary poet Mayakovsky which Lenin had any time for was *Prozasedavshiyesya* (*On Meetings*) – the first famous satire on the growing Soviet bureaucracy; it ends with an ardent wish that, one day, a meeting will be called to pass a resolution to do away with all meetings.

The unwillingness of officials to diverge from the rule-book seems to be at its worst in the Soviet Union, although it is certainly a hazard of bureaucratic organisations everywhere. It may often be the result of a poorly written rule-book. It is probably exacerbated by the Soviet neglect of autonomy. Just as this may impair initiative in intellectual work, so it may also hinder the development of an independent reasoning attitude to the carrying out of rules.

In discussing those officials who do not find it difficult to say '*nyet*' unflinchingly in the face of persuasion by members of the public, one must not neglect to mention the role of fear in Soviet society. As was seen, discipline in Soviet schools is maintained largely by the carrot of praise for good behaviour or good work, but also by the hard stick of shaming in front of fellow pupils. Thus an element of fear-manipulation has a planned part in the Soviet teacher's disciplinary methods; this persists into adult life, where recalcitrant behaviour is also given publicity on factory or trade union notice-boards, for example. It is not, of course, such a powerful and obvious motivating factor in the regulation of behaviour as it was in the Stalin period – when even petty sins of omission or commission were liable to interpretation as 'wrecking' and the high probability of a consequence of forced labour or death – but it is still certainly one element lying behind the often unreasonable adherence to rules in Soviet society.

Since attachment to Soviet values is taught not so much by fostering autonomous thought as by constant repetition of the desired views, the language used, sadly enough, gradually tends to become debased and loses impact and real meaning. In a similar way English too has been weakened in this century though by advertising rather than propaganda. 'Sun Shower is a Van Gogh of a scent. Vibrant. Bright. Brimming with abandon.' This is as harmful to language as 'Before Communism, which was once only a dream, became the greatest force in contemporary life, a giant's path had to be traversed, a path spilt over with the blood of fighters for the people's happiness, a path of glorious victories and temporary defeats.' (*Programma KPSS* 1976:1–2.) Both are enfeebling through their excessive hyperbole and also because their stock phrases are continually being repeated in only slightly varying forms in their respective societies. The situation is summed up by Yevtushenko's feelings as he watches a crowd of ordinary Moscow workers: 'These people had no use for fine empty words. They had heard too many and had ceased to believe them.' (Yevtushenko 1965:75.) The natural next step is to suspect that those who use the lofty words are themselves not honest. Many must mistrust the writers of Party propaganda in the same way that Ivan Nikolaich doubts the sincerity of the hack poet Ryukhin in Bulgakov's *The Master and Margarita*: 'Look at his mean face and compare it with all that pompous verse he writes for May Day...all that stuff about "onwards and upwards" and "banners waving"! If you could look inside him and see what he's thinking you'd be sickened!' (Bulgakov 1971:76–7.) Similarly, the incident below shows how sincerity only entered into a meeting after the standard set of cliches had been said. It is noteworthy that genuine enthusiasm here is shown as being communicated by simple language from the heart rather than the lists of Party slogans.

There was a general meeting and our Chairman spoke. It made you fair sick to hear him drooling away about 'assuming responsibilities' and doing things 'on the basis of this and that', and all the other stock clap trap. I don't know why, but all those empty words just bounced off me like hail off a steep tin roof. But after he'd got all that off his chest he turned to talking like an ordinary human being. He said we'd got to catch all the fish we could because it was up to us to get the onion in for the co-op, and, if we did that, next year we would be able to have a big Atlantic-going trawler. (Aksenov 1962: 184.)

It is symbolic that, in *The Holy Well*, Valentin Kataev has a recurrent nightmare image of a talking cat dying while being trained to reproduce the latest jargon word 'neo-colonialism' (Kataev 1967).[1] It may be that the problem of writers' sincerity could only be solved by an abandonment of the system of censorship. But the problem of repetitive, debased language could be eased by a greater originality on the part of authors and journalists. *Pravda* makes this very point – though in relation to the somewhat stale posters frequently seen on classroom walls, when

[1] See also Yashin, *Rychagi*, London, 1965, striking example of this point.

it urges an additional sparkle and freshness (*Pravda*, 13 October 1968).

Not encouraging independent thought and insisting on one unreasoning 'correct' attitude also causes problems when that 'correct' view alters. A striking example of how this affects education is given by George Counts: he compares four versions of the allied landings in Normandy as described in subsequent editions of Soviet school history textbooks (1945, 1946, 1951 and 1956). In the first account, children read of

a brilliant success of our allies. It cannot be denied that the history of warfare knows no other undertaking equal in breadth of design, grandeur of scale and mastery of execution.

The writers become steadily less enthusiastic until, in the 1956 version, it is hard to recognise the same event:

England and the United States of America, in the course of three years of war, delayed in every way the opening of a second front in Europe against the German troops. But when, after the tremendous victories of the Soviet Army, it became clear that the Soviet Union with its own forces could occupy the entire territory of Germany and liberate France, England and the USA decided to open a second front in Europe. (Counts 1957.)

Such periodic modifications of 'the truth' must cause confusion – although it must be remembered that this tends to happen much less now than it did in the thirties and forties. The most dramatic instance of this revision was, of course, the denunciation of Stalin at the Twentieth Party Congress. This, of course, was a case of truth superseding myth. Suddenly the kindly father of all little children became the perpetrator of dreadful crimes. The shock of this is said to have been a major factor leading the writer Fadeyev, a prominent executor of Stalinist literary policies, to shoot himself. While few reacted so violently, most people, especially the impressionable youth, must have been profoundly disturbed and must have found the necessary readjustment of outlook a distressing process.

Khrushchev's fall from power, the switch in official attitudes towards China and the gradually more conciliatory approach to the USA are more recent examples of switches in the Party line which must have brought some conflict in the minds of many

Soviet citizens. It was changes such as these that could engender
the state of mind which called forth the following poem.

> I don't believe a thing today –
> I don't believe my eyes
> I don't believe my ears
> But let me touch it, then I'll believe it's true – maybe.
>
> I remember sullen Germans,
> The sad prisoners of nineteen-hundred-forty-five,
> Standing – during interrogation – with their hands on their
>     seams.
>
> I asked, they answered :–
> 'You believe Hitler?' – 'No, I don't.'
> 'You believe Goering?' – 'No, I don't.'
> 'You believe Goebbels?' – 'O, propaganda.'
> 'And what of me?' – (a brief silence)
> 'Mr Commissar, I don't believe you.
> All propaganda. The whole world is propaganda.'
>
> Four syllables: pro-pa-gan-da
> Still resound in my ears today:
> All propaganda. The whole world's propaganda.
> If I were changed to a child once more,
> Learning again in a primary school,
> And they told me this:
> The Volga flows into the Caspian Sea!
> I would believe it, of course, but first
> I would find that Volga,
> Would go down that stream to the sea,
> Would wash in its turbid water,
> And only then would I believe.
>
> Horses eat oats and hay!
> It's a lie. In the winter of forty-eight
> I lived in the Ukraine which was as thin as a rail.
> Horses at first ate straw,
> Next – the skimpy straw-roofs,
> And then they were handed to Kharkov to the city dump.
> I saw them with my own eyes:
> Austere, serious, almost important-looking
> Silently, unhurriedly walking in the dump.

They used to walk, then they used to stand. . .
After which they fell and lay a long time.
And the horses took a while to die. . .
Horses eat oats and hay!
No! It's not true! It's a lie. Propaganda.
All propaganda. The whole world's propaganda.
(Markov and Sparks 1966:817–19.)[2]

This poet would clearly advocate teaching through the encouragement of autonomous reasoning rather than through slogans –
especially slogans based on myth.

A training in autonomous thought might help to obviate the
four problems outlined above – the lack of intellectual originality,
lack of flexibility in adherence to rules, debasement of language
and inability to cope intellectually with changes in the Party line.
The constraint impeding the adoption of such a solution would
appear to be a seemingly inconsistent fear that the individual
would not draw the desired conclusion. It would seem that a
society which wishes to create a secular morality without running
across the problems above must not have such fears and must be
prepared somehow to encourage autonomous thought. The cost
will be that some will reject the current authorities' views but this
after all should only help the dialectic progress of society.

## Myths and reality

Durkheim stressed the need for a modern secular morality to
provide itself with sources of authority and inspiration equivalent
to those supplied to a morality based on religion by God and
divine heroes. But he insisted that science and reason should be
the sources of the new authority and inspiration of morality;
nowhere would he permit anything untrue or irrational to be
communicated to the growing generation. No 'foundation myth'
was to be developed. Throughout this study of writing for Soviet

2 The Western compilers of this anthology withheld the author's name – an
indication of the widespread awareness of the role of fear in Soviet society
which is perhaps especially powerful amongst those working in the field of
the creative arts. (The statements 'the Volga flows into the Caspian Sea'
and 'horses eat oats and hay' are standard truisms, comparable to the
English 'two and two make four': they hark back to a Chekhov story in
which a schoolmaster is heard dictating them to his class.)

children, it has become apparent that, although Soviet authorities, along with Durkheim, highly praise science and reason, they have none the less permitted, indeed opted, for the inclusion of certain irrational elements in the depiction of life which they offer children.

Firstly, in the classroom and in the reading matter prepared for him, the Soviet child is presented with a very sunny view of the world. Up to the frontier, it is a place where everything is just and where good always triumphs. It would seem that some distress, even trauma, must be experienced when the thoughtful child realises for the first time that the world is not such a simple and universally happy place.

Doronin poses the conflict in sharp terms in Solzhenitsyn's *The First Circle*: 'It's just that they din all these beautiful words in your ears when you're a kid at school, and then you find that you can't move an inch without pulling strings or giving bribes.' (Solzhenitsyn 1971:282.)

A film, *Tri dnya Viktora Chernysheva* (*Three Days in the Life of Victor Chernyshev*), caused a stir when it appeared in the USSR in 1968; it openly suggested that the reason for disenchantment among some Soviet young people was the contrast between the glorious future they had been promised and the realities of daily life. The climax of the film comes when the disillusioned hero is asked: 'What does the future hold for you, Viktor?' He replies drily: 'I'll be drafted into the army.' (*Ogonek*, August 1968.)

Non-fictional sources also have put the problem into words. A very interesting correspondence was carried on in the central youth newspaper in 1971 on the subject of hooliganism. One writer, a People's Artist of the USSR, defended hooligans:

If you begin to talk to them you will be convinced that they are not coarse brutes (*khamy*); they simply do not understand what is not done. No one has taught them how to behave.

Another correspondent objected to this, replying:

They have been taught. Dear me, they have been taught. They have been taught at length and painstakingly from good books. They have been crammed with wise judgments and selected examples from life. But the blunt matter is that, as well as greying literature-mistresses, there are also forces in life which produce quite a different impression of the world. (*Vospityvat' vospitannost'* 1971:18.)

There is, then, some evidence to support the hypothesis that there will be some conflict in Soviet youth caused by the clash between life in literature and life in reality. This conflict could be eradicated only by a radically new official approach to literature – and this shows few signs of coming about at the moment. Some steps towards grappling with this problem within the educational system have been made, however, by L. S. Aizerman, for example, in an article in the teachers' press entitled 'To Older Pupils – about Duty and Responsibility'. In it, the teacher is urged to point out to his pupils, through the medium of the literature lesson, that life will not always be easy, that decisions may sometimes be painful and that the individual may actually feel conflict at having to act for the good of the collective (*Literatura v shkole* 1971: No. 1, pp. 18–20). I. S. Kon, a major Soviet sociologist, also acknowledges this problem.

A person who has just realised that life is more complicated than a newspaper leader, that swindlers, careerists and villains succeed as well as good men, may hasten to reject his former ideals. 'They have deceived us', he says, 'elevated ideals are only for naive children, and life must be taken as it is; if you live with wolves, you must howl with the wolves.' (Kon 1960:45.)

The tendency of the schools, in particular, to protect children from the negative aspects of Soviet life does get criticised:

Pedagogical theory recommends, and schools in their work follow, the principle of character-education through positive influences and examples. On this basis, 'strategies and tactics', a programme and methods have been worked out and scientific, academic and popular literature and the educational press shaped. As far as education from negative examples and phenomena is concerned, the problem has been worked out much more weakly and the school does not programme this work but, most often of all, strives simply to protect the pupil from encountering the negative sides of life and keeping him in ignorance of the existence of such things. To the extent that the school and family succeed here, the child gets an idealised impression of life and is unprepared to react correctly to its negative sides, especially at the time when he is entering upon an independent life. (Arkhangel'sky 1967:219–20.)

The problems created by the 'varnishing' of life in literature are, therefore, beginning to be both acknowledged and discussed by the Soviet press – although the process begetting the problem continues.

There has developed in Soviet society one even more striking contrast between life as it is in reality and as it is depicted in literature – a phenomenon which is, at the same time, one of the most remarkable contradictions in Soviet ideology: the endowment of the political doctrine of Leninism with the features of a religion. Max Weber has adumbrated four major features common to all world religions: these are shown below and, alongside them are Soviet equivalents identified in the children's literature examined and propagated throughout Soviet society.

| Characteristics of religion (see Weber 1971) | Characteristics of Soviet ideology |
| --- | --- |
| Rationalisation of suffering | Rationalisation of sacrifices for the building of Communism |
| Acceptance of certain people as spiritual advisors (the 'rationalisation of hierocracy') | Acceptance of top Party people as 'leaders, teachers and inspirers of victories' |
| Messianic promises | Prediction of a Communist future |
| Central figure of a saviour | Lenin – 'with whose name we are invincible' |

Other important functions traditionally fulfilled by a church have also found Soviet counterparts – for example, *rites de passage*. The momentous occasions of a citizen's life have been deliberately replaced by new Soviet ceremonies.[3] Planting a tree at a child's birth is shown as an attractive alternative ritual to baptism. His first day at school is made into a day of colour and gaiety by the teachers and older pupils. The youth movement has its own solemn induction ceremonies. The young person's reaching the age of legal responsibility at sixteen is celebrated by the official presentation of the internal passport which every Soviet townsman must carry after leaving the age of minority. In many cities, marriages can be performed in a Wedding Palace where

[3] See, for example, *Komsomol'skaya pravda*, 17 April 1975, which tells of replacing a popular church rite (confirmation) with a new Soviet coming-of-age ceremony.

the bride can wear white and the marriage receives a ceremonial state blessing. The love of spectacle is also catered for by counter-religious processions and festivals. There are often organised to coincide with religious feast days.[4]

The basic function previously fulfilled by religion but now intended to be taken over by Leninism is the provision of a purpose for the individual to strive towards. This is not done in totally rational scientific terms. Soviet man is exhorted repeatedly to justify his existence in terms of the Communist cause, giving a worth to all work and a point to any short-term suffering.

In the children's literature there are, as has been seen, constant examples of the treatment of Lenin as the pattern of ideal behaviour and as an inspiration to contemporary Soviet people. He indeed is shown to embody all the characteristics of the New Soviet Man. He is dedicated to the cause of Communism and works for it to the utmost of his strength, yet he is also humane and modest.

Lenin is not only presented as an inspiration of labour and self-discipline, he is also a substitute for religion's function of giving solace in time of need. A youth song refers to Lenin who is 'always with you, in joy and hope and grief'. Ten-year-olds, it will be recalled, are recommended to visit the mausoleum when-ever they are passing through a difficult period in their life and whenever some especially important decision has to be taken. Thus Lenin is offered as the shepherd who safely guards his flocks, as the staff on which one can always lean and find support.

While Lenin certainly promoted the goal-directedness of Soviet society, he is known to have resisted in his lifetime any attempts to make a cult out of his personality and bitterly opposed any signs of myth-making. Herein lies what seems to be a major contradiction in the Soviet world-view – promoted, as has been seen, as a basic part of a Soviet 'foundation myth'.

Thus there is evidence that the Soviet authorities have deliber-ately created a 'foundation myth' in order to legitimate their own position and to make the people more malleable. Before briefly summing up the nature of the Soviet 'myth' it must be

---

[4] See, for example, *Turkmenskaya iskra*, 17 October 1975, which calls for the setting-up of replacement ceremonies to erase the 'harmful features of past traditions'.

pointed out that by using the term 'myth' the writer does not necessarily wish to imply that it is wholly untrue or to condemn it solely because it is not the whole truth. A myth may be untrue but it may also be a simplification of the truth – in a way that comes naturally when one's audience is children. Moreover, even when a myth may be untrue, it may have an aesthetic or symbolic beauty that justifies its existence, for example, the legend of Adam and Eve. It is what is done in the name of the myth that is important. It is, for instance, hard now for the Englishman to justify aggression in the name of a glorious Empire upon which the sun never sets. Most people in the West probably do not agree with many of the elements of the Soviet myth although we are probably not as free of acceptance of our own society's myths as we may imagine.

The major Soviet myths, as highlighted by its children's literature, are as follows:

Soviet society is the most democratic, just, humane, productive and non-exploitative in the world because it is socialist and therefore lacks class contradictions.

The Party is the Party of Lenin. It embodies today the precepts of 'the most humane of men' and is thus infallible, omnipotent, solicitous and carries out the will of the masses.

Lenin's Party was like today's Party. It was leader-oriented, 'hero'-led, patriotic and highly disciplined.

Contemporary Soviet society is in a process of transition from socialism to Communism and a united effort will soon bring Communism to the Soviet Union.

One's attitudes to these myths must be conditioned largely by the extent to which one considers that the nature of contemporary Soviet society and the ends towards which it is progressing justify them. Nevertheless the very existence of what can be called either simplifications or distortions depending on one's viewpoint cannot but lead to a certain cynicism among at least a section of the adult Soviet population. It would seem wise for a society developing a secular morality to try to avoid distortion in its myths even if simplification is sometimes necessary but also to try to stop myths becoming rigid dogma and thus eventually degenerating into mere ritualistic meaninglessness.

Although, as has been seen, a fair measure of success has been achieved in certain areas, Soviet schoolchildren have not grown as smoothly into the Builders of Communism as was hoped. A Hobbesian philosopher might account for this by the basic and unchangeable evil of man's nature. A Stalinist would have dismissed acts of delinquency as 'relics of the past', perhaps quoting the old Russian proverb that points out how, even with a large bucket, it takes a long time to empty even a small lake. There may be an element of truth in both views – and other explanations are certainly possible. Soviet life is in many ways demanding, unequal and lacking in amenities and can thus generate discontent. 'Non-Soviet' behaviour may undoubtedly in some instances, too, be a reaction against the relentless reiteration of the official precepts; it may also be explicable in terms of alternative socialising influences – parents who listen to foreign broadcasts, a religious grandmother or an alcoholic father, say, even access to *samizdat* literature – all of which are circumstances largely outside the effective control of the state.[5]

Within the Soviet character-education system itself, however, there are also factors giving rise to certain ambiguities; the previous chapter highlighted the conflict between the value of patriotism and that of internationalism, the double-think about the nature of work in Soviet society and the age-old conflict of the collective and the individual. This chapter has broadened the focus to draw in two problems of perhaps wider social implication. The first question is that concerning autonomy or independent thought and the second has to do with the relationship between myth and reality. It seems to the author that better answers will have to be found to these questions before a truly satisfactory secular morality is established.

It is appreciated – and regretted – that much of this work has tended to stress the failures rather than the successes, the contradictions rather than the achievements of the Soviet character-education process. There is much in Soviet child-socialisation that

[5] This is an explanation of persisting deviant behaviour that is currently favoured by Soviet scholars; there are corresponding attempts on behalf of the authorities to eradicate continuing sources of alternative influences. Thus, for example, non-teaching school-staff (e.g. furnacemen) are encouraged to take courses to enable them to support the work of the teacher in the character-education process. (See *Uchitel'skaya gazeta*, 12 January 1971.)

is, in the writer's opinion, good and admirable. If there has been an over-emphasis on the negative it is with the hope that others attempting to create a secular morality will be able to avoid some of the pitfalls encountered by those who have been pioneers in this field.

# Bibliography

Abdullina, O. A. 'O metodike izucheniya urovnya nravstvennykh znaniy povedeniya uchashchikhsya VI–VII klassov.' ('On methods of studying the level of moral knowledge of behaviour in pupils of the VI–VII classes.') *Sovetskaya pedagogika*, 1971, No. 1.

Aksenov, V. *A Starry Ticket*. London, 1962.

Aksenova, E. S. (ed.) *Detskaya literatura 1970-go goda. (Children's Literature of the year 1970.)* Moscow, 1971.

Aleksin, A. *Govorit sed'moy etazh. (Seventh Floor Speaking.)* Moscow, 1959.

Angelov, S. *Marksistskaya etika kak nauka. (Marxist Ethics as a Science.)* Moscow, 1973.

Arkhangel'sky, I. M. (ed.) *Dukhovnoe razvitie lichnosti. (Spiritual Development of the Personality.)* Sverdlovsk, 1967.

Artomonov, S. *Bunt na korable ili povest' o davnem lete. (Mutiny on Board or A Tale of a Distant Summer.)* Moscow, 1971.

Barghoorn, F. *Politics in the USSR*. Boston, 1966.

Barrington Moore, J. *Social Origins of Dictatorship and Democracy*. London, 1967.

Baruzdin, S. *Shel po ulitse soldat. (A Soldier went along the Street.)* Moscow, 1969.

Bawden, N. *Squib*. London, 1973.

Bawden, N. 'Kids Stuff'. *The Guardian*, 6 February 1974.

Belinsky, V. G. *Izbrannye pedagogicheskie sochineniya. (Selected Pedagogical Writings.)* Moscow, 1948.

Bogdanov, N. 'Literary characters influence the life of Soviet children'. *Journal of Educational Psychology*, November 1961, Vol. 35, pp. 162–4.

*Bol'shaya sovetskaya entsiklopediya. (Great Soviet Encyclopaedia.)* Moscow, 1957 and 1972.

Bondarevskaya, E. V. and Krupenya, Z. B. 'Issledovanie osobennostey otsenochnykh suzhdeniy starshikh shkol'nikov'. *Sovetskaya pedagogika*, 1970, No. 2.

Bronfenbrenner, U. *Two Worlds of Childhood: US and USSR*. London, 1971.

Brzezinski, Z. and Huntington, S. P. *Political Power: USA/USSR*. London, 1964.

Bulgakov, M. *The Master and Margarita*. Fontana, 1971.

Chekhov, N. V. *Materialy po istorii russkoy detskoy literatury s 1750-go do 1850-go. (Materials on the History of Russian Children's Literature from 1750 to 1850.)* Moscow, 1927.

Chernyavskaya, Ya A. *Sovetskaya detskaya literatura.* (*Soviet Children's Literature.*) Minsk, 1971.

Chikin and Grushin. *Ispoved pokoleniya.* (*Testament of a Generation.*) Moscow, 1962.

Chukovsky, K. *From Two to Five.* California, 1963.

Chukovsky, K. *Mukha-Tsokotukha.* Moscow, 1967.

Counts, G. S. *I Want To Be Like Stalin.* London, 1948.

Counts, G. S. *The Challenge of Soviet Education.* New York, 1957.

Durkheim, E. *Moral Education.* London, 1973.

D'yachenko, N. N. *Professional'naya orientatsiya i vovlechenie molodezhi v sistemu professional'nogo–tekhnicheskogo obrazovaniya* (*Vocational Guidance and Attracting Young People into Trade and Technical Education.*) Moscow, 1971.

Eysenck, H. *Sense and Nonsense in Psychology.* Penguin, 1958.

Filippenko. 'O preodolenii religioznykh perezhivaniy.' ('On the overcoming of religious experiences.') *Bibliotekar'*, 1972, No. 2, pp. 28–31.

Fisher, M. *Intent Upon Reading.* Leicester, 1961.

*Flazhok.* (*Little Flag.*) Moscow, 1971.

Florinsky, M. *Russia.* New York, 1966.

Frank, J. *Your Child's Reading Today.* New York, 1954.

Frumin, I. M. *Organizatsiya raboty sovetskoy biblioteki.* (*Organisation of Work in a Soviet Library.*) Moscow, 1969.

Gaidar, A. *Timur i ego komanda.* (*Timur and his Team.*) Novosibirsk, 1968.

Garaudy, R. *Marxism in the Twentieth Century.* London, 1970.

Golitsyn, S. *Sorok izyskateley.* (*Forty Explorers.*) Moscow, 1966.

Golod, S. I. *Sotsial'nye problemy polevoy morali.* (*Social Problems of Sexual Morality.*) Leningrad, 1968.

Gor'ky, M. *Starukha Izergil'.* (*The Old Woman Izergil.*) Moscow, 1895.

Gouzenko, S. *Before Igor.* London, 1961.

Grant, N. *Soviet Education.* Penguin, 1968.

Greenstein, F. I. *Children and Politics.* New Haven, 1969.

Gurova, R. G. 'Ob odnom konkretnom issledovanii.' ('On one concrete experiment.') *Sovetskaya pedagogika*, 1971, No. 1, pp. 41–51.

Hazard, P. *Books, Children and Men.* Boston, 1960.

Hollander, P. *American and Soviet Society.* Englewood Cliffs, NJ, 1969.

Hurlimann, B. *Three Centuries of Books.* London, 1967.

Indursky, S. et al. *Doma, na rabote, v Iyudyakh.* (*At Home, at Work, with People.*) Vol. 2. Moscow, 1972.

Kamenka, E. *Marxism and Ethics.* London, 1970.

Karpinskaya, N. S. *Khudozhestvennoe slovo v vospitanii detey.* (*The Artistic Word is the Character Education of Children.*) Moscow, 1972.

Kataev, V. *The Holy Well.* London, 1967.

Khanchin, V. S. 'Kriterii moral'nosti i urovnya nravstvennoy vospitannosti shkol'nika. ('Criteria of morality and the level of moral development in the schoolchild.') *Novye issledovaniya v pedagogike*, 1970, No. 2, pp. 48–53.

*Khrestomatiya dlya detey starshego doshkol'nogo vosrasta.* (*Anthology for Children of Older Pre-school Age.*) Moscow, 1972.

Kibareva, A. *Zhivye stranitsy.* (*Living Pages.*) Moscow, 1969.

Kolotinsky, P. N. *Opyt dlitel'nogo izucheniya mirovozzreniya uchashchikh sya vypusknykh klassov.* (*An Experiment in the Extended Study of the World-view of Pupils in the Top Classes.*) Krasnodar, 1929.

Kon, I. S., in *Obshchestvo i molodezh'.* (*Society and Youth.*) Moscow, 1973.

Kon, L. *Sovetskaya detskaya literatura (1917–29).* (*Soviet Children's Literature (1917–29).*) Moscow, 1960.

Krupskaya, N. *O kommunisticheskom vospitanii.* ( *On Communist Character Training.*) Moscow, 1956.

Krupskaya, N. *Pedagogicheskie sochineniya v 10 tomakh.* (*Pedagogical Writings in 10 volumes.*) Moscow, 1963(a).

Krupskaya, N. *Nash samy lushchiy drug.* (*Our Very Best Friend.*) Moscow, 1963(b).

Krupskaya, N. *Izbrannye pedagogicheskie sochineniya.* (*Selected Pedagogical Writings.*) Moscow, 1968.

Lane, D. S. *The End of Inequality?* Penguin, 1971.

Lane, D. S. and O'Dell, F. *The Soviet Industrial Worker: Social Class, Education and Control.* London, 1978.

Lenin, V. I. *Polnoe sobranie sochineniy.* (*Complete Collected Works.*) Moscow, 1963.

Lisovsky, V. G. and Ikonnikova, S. N. *Molodezh' o sebe i o svoikh sverstnikakh.* (*Young People on Themselves and their Contemporaries.*) Leningrad, 1969.

Lukacs, G. *Political Writings 1919–1929.* London, 1972.

Lyublinskaya, A. A. *Detskaya psikhologiya.* (*Child Psychology.*) Moscow, 1971.

Machiavelli, N. *The Prince.* Penguin, 1972.

Makarova, V. (ed.) *O literature dlya detey.* (*On Literature for Children.*) Leningrad, 1973.

Maksimov, V. *Proshchanie iz niotkuda.* (*Farewell from Nowhere.*) Frankfurt, 1974.

Marcuse, H. *Soviet Marxism.* Penguin, 1971.

Markov, V. and Sparks, M. (eds.) *Modern Russian Poetry.* London, 1966.

*K. Marx and F. Engels on Religion.* Moscow, 1955.

Mayakovsky, V. *Izbrannye proizvedeniya.* (*Selected Works.*) Leningrad, 1963.

Medvedeva, M. 'Russian children's literature on the contemporary stage.' *International Library Review,* 1971, No. 3.

Medvedeva, M. 'Scientific work on children's reading and library work with children.' *Unesco Bulletin for Libraries,* 1972, Vol. 26, No. 4, pp. 207–8.

Meyer, A. *The Soviet Political System.* New York, 1965.

Milner-Gulland, R. 'Left Art in Leningrad.' *Oxford Slavonic Papers* (NS), 1970, No. 3.

Montelli, A. *Razvedka v oblast' interesov shkol'nikov vtoroy stepeni.* (*Research into the Areas of Interest of Schoolchildren of the Second Grade.*) Leningrad, 1930.

Murray, J. *The Union of Soviet Writers.* Ph.D. thesis, Birmingham, 1973.

Musatov, A. *Stozhary.* (*Old Timers.*) Moscow, 1948.

*Narodnoe obrazovanie, nauka i kultura v SSSR.* (*National Education, Science and Culture in the USSR.*) Moscow, 1977.

Nash, R. 'History as she is writ.' *New Society,* 1972, Vol. 21, No. 514.

*Nasha rodina.* (*Our Motherland.*) Moscow, 1971.

Nekrasov, V. 'On both sides of the ocean.' In Blake, P. and Hayward, M. (eds) *Halfway to the Moon.* London, 1964.

Neuburg, P. *The Hero's Children: The Post War Generation in Eastern Europe.* London, 1972.

Nikishov, S. I. *XXIV S"ezd KPSS i zadachi ateisticheskogo vospitaniya.* (*The Twenty-fourth Congress of the CPSU and Tasks of Atheist Education.*) Moscow, 1972.

Ogryzko, I. I. *Deti i religiya.* (*Children and Religion.*) Leningrad, 1970.

Omel'yanenko, V. G. *Tekhnicheskiy progress i sovremennye trebovaniya k urovnyu kvalifikatsiy i podgotovke spetsialistov.* (*Technical Progress and Contemporary Demands on the Level of Qualifications and Training in Specialists.*) Moscow, 1973.

*O partiynoy i sovetskoy pechati.* (*On the Poetry and Soviet Press.*) Moscow, 1954.

*Osnovy kommunisticheskoy morali.* (*Foundations of Communist Morality.*) Moscow, 1973.

Ostrovsky, N. *Kak zakalyalas' stal'.* (*How the Steel was Tempered.*) Moscow, 1935.

Ozhegov, S. I. *Slovar' russkogo yazyka.* (*Dictionary of the Russian Language.*) Moscow, 1968.

Panteleev, L. *Izbrannoe.* (*A Selection.*) Moscow, 1967.

Plato. *The Republic.* Penguin, 1973.

Petrova, V. I. 'Nekotorye voprosy diagnostiki nravstvennogo razvitiya detey.' ('Some questions on the diagnosis of the level of moral development of the child.') *Novye issledovaniya v pedagogicheskikh naukakh,* 1971, No. 4.

Polevoy, B. *Povest' o nastoyashchem cheloveke.* (*Story of a Real Man.*) Moscow, 1947.

*Programma KPSS.* (*CPSU Programme.*) Moscow, 1969 and 1976.

*Programma vos'miletney shkoly, nachal'nye klassy.* (*Syllabus of the Eight-year School: Primary Classes.*) Moscow, 1971.

*Pyaty s"ezd pisateley SSSR.* (*Fifth Congress of the Writers of the USSR.*) Moscow, 1972.

Rapp, H. 'Soviet Literature for Children.' In Kent Greiger, H. (ed.) *Soviet Society: A Book of Readings.* London, 1961.

Ready, T. M. *The Little Hermit.* London, 1853.

Reich, W. *What is Class Consciousness?* Socialist Reproduction undated (originally published Denmark 1933).

Schwarcz, H. J., in Fenwick, S. I. (ed.) *A Critical Approach to Children's Literature.* Chicago, 1966.

Schwartz, J. 'The Elusive New Soviet Man.' *Problems of Communism,* September/October 1973.

Slepenko, I. N. *Vospitanie kollektivizma v trude.* (*Education in Collectivism in Labour.*) Moscow, 1958.

Slonim, M. *From Chekhov to the Revolution.* New York, 1962.
Smirnov, S. *Izbrannoe na ves' al'favit.* (*Selection through the Alphabet.*) Moscow, 1968.
Smirnova, V. *O detyakh i dlya detey.* (*On Children and for Children.*) Moscow, 1958.
Smith, D. *Fifty Years of Children's Books 1910–1960.* Illinois, 1963.
Solzhenitsyn, A. *Cancer Ward.* Penguin, 1971.
Solzhenitsyn, A. *The First Circle.* Fontana, 1971.
Solzhenitsyn, A. *For the Good of the Cause.* Sphere, 1971.
Solzhenitsyn, A. 'Letter to the Soviet Leaders.' *The Sunday Times,* 3 March 1974.
*Sovetskaya detskaya literatura.* (*Soviet Children's Literature.*) Moscow, 1952.
Stillman, E. (ed.) *Bitter Harvest.* London, 1958.
Tendryakov, V. *Izbrannye proizvedeniya* (*Selected Works.*) Moscow, 1963.
Thwaite, M. F. *From Primer to Pleasure in Reading.* London, 1972.
de Tocqueville, A. *Democracy in America.* New York, 1961.
Trease, G. *Tales out of School.* London, 1964.
Trinkner, C. L. (ed.) *Better Libraries make Better Schools.* Hamden, CT, 1962.
Trotsky, L. *Their Morals and Ours.* New York, 1966.
Tucker, E. S. *Boys will be Boys.* London, 1957.
Turchenko, V. N. *Nauchno-tekhnicheskaya revolyutsiya i revolyutsiya v obrazovanii.* (*The Scientific-Technical Revolution and the Revolution in Education.*) Moscow, 1973.
Ukh'yankin, S. P. *Pionery Timurovtsy.* (*Pioneers and Timurites.*) Moscow, 1961.
van der Post, L. *Journey into Russia.* Penguin, 1964.
Vasil'ev, V. *et al. Vashemnenie?* (*Your Opinion?*) Moscow, 1967.
Vasil'eva, M. S. (ed.) *Chtenie v tret'em klasse.* (*Reading in the Third Class.*) Moscow, 1971.
Vaughan James, C. *Soviet Socialist Realism.* London, 1973.
Verba, I. A. and Pikovsky, V. I. *Vospitanie patriotov-internatsionalistov.* (*Education of Patriots and Internationalists.*) Moscow, 1973.
Vishnevsky, V. *Optimisticheskaya tragediya.* (*An Optimistic Tragedy.*) Moscow, 1933.
Vodzinskaya, V. V. *Molodezh' i trud.* (*Young People and Labour.*) Moscow, 1970.
*Vospityvat' vospitannost'.* (*Educating Character.*) Moscow, 1971.
Voynich, E. L. *The Gadfly.* New York, 1897.
Weber, M. *The Theory of Social Economic Organisation.* Oxford, 1947.
Weber, M. *The Protestant Ethic and the Spirit of Capitalism.* London, 1971.
Yashin, A. *Rychagi.* (*Levers.*) London, 1965.
Yevtushenko, Ye. *A Precocious Autobiography.* Penguin, 1965.
Zankova, L. V. *Novaya sistema nachal'nogo obucheniya.* (*New System of Primary Education.*) Moscow, 1967.
Zhdanov, M. *On Literature, Music and Philosophy.* Moscow, 1950.

Zoshchenko, M. *Izbrannye proizvedeniya* (*Selected Works.*) Leningrad, 1968.
*Zvezdochka.* (*Little Star.*) Moscow, 1971.

## SOVIET PERIODICALS USEFUL IN THIS STUDY

*Bibliotekar'*
*Detskaya literatura*
*Doshkol'noe vospitanie*
*Izvestiya*
*Komsomol'skaya pravda*
*Koster*
*Literatura v shkole*
*Literaturnaya gazeta*
*Murzilka*
*Narodnoe obrazovanie*
*Novye issledovaniya v pedagogicheskikh naukakh*
*Novye issledovaniya v pedagogike*
*Ogonek*
*Pioner*
*Pionerskaya pravda*
*Pravda*
*Sem'ya i shkola*
*Sovetskaya pedagogika*
*Uchitel'skaya gazeta*
*Voprosy filosofii*

# Index

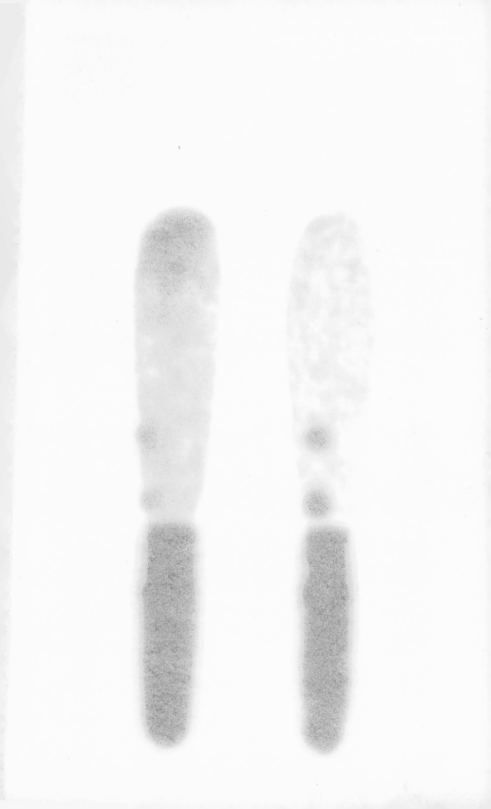

## DATE DUE

| | |
|---|---|
| | |
| | |
| | |
| | |
| | |
| | |
| | |
| | |
| | |
| | |
| | |
| | |
| | |
| | |
| | |
| | |

GAYLORD                                    PRINTED IN U.S.A.